ACQUIRED BRAIN INJURY IN CHILDHOOD AND ADOLESCENCE

ACQUIRED BRAIN INJURY IN CHILDHOOD AND ADOLESCENCE

A Team and Family Guide to Educational Program Development and Implementation

Edited by

ALAN L. GOLDBERG, PSY.D.

CHARLES C THOMAS · PUBLISHER
Springfield · Illinois · U.S.A.

Published and Distributed Throughout the World by

CHARLES C THOMAS • PUBLISHER
2600 South First Street
Springfield, Illinois 62794-9265

© *1996 by* CHARLES C THOMAS • PUBLISHER

ISBN 0-398-06589-6   (cloth)
ISBN 0-398-06590-X   (paper)

Library of Congress Catalog Card Number: 95-51316

With THOMAS BOOKS *careful attention is given to all details of manufacturing
and design. It is the Publisher's desire to present books that are satisfactory as to their
physical qualities and artistic possibilities and appropriate for their particular use.*
THOMAS BOOKS *will be true to those laws of quality that assure a good name
and good will.*

Printed in the United States of America
SC-R-3

Library of Congress Cataloging-in-Publication Data

Acquired brain injury in childhood and adolescence : a team and family
   guide to educational program development and implementation / edited
   by Alan L. Goldberg.
       p.   cm.
     Includes bibliographical bibliographical references and index.
     ISBN 0-398-06589-6 (cloth). — ISBN 0-398-06590-X (paper)
     1. Brain-damaged children—Education—United States.   2. Brain-
   damaged children—Rehabilitation—United States.   I. Goldberg,
   Alan L.
   LC4596.A37   1996
       371.91′6—dc20   95-51316
                                                             CIP

CONTRIBUTORS

MARTHA M. BERGLAND, Ph.D.
Mankato State University
Mankato, Minnesota

ERIC C. BROUSAIDES, J.D.
Private Practice
Greenbelt, Maryland

SALLY B. COHEN, M.Ed.
Private Consultant
Pittsburgh, Pennsylvania

RICHARD E. EKSTRAND, J.D.
Private Practice
Greenbelt, Maryland

ALAN L. GOLDBERG, Psy.D.
Private Practice
Tucson, Arizona

LAURIE E. GRAHAM, Ph.D.
Orcutt Union School District
Santa Maria, California

PATRICIA L. JANUS, M.Ed.
Montgomery County Public Schools
Bethesda, Maryland

MARTHA LYONS-HOLDEN, M.S. + 6th year
Orcutt Union School District
Santa Maria, California

MARCIA R. NORDLUND, M.Ed.
SASED
Westmont, Illinois

JAMES A. PASINO, Ph.D.
Rancho Los Amigos Medical Center
Downey, California

DIANA P. TOGNAZZINI, Ph.D.
Santa Maria Joint Union High School District
Santa Maria, California

This book is dedicated to our mentors. These include teachers, colleagues, friends, and significant others who have influenced our lives and motivated us for this scholarly undertaking. But, most of all, it is dedicated to the brave individuals who have acquired brain injuries. These individuals, along with their families, have taught us valuable lessons about faith, courage, and humility.

FOREWORD

Mark Ylvisaker, Ph.D.
Albany, New York

I am pleased to introduce this fine textbook to what I hope will be a large and varied audience. Brain injury acquired during childhood and adolescence is an enormous public health and public education concern, which has only recently received attention in the special education literature. Although schools have always been the largest providers of services, including rehabilitation services for children with acquired brain injury, the critical role of schools was not officially recognized until traumatic brain injury was added as a disability category in federal special education law. Shrinking health care budgets and ever-decreasing lengths of stay in children's hospitals and rehabilitation centers have punctuated the need to focus program development efforts in schools. Within this historical setting, Alan L. Goldberg's book is a welcome addition to the small body of publications designed to increase professionals' understanding of the educational dimensions of acquired brain injury.

Goldberg has assembled a group of authors who write from years of experience in the trenches, giving the book a welcome practical orientation. The book's goal is not simply to help readers understand the often tricky realities of acquired brain injury in children, but more importantly to help them work effectively with these children and their families. Each chapter rewards its careful reader with approaches, techniques, and procedures that are useful for some students within this very diverse disability category. Furthermore, the book sheds needed light on the often confusing and fragmented systems within which children with brain injury are served.

In Chapter 1, Pasino provides a digestible summary of basic information related to brain injury and its varied effects on behavior. Causes of acquired brain injury and its pathophysiology, measures of severity and of outcome, and factors that affect outcome are presented along with a brief introduction to assessment and intervention. The chapter effectively introduces themes that may not be familiar to those who lack specific training in this area. In Chapter 2, Ekstrand and Brousaides review the history of special education law and provide useful detail, including summaries of critical court decisions about brain injury and the law. This chapter is important reading for school administrators and people who find themselves playing the role of advocate for children and adolescents with brain injury. It is supplemented by Graham, Tognazzini, and Lyons-Holden's discussion of the history of special education and its procedural regulations.

In Chapters 4, 5, and 6, Nordlund, Graham, and Goldberg review the options for educational service delivery for students with brain injury, appropriately highlighting the use of consultation models to support students in the least restrictive educational environment. This is followed by practical discussions of educational program development (Cohen, Chapter 7), school reentry and staff training (Janus, Chapter 9), and transitions from school to adult life (Bergland, Chapter 8). The critical role of parents, how to support them, and how to work collaboratively with them are the focus of Janus' discussion in Chapter 10. These themes are effectively illustrated in Cohen's extended case study in Chapter 11.

Goldberg and the other authors are to be congratulated and thanked for taking time out of their demanding lives as practicing clinicians, teachers, administrators, and attorneys to share important information about a group of students who need to be served by well-informed staff. Their book is a large step in the direction of providing professionals with the information and tools needed to meet this goal.

PREFACE

Brain injuries continue to be a leading cause of death and disability in individuals of school age. Over 150,000 children are hospitalized with a traumatic brain injury in the United States each year, with approximately 29,000 of these individuals becoming permanently disabled (National Pediatric Trauma Register, 1993). When one considers that individuals who have sustained brain injuries most often have normal life expectancies, with large numbers (including those who are permanently disabled) being on-going consumers of rehabilitative services, the social and economic impact can be justifiably seen as staggering. The numbers swell even more when broad definitions of brain injury are utilized. Many conditions can be classified under a broad definition, with strokes, brain tumors, arteriovenous malformations, and aneurysms being just a few of the diagnoses which can be added to the commonly used category of brain injuries caused by an external force to the head. The majority of the acquired brain injuries share a number of common characteristics which make them compatible in terms of educational service delivery. Use of a broader definition also provides for a larger group, thereby enhancing lobbying power for ever-shrinking dollars to fund services.

This book utilizes a broad definition of brain injury, acquired after birth. Chapters have been written by a diverse group of professionals representing differing perspectives on educational service delivery. We have met through our common concerns for the rehabilitation and education of children and adolescents. We hope that this book will be a useful compendium of information for parents, educators, attorneys, rehabilitation professionals, and vocational specialists. Chapters can be read individually for information concerning a specific topic, or the book can be read as a whole to broaden perspectives and gain an overview of a variety of issues important to the education and rehabilitation of youths who have sustained injuries to the brain.

A.L.G.

CONTENTS

ACQUIRED BRAIN INJURY IN CHILDHOOD AND ADOLESCENCE

Chapter 1

NEUROPSYCHOLOGICAL ASPECTS OF ACQUIRED BRAIN INJURY IN CHILDREN

JAMES A. PASINO

INTRODUCTION

In the not too distant past, pediatric brain injury was not well appreciated, nor was it very well recognized outside the homes of families stricken with this tragic event, or beyond the walls of school classrooms where teachers struggled to educate these children. Educational placements for children challenged by brain injuries were often with the mentally retarded, emotionally disturbed, or severely developmentally disabled. Before the National Head Injury Foundation was established, adult brain injury was a silent epidemic while pediatric brain injury was barely recognized at all.

Pediatric brain injury is not uncommon, with estimates indicating that one out of every thirty newborns will suffer significant brain injury before he or she is of driving age (Allison, 1992). Fortunately, today there is a rapidly growing awareness of the scope of the problem, with increasing understanding of the diagnosis and treatment of pediatric brain injury. In part, this is manifested in the passage of Public Law 101-476, the Individuals with Disabilities Education Act (IDEA), which, for the first time, recognized children with traumatic brain injury as a group with disabilities categorically eligible for special education services (Federal Register, 1991). However, the people having the second greatest long-term contact with these children, our educators, often are omitted from the research, treatment, and funding processes.

The purpose of this chapter is to provide treaters and educators of children with information on neuropsychological issues surrounding pediatric brain injury. Topics discussed are: (1) the child as patient, (2) dynamic brain function, (3) neurodevelopment, (4) mechanisms of injury, (5) assessment of severity of injury, (6) mechanisms of recovery, (7) measures of outcome, and (8) the continuum of care.

THE CHILD AS PATIENT

Psychological Factors

With primary emphasis on brain injury in pediatric populations, one would not want to overlook the most salient issue; we are discussing children who, by definition, have special needs and demand considerations different from adults.

Many of us have had the experience of a young child in the doctor's waiting room screaming in distress, the fearful and anxious anticipation of a child about to be taken by a gentle but alien therapist, and the questions and worry about not being in the same class as the other children in the neighborhood and the clinging, tugging, holding, and complaints of not feeling well that come in the aftermath. In older children, stressful events may be met with angry, avoidant, sullen, and withdrawn behavior, conduct disorder, or academic decline. For either age group, these children are attempting to cope with the ravages of anxiety without adult coping skills and cognitive capabilities to help them out.

Compared to adults, children rely on incompletely formed and emerging ego functions. Their confidence and trust in themselves, stable ideas about who they are, and clear understanding of their relationships with parents and community are vaguely defined and unstable. Cognitively, they lack depth in fund of experience and past learning, and depending on age, may process their world in terms of myth, absolute physics and morality, or stereotype and overgeneralize. For example, how often have you been successful in convincing a child that smaller or less is better, and that the moon does not follow him/her home, or with an older child, that he/she is unique and does not need to worry about looking like, or being as physically agile and attractive, as the other kids?

Children are different from adults in that they change rapidly, not only cognitively and psychologically, but in terms of competence in adaptive skills. Children use toys and play as media to identify, express, fulfill, and soothe themselves. Arrests and delays in new learning and development can threaten or obliterate the opportunity for skill acquisition and produce lifelong disability. But most importantly, children are constantly faced with anxiety and conflict surrounding separation and dependency.

The treatment of any child, be it medical, rehabilitative, psychological, or educational, needs to spring from a firm grasp on normal physical and psychological development.

Structural Considerations

While the adult brain is relatively stable, the child's brain is in a constant state of change, increasing rapidly in size, weight, and functional complexity. The child's brain, while much smaller than an adult's, is proportionally much larger in relationship to body size. Substantial myelination occurs during the first two years and synaptic and dendritic changes occur through maturation and stimulation. The child's skull is more flexible and pliable. The arachnoid space is much closer to the dura in children than in adults.

Some authors believe that the structural differences between the adult and child brain may actually increase the risk of brain injury in children (Lehr, 1990). Because of increased blood volume, cerebral swelling is more frequent following injury (Zimmerman and Bilanuik, 1981) increasing intracranial pressure and causing secondary sites of injury. The ability of the child's brain to move more freely within the skull may dispose it to more diffuse injury to nerve fibers. Immature and shallow convolutions in the child's brain may dispose it to greater shearing effects (Gurdjian, 1971). In children with mild or trivial injuries, deterioration not infrequently follows a lucid symptom-free period. With little or no loss of consciousness, children can show significant pathology on CT and MRI scans (Levin, et al., 1989). However, on the issue of structural differences in children versus adults, there exists a body of conflicting evidence showing both greater and diminished effects of brain damage on children, as compared to adults.

Preinjury Factors

A child's premorbid or preinjury functioning is a critical constellation of factors that bears directly on diagnosis, treatment, and outcome. In terms of practical suggestions in understanding where the child with acquired brain injury has been and where he/she comes from, the following areas should be thoroughly explored.

1. *Level of Behavior Controls:* An examination should be conducted of the preinjury status of age appropriate impulse control, attention, inhibitory, self-regulating, and monitoring systems.
2. *Developmental Status:* It is important to be alert to signs of CNS immaturity and delays in timely achievement of milestones and developmental challenges.
3. *Sensory Integration:* An area for exploration is evidence regarding ability for self-expression through use of voluntary muscles and integration of sensory information into smooth schemas of action.
4. *Learning Skill:* The style of the child's preinjury cognitive processing should be examined along the parameters of visual versus auditory,

nonverbal versus verbal, and field dependent versus field independent. Any evidence of pre-onset or familial learning disability deserves close inspection.

5. *Social and Emotional Maturity:* The question should be posed as to whether or not there is evidence of anxiety, excessive opposition, self blame, depression, conduct disorder, overdependency, or social isolation.

6. *Adaptive Behavior:* Sometimes overlooked is a structured interview of parents, caretakers, and educators to determine preinjury skill status in communication, activities of daily living, community activities, and socialization.

7. *Home and Community Environment:* An assessment needs to be taken regarding the nature of parent-child interactions, stability of primary care givers, opportunity for social and cognitive stimulation, quality of nutrition and access to health care, possible exposure to environmental toxins, and effects of cultural differences and poverty.

DYNAMIC BRAIN FUNCTION

In the author's experience, the best place to start a discussion of brain function is to define a few terms typically used by medical practitioners, which at one time certainly baffled the author.

If you were to look at yourself sideways in a mirror, the top of your head would be described as "superior," while the bottom of your feet would be "inferior." Your front would be "anterior" while your back would be "posterior." Taking this a bit further, if you looked straight ahead through your face, that would be a "coronal" view. Looking through your head from the side would be a "sagittal" or "lateral" view, while looking down on your head from above would be a "horizontal" view. So, the next time you read a medical report and attempt to understand a child's brain damage, at least you will know something about where the location of the damage is and from what viewpoint it is being looked at.

Anatomy and Physiology

Starting with the basics, and proceeding on the inferior/superior axis and working up (e.g., from bottom to top), the central nervous system includes the spine, brain stem, cerebellum, basal ganglia, diencephalon, and cerebrum.

The brain stem mediates postural reflexes, arousal and attention. The cerebellum is an area of motor coordination. The basal ganglia control fine motor movements. The diencephalon (the area of the brain that contains all the words with "thalamus" in them) is responsible for transmitting information regarding sensation and movement and controls the endocrine system. The cerebrum, composed of four lobes (frontal, temporal, parietal, occipital) divided from anterior to posterior into left and right hemispheres, forms the cortex which is involved in higher mental processes. Another important structure located in the central area of the brain is the hippocampus, whose function is to consolidate recently acquired information and turn short-term memory into long-term memory.

Other anatomical terms you may encounter are "white matter" and "grey matter." Grey matter is the cell bodies or neurons of the cortex. White matter is the fibers (axons and dendrites) that transmit neural impulses between cortical points, hemispheres, and lower levels of the brain.

Before moving on to dynamic brain organization and function, a few more topics require discussion.

Within the skull, there are three membranes that protect the brain. The pia mater is closest to the brain. Separating the pia mater from the second membrane, the arachnoid, is the arachnoid space. The arachnoid space is filled with circulating cerebral spinal fluid (CSF). The third membrane, the dura, is a lining on the inner surface of the skull.

As just mentioned, within the brain there is a system of circulating CSF. CSF is a colorless fluid which provides a cushion for the brain and a pathway for chemicals to reach and possibly be excreted from the brain. In the central area of the brain extending laterally and inferiorally are four ventricles that produce CSF. Enlargement of the ventricles can indicate atrophy (loss of brain tissue), and blockage of CSF pathways (hydrocephalus).

Blood supply is critically important to brain function. The brain itself has no metabolic or oxygen reserves. Compromise or disruption in blood flow may rapidly lead to loss of consciousness and permanent brain damage.

Function and Organization

Part to Part

On a single function or "part to part" basis, cerebral organization can be viewed most globally, from the standpoint of left and right, or dominant and nondominant cerebral hemisphere organization. Simply put, left hemisphere function is more "digital," that is, rich in logic, spoken and written language, calculations, and getting things started. The right hemisphere is more of an "analogue system," that is, concerned with nonverbal thinking, intuition, and the emotional quality of language and behavior. Hemispheric specialization is usually in full swing by two years of age. Still part to part, but more localized, is organization at the level of the cortical (cerebrum) structures. The frontal lobes plan for the future, organize action, control movement, and produce speech. The temporal lobes hear and interpret language and music. Parietal lobes receive and process data from the senses. Occipital lobes specialize in vision.

A somewhat peculiar feature in the organization of the brain is the crossed brain phenomena. Simply put, each of the brain's hemispheres responds to sensory stimuli from the contralateral (opposite) side of the body, and controls the musculature on the contralateral side of the body. Why and how this occurs is a topic in and of itself. However, this should help clear up why a child with a left hemiparesis is often described as having right hemisphere involvement or dysfunction.

Dynamic Functional Organization

Single function localization, which implies a one-to-one correspondence between brain site and behavior, is no longer adequate or accepted as a model for brain organization and function. It is true that the human CNS is highly specialized for function. However, this has been misunderstood to suggest that specific portions of the brain act independently. The functional systems theory of brain organization, as proposed by Luria (1970, 1973), is currently accepted by most neuropsychologists as a model to describe brain function and organization.

Functional Units or Blocks

Luria's dynamic functional system organizes the brain into three major blocks or units: unit I, the subcortical block; unit II, the posterior cortical block; and unit III, the anterior cortical block. In order to visualize this model, look at a sagittal section of the brain. Right at about the middle of the brain (actually a fold in the brain called the central sulcus), everything posterior would be block II (temporal, parietal, and occipital lobes) while everything anterior would be block III (frontal lobes). Block I involves the brain stem and diencephalon. Block I controls arousal, block II processing and integration of sensory input, and block III, planning and output.

Primary, Secondary, and Tertiary Systems

To take Luria's model one step further, the three lobes of block II, and the one lobe of block III, are organized into primary, secondary, and tertiary zones. Briefly put, block II primary zones accept direct information input from auditory, vision, and body senses. This specific sensory information is then passed on to the secondary zones where it becomes organized and coded into meaningful wholes. While the primary zones are concerned with sensation, secondary zones are concerned with perception. The tertiary zones serve to simultaneously analyze and integrate information across different sense modalities. Anatomically, the tertiary zones lie at the borders of the parietal, temporal, and occipital lobes and to some extent are seen as overlapping (Walsh, 1987). This is believed to be responsible for cross-modality processing and mediation of the skills of reading, writing, grammar, and logical analysis (Das et al., 1979; Golden, 1981).

The primary zone of block III is the motor strip (located just anterior to the central sulcus) and is the final motor command area. This area directs specific muscles needed to perform motor acts including speech. The secondary zone is the premotor area where motor programs are organized and prepared for execution by the motor strip. The tertiary zone is where intentions are formed. This area, also referred to as the prefrontal lobes, is where attention and arousal are regulated, long-term planning occurs, decision making is carried out, impulses are controlled, judgements are made, problem solving is executed, and the nuances and tenants of social convention are understood.

By way of example, think of a child sitting in class observing a blackboard lesson. In the primary zones are the actual sensory representations of the movements of the teacher, the sound of her voice, and the visual symbols and auditory representations of topography and language. In the secondary zones is the perception of the different sensory experiences as a geography lesson. In the tertiary zones, information is analyzed and integrated into the realization that the teacher is discussing Asia verbally and by illustration, and that he or she (the child) does not understand the lesson. These events could then lead to the intention to formulate a question, and carry out the intention motorically by raising his or her hand and appropriately verbalizing the question within the social context of the classroom. A lesion in the primary area may produce a distortion or neglect in the visual field. A lesion in the secondary area might produce a perceptual deficit making the child unable to identify the visual topographical representation as a map. A lesion in the tertiary area might cause the child not to recognize the significance of the situation if he or she was to act inappropriately.

To summarize, for those of you who like computer analogies, block I turns on the brain (arousal, consciousness, activation of cortical function), block II sorts, records, codes, and processes information, and block III formulates programs of behavior and executes the programs.

NEURODEVELOPMENTAL ISSUES

Plasticity

For quite some time, scientists and practitioners thought of children as having brains that were resilient and could readily adapt and reorganize after injury. The term for this is commonly referred to as "plasticity" (Kennard, 1942).

To summarize, it was felt that the younger the injured brain, the greater the preservation of function and the better the outcome. The reason for this is that a younger brain is less mature and specialized in function and more likely able to take over for damaged areas. Since not as much of the young brain is committed to specific functions, it is more flexible or plastic (capable of being molded) than an older brain.

While it may seem that older brains do not fare as well following cerebral insult as younger brains, Lehr (1990) points out a significant body of evidence indicating that the role of plasticity in early brain damage is contradictory, and that there are factors such as age at onset, insult occurring during a critical period of development, lesion size and location, and pre and postonset experiences that determine the degree of plasticity.

Singer (1992) reports that children may be just as vulnerable to consequences of brain damage as adults, but that it may take much longer for the effects of brain damage to be appreciated. It is this author's experience that it is not uncommon to see late manifest deficits which can be correlated with brain injury in the perinatal period or young childhood.

Young children with neuropsychological deficits may present with a subclinical or asymptomatic picture until there is a demand for more complex, integrated processing. In the absence of clear-cut neuromotor deficits, and the presence of less conspicuous symptoms of inattention, learning problems, and physical and behavioral overreactivity, a child's neuropsychological impairments may go unappreciated or misunderstood. The need for thorough long term serial assessment is indicated.

Perinatal Maturation

Even before the birth of the child, he or she is subject to faulty neurodevelopment at the structural level. Briefly, common anomalies are: (1) abnormal growth in the size of the brain (usually associated with mental retardation), (2) malformation of the cortex (e.g., few and coarse gyria or folds in the brain often associated with severe retardation), (3) malformation associated with hydrocephalus (e.g., obstruction of the aqueduct that allows for CSF circulation often resulting in learning and behavioral problems with lower perceptual functioning compared to verbal skills), and (4) anomalies of the neural tube (e.g., spina bifida, a protrusion of the spinal cord and meninges through a defect in the bony encasement of the cord not infrequently resulting in more subtle intellectual and perceptual deficits) (Hynd and Willis, 1988).

CNS compromise can occur during the perinatal period. For example,

Emory (1991) points out one of the most common causes of nonprogressive neurological deficit in children is perinatal hypoxia or hypoxic-ischemic perinatal brain injury (oxygen deprivation). From a developmental standpoint, perinatal hypoxia in the full-term infant seems to affect primarily the cortex while insult to premature infants seems to have a locus of damage at the subcortical level, including the tissue surrounding the ventricles and the brainstem.

The practical utility of looking into perinatal maturational factors is that term-injured infants seem to fare worse in terms of exhibiting signs of attention deficit, hyperactivity, and learning disability, while preterm infants seem to fare worse in terms of motor disability and more global impairment. Careful review of perinatal history in children who demonstrate subtle deficits can produce data that has significant diagnostic, treatment, and educational implications.

Neurodevelopment

Overall, neurodevelopment parallels rather closely the work of Piaget and Inhelder (1969). Golden (1981) has enhanced the discussion of neurodevelopment of the child from the standpoint of brain behavior relationships, while authors such as Ewing-Cobbs and Minor (1989) and Lehr (1990) have discussed the impact of injury at different stages of brain maturation. While specific descriptions vary, the concepts are similar.

The Infant

The world of the infant is alive with rapid organized development of sensory capabilities, perceptual and attention skills, primary motor competence, and social responsiveness. Unlike the writings of the British philosopher John Locke (1690) and the American psychologist William James (1890), the infant is neither a blank tablet on which the pen of experience writes nor a helpless organism assailed by a bundle of chaotic sensory experiences.

The newborn develops competence in visual accommodation, visual acuity, auditory discrimination for pitch and loudness, selection and filtering of visual and auditory stimuli (e.g., attention based on brightness, movement, pattern), attenuation of cry, selective discrimination and response to human voice. Regulation of feeding, sleep, temperature, and elimination develop. Physical maturation proceeds in a proximodistal direction (i.e., the child learns motor control of his or her body from the center to the periphery).

This is a period of maturation of the arousal unit (brainstem) which is nearly fully complete by 12 months of age. While the four major regions of the brain show synchronous development, the early stages of development are specifically characterized by an orderly sequence in which primary motor and sensory areas of the brain (motor area located just anterior to the central sulcus; sensory area just posterior to the central sulcus) gain competence, followed by development of the primary visual area at the back of the head in the occipital lobe, and the primary auditory area at the side of the head in the temporal lobe. This is also a period when the cells of the motor and sensory system develop a sheath of myelin (myelination) which keeps the transmission of nerve impulses channeled along neural fibers and reduces the random spread of impulses from one neuron to another.

Preschoolers

The child at the level of primary zone development can control basic body movements and can hear and see. However, before the child can perform more complex behaviors such as coordination of movement, visual and auditory recognition, and form associations between words as symbolic representations of objects and actions, the secondary association areas of the cortex must develop and the hemispheres differentiate into verbal and nonverbal systems. This continuation of cortical development enables the two year old to integrate information from the environment and his or her own movements into more complex patterns of behavior. The preschool child can be viewed as making the shift from "sensing" to "knowing" from "prespeech" to words, and from gross to fine motor skills.

Lesions to the brain during these early developmental periods can have very damaging immediate and far reaching consequences. Skills undergoing rapid change at the time of injury are usually quite impaired (Fletcher, 1987). Because of the rate of rapid change, the prognosis in infants and toddlers is more unfavorable than in school age children and adolescents. In young children, interference in the development of primary and secondary association areas may seriously alter the child's basic ability to accurately register sensory data, perceive the data's meaning, and translate it into speech and other motor activity. Even more seriously, childhood brain injury can not only alter or interrupt, but can also halt key stages of cerebral development (Allison, 1992). As discussed earlier in this chapter, the true extent of the functional disability following brain injury may not manifest itself until that part of the brain that was damaged is challenged for development of a required skill complex.

Childhood

School-age children make a gradual shift towards abstract thinking, becoming less dependent on concrete, real life, sensory, and stimulus bound material for learning new concepts. Piagetian concepts such as relational thinking (rearranging a row of candies does not affect their number) begin to emerge (Piaget and Inhelder, 1969). Thinking starts changing from artificialisms (*the moon followed me home*) to physical causality (*the moon spins around the earth*). School-age children rapidly master more complex physical activities and develop more sophisticated networks of neighborhood and community social relationships. From the viewpoint of Luria's model, this is period of tertiary cortical development where the brain "links up" the perceptions of auditory, visual, and tactile sensations which underpin the learning of reading, writing, arithmetic, causal reasoning, problem solving, and complex spoken language.

Lesions to the brain during this period may not only produce serious and persistent intellectual deficits, but lay the child bare to the onset of behavioral disorder, social ostracism, special education placement, and fragmentation of a fragile and emerging self-concept and self-esteem. On the brink of the child's final journey towards independence and self direction, he/she can be thrown into confusion and chaos that he/she does not have the cognitive or personality-based resources to emerge from. The child has the ability to process that something terrible has happened to him/her, but lacks the skills and stored experiences to appreciate the nature of the injury and what it will encompass to recover. It is at this stage of development that the emotional impact of the psychological and physical sequelae of brain injury is first felt and understood.

Adolescence

While later childhood saw the organization of the tertiary zones of the sensory unit (block II), adolescence gives testament to the development of the tertiary areas of the prefrontal lobes. Beginning at about age 13, this neurodevelopmental period continues into early adulthood.

There is a striking difference between childhood and adolescence that is well illustrated in the psychological response to injury: the child knows something terrible has happened; the adolescent asks "why?".

There is a change in thinking from concrete to hypothetical. There develops more complex problem-solving skills, mental flexibility, planning, monitoring of one's own thinking, self-regulation, and consideration of long-term consequences of behavior. There develops the ability to appreciate concepts such as honesty, courage, love, and loyalty. Vocational ideas, once couched in terms of myth and stereotype, become more crystallized in light of developing self-concept and appraisal of abilities. Development of self-identity is in full earnest encompassing psychological, social, physical, and sexual areas. Self-definition in terms of "roles" takes on new significance. The developmental challenges of: (1) resolution of dependency versus independence, (2) generation of personal and social goals that match the views of oneself, and (3) integration of expectations and perceptions of others into oneself are met and resolved.

While injury during this neurodevelopmental period seems to produce less pronounced intellectual deficits, neuropsychological disorders are very likely to mimic disorders in social maturation, making it difficult to sort out the nature and basis of problem behavior (Golden, 1981). This is also a period where injuries sustained at earlier neurodevelopmental stages are likely to manifest themselves.

Before leaving a formal discussion of neurodevelopmental factors, one final issue requires attention. Even though neurodevelopment and cognitive development are compatible and progress through fairly orderly stages of events, physical maturation of the brain is not as steady as one might be led to believe. For example, the parietooccipital region of the brain shows its peak development between the ages of one to six. However, maturational peaks continue over the next 15 years. Similarly, the frontotemporal region shows accelerated development during the age periods of one to five, slower maturation from ages seven to 10, and rapid maturation between ages 15 and 21. The temporal region of the brain matures rapidly ages one to six and 13 to 17. However, there continues to be a correlation between these variable periods of actual physical maturation and cognitive development (Hudspeth, 1992).

MECHANISMS OF INJURY

In infants and children, there are a multitude of factors and disorders that may account for impaired neuropsychological functioning. For example, detrimental prenatal influences on patency of brain function may be parental drug addiction, fetal alcohol syndrome, maternal malnutrition, maternal infection such as herpes and rubella, fetal AIDS syndrome, intraventricular hemorrhage, and exposure to teratogens. Unwanted birth events may be prematurity, low birth weight, birth trauma, and perinatal asphyxia. Adverse neonatal disorders might be respiratory distress syndrome, bronchopulmonary dysplasia, floppy baby syndrome, failure to thrive, exposure to teratogens and toxins, seizure disorder, hypothyroidism, and hydrocephalus. Examples of genetic disorders are Trisomy 21, Fragile X, Cri du chat syndrome, and Wilson's disease. Examples of infections and diseases that can affect neuropsychological functioning are meningitis, neoplasms, chronic otitis media, encephalitis, intracranial abscess, cytomegalovirus, toxoplasmosis, and allergies. Closed, crush, and penetrating injuries to the head are examples of traumatic brain injuries that can result in neurological impairments.

Children with behavioral and developmental disorders can exhibit neuropsychological deficits. Examples are ADHD (attention deficit-hyperactivity disorder), autism, seizure disorders, specific learning disabilities, conduct disorders, affective and anxiety disorders, and childhood schizophrenia. Additionally, psychoactive substances such as seizure medications, antidepressants, neuroleptics, and ADHD medications can alter neuropsychological functioning. While often not recognized as psychoactive, many cold and allergy medications, over the counter as well as prescription, contribute to attention and processing problems. Now readily available in many primary grade schools, illicit substances should not be overlooked when exploring and understanding neuropsychological impairment.

In-depth discussion of all mechanisms responsible for impaired neuropsychological functioning is well beyond the scope of this chapter. However, the more commonly encountered sources of acquired brain injury will be reviewed.

Traumatic Brain Injury

Trauma to the brain is a leading cause of death and morbidity in the United States. The National Pediatric Trauma Registry (NPTR) (DiScala, 1991 and 1992) reports alarming statistics for the period October 1988 through October 1990. In the age group birth to 19, on an annual basis, 7000 children die, 150,000 are hospitalized, and 29,000 are permanently disabled.

Overall, boys are almost twice as likely than girls to be injured. Injury rates, by age, peak between 15 and 19 years of age for both sexes, steadily declining thereafter to about age 60. It is estimated that the cumulative risk of brain injury for children through age 15 is about 4 percent for boys and 2.5 percent for girls (Pipitone, 1992).

The NPTR reports that blunt trauma in the P.M. hours continues to be the major component of injuries affecting children. However, there has been a recent increase in the incidence of penetrating missile injuries (gunshot wounds), 70 percent of which are intentional. This finding certainly reflects the experience of the author at Rancho Los Amigos Medical Center, where a significant number of gang-related gunshot wound patients are rehabilitated.

In the NPTR sample, 26 percent of brain injuries were related to falls, 18 percent MVA's (motor vehicle accident: 60 percent of all injured children were not restrained by seatbelt or car seat), 17 percent pedestrian, bicycle 8 percent, stabbing and gunshot wounds 5 and 5½ percent respectively, 1 percent motorcycle and ATV (all terrain vehicle) each, and about 18 percent from other causes. The highest mortality was associated with gunshot wounds followed in order by beatings (child abuse), pedestrian, and MVA. In children, limited to the birth to five age group, child abuse accounted for about 18 percent of all injuries.

Aside from neurodevelopmental issues previously discussed, the question arises: Why is brain injury so devastating? After all, if you are struck only in the back of the head and suffer a localized subdural hematoma (a bleed occurring between the dura mater and membranes covering the brain itself), why is there such serious impairment? When the author first began treating people with brain injury, there was no CT scanning, but there was a general (and false) belief that injuries were much more localized than they actually were. In fact, traumatic brain injury subjects the brain to at least four mechanisms of injury producing a number of sites of insult resulting in diffuse brain damage.

When the brain strikes an object, for example, the dash of a suddenly stopped auto or the pavement beneath the wheels of a moving bicycle, there is a primary site of initial impact, for example, the forehead. However, in a split second, the head is thrown backwards with the brain violently compressing against the back of the head. This is known as the coup-contrecoup effect, leaving both localized anterior and posterior portions of the brain damaged. However, that is only the beginning. Once the brain is set into violent motion, catastrophic consequences occur.

Since the brain is "attached" at the brain stem, during impact it does not simply move anterior to posterior on a straight even plane. As the brain moves, there is a rotational shearing effect that tears blood vessels and white matter while causing shearing strains throughout the entire brain. As the brain slides against the bony rough prominences at the base of the skull, the inferior aspect of the brain is subject to further tearing and laceration.

Because of the massive strain put on the brain stem, it too, hemorrhages. Swelling and pressure rapidly build inside the unforgiving confines of the skull, causing structures in the brain to compress, inflicting further damage. As pressure continues to increase, cerebral blood flow is compromised, causing generalized and wide spread damage. Even in mild traumatic brain injury, there are a multitude of small, sometimes microscopic, lesions throughout subcortical structures causing significant changes in attention and cognition.

Hypoxic-Ischemic Encephalopathy

The normal brain depends on the constant availability of oxygen and glucose for energy production. The supply of these two substances and other cofactors depends on adequate cerebral blood flow. Any event that interferes with this process places the patency of the brain at great risk secondary to cerebral tissue damage that could be permanent.

The brain is very vulnerable to even brief interruptions of blood flow or oxygen because it possesses no reserves or nutrients of its own and because of its very high rate of metabolism. If the brain's oxygen supply is insufficient (hypoxic) because of decreased delivery (deficiency in the amount of blood perfusing the brain, i.e., ischemia) and/or decreased availability (ventilation difficulties, i.e., asphyxia), consciousness is quickly lost. If oxygen deprivation lasts longer than one to two minutes, encephalopathy (disturbed brain function resulting in altered consciousness, behavioral changes, or seizures) may persist for hours or permanently. Total ischemic hypoxia lasting longer than four minutes results in severe irreversible brain damage (Parke, 1990). In the neonate, perinatal asphyxia is a leading cause of hypoxic-ischemic encephalopathy. In children, major causes are near drowning, choking, and suffocation. Subacute chronic hypoxia, as occurs in congestive heart failure, anemia, or pulmonary or obstructive airway disease, may also cause encephalopathy.

Perinatal Asphyxia

Neonatal hypoxic-ischemic injuries are due to intrauterine or intrapartum asphyxia in 90 percent of instances, and when clinically present at birth (alterations in alertness, muscle tone, respiration; irritability and feeding difficulty; high-pitched cry and tremulousness; seizure), reflect significant central nervous system insult (Volpe, 1987). Clinical symptoms that persist beyond the first week of life foretell a future of serious outcome 20 to 30 percent of the time. If there are persistent seizures and neurological abnormalities, 70 percent will be handicapped (Levine, 1983). While there is variation based on whether the infant is premature or full-term, periventricular and intracerebral hemorrhage may be seen as complications which could further compromise outcome.

Utilization of the Apgar score (measures of appearance, pulse, grimace, activity, and respiratory effort; maximum of two points for each measure, a score of 10 being the maximum; Ehrenkranz, 1990) as an index of cardiorespiratory and central nervous system well-being in the neonate is generally accepted (Levine, 1983). Menkes (1990) reports that the Apgar score has been used to measure the severity of initial hypoxic-ischemic insult, and that Apgars taken at one and five minutes may imply hypoxic insult, but that value of doing so may be limited. However, Menkes (1990) does note that extended Apgars taken at 10 and 20 minutes hold value in predicting neurologic outcome.

Drowning

Submersion injuries are second only to motor vehicle related injuries as a cause of death for persons over the age of five. The nonboating drowning death rate is highest for children one to two years of age with one-third occurring in swimming pools (Wilson, 1990). Native Americans, the poor, and rural residents have the highest overall drowning rates. The rate for blacks is twice as high for whites, except for the very young for whom swimming pool drownings are prominent secondary to the availability of pools, hot tubs, and spas. Children who survive, referred to as "near drowning" victims, often face life long physical and mental handicap.

There are several factors such as duration of anoxia, length of coma, age of the subject, and body temperature, that determine the extent and permanence of cerebral anoxia secondary to near drowning. Secondary factors of cerebral edema (swelling) and increase in intracranial pressure are additional mechanisms of injury. Areas of the brain most sensitive to anoxia are the middle cortical areas of the occipital and parietal lobes, the hippocampus, caudate nucleus (basal ganglia), and cerebellum.

Cerebral Palsy

Infants who have suffered perinatal asphyxia or other birth trauma may experience various sequential changes of muscle tone and an abnormal evolution of postural reflexes. Most often, a gradual change occurs from generalized hypotonia (diminished tone of the skeletal muscles; diminished resistance to passive stretching) to periods of spasticity (increased abnormal muscle tone with heightened deep tendon reflexes). This group of motor disorders arising from brain lesions typically in the cerebral hemispheres, brain stem, and cerebellum, is collectively called cerebral palsy (CP). There are four major types of CP. Spastic CP is characterized by tense, contracted muscles. Extrapyramidal CP presents with uncontrolled, abnormal movements. Hypotonic CP is demonstrated in generalized muscular laxness or loss of muscle tone. Mixed forms of CP typically are present with a mixture of spasticity and extrapyramidal movements.

Intellectual impairment is often severe in children with spastic quadriparetic CP. Children with spastic diplegic CP fare better, with one study showing a little more than half having IQ's above 70 (Veelkin, 1983). Ingram (1964) reported that in these cases, the more severe the motor deficit, the greater the intellectual impairment.

In a considerable number of children with extrapyramidal CP, delayed language development and gross motor handicaps can cause underestimation of intellectual capacity (Menkes, 1990). In a study by Crothers and Paine (1959), 65 percent of children with extrapyramidal CP had IQ's over 70 with 45 percent 90 or better. Kyllerman (1982) found 78 percent of such children to have IQ's 90 or higher. CP children are not uncommon in special education programs and their intellectual potential should not be underestimated.

Meningitis and Encephalitis

Meningitis

Meningitis is an inflammation in the layers or membranes (meninges) of the CNS caused by bacteria, fungi, or viruses. Hemophilus influenzae is the leading cause of meningitis in the United States, resulting in 8,000 to 11,000 cases annually. Meningitis caused by Hemophilus influenzae occurs almost exclusively in children under age six and is the most common form of bacterial meningitis in this age group (Menkes, 1990). Green and George (1979) report that in all forms of bacterial meningitis, about 80 percent of cases are pediatric.

Signs and symptoms of meningitis are fever, headache, nausea and vomiting, nuchal (back of the neck) and spinal rigidity, altered mental state, convulsions, cranial nerve palsies, and in some cases, cerebellar ataxia. Diagnosis is by examination of CSF (cerebral spinal fluid). Potentially severe complications are ventriculitis (infection of the ventricles), hydrocephalus, and subdural effusion (escape of fluid and cellular debris). Electrolyte disturbances may be present and there may be a recurrence of meningitis.

Prognosis depends on four factors (Smith, 1988). They are: (1) nature of the infectious agent, (2) age of patient (younger children do poorer than older children), (3) duration of symptoms before diagnosis and institution of treatment, and (4) type and amount of antibiotic used. In a review by Dodge and Swartz (1965) of major complications, mental retardation, seizures, and bilateral deafness occurred with the highest frequency. Sell (1983) reported long-term sequelae of bacterial meningitis in children as 15 to 27 percent language delay, about 10 percent hearing impairment, 10 percent intellectual deficits, 2 to 8 percent seizures, 3 to 7 percent motor impairment, and 2 to 4 percent visual impairment.

Encephalitis

Encephalitis is a term that describes an inflammatory condition of the brain. It can be acquired pre or postnatally. The inflammation is largely caused by infection from three groups of viruses known as arboviruses (arthropod borne), herpes viruses, and enteroviruses (viruses from the intestinal tract) (Tsai, 1990). However, encephalitis may be indirectly related to vaccination and various childhood infections such as measles, mumps, and chicken pox. Incidence of encephalitis in the United States is about 1,400 to 4,300 cases annually (Ho and Hirsch, 1985). Adler and Toor (1984) note that up to 50 percent of acute cases of encephalitis have no known cause.

Of greatest significance in the United States are the arboviruses that give rise to California, St. Louis, western equine, and eastern equine encephalitis (Weil, 1990). California encephalitis is a relatively mild disease with low mortality and low incidence of permanent neurologic residual. However, in some cases, there may be late problems with development of personality characteristics similar to organic hyperkinetic syndrome. St. Louis Encephalitis is of intermediate severity between California and equine encephalitis. In equine encephalitis, damage is seen in the basal ganglia and cerebral white matter with foci of demyelination and necrosis. In the eastern form of equine encephalitis, the mortality rate is about 60 percent in children under 10 years of age (Johnson, 1982). Severe outcomes are reported such as mental retardation, motor dysfunction, deafness, and seizures.

Intracerebral Abscess

An intracerebral abscess is an encapsulated area of infection within the brain. Infection can spread from a variety of sources or from an adjacent infection (e.g., otitis media mastoiditis). The cause is often unknown but seems to occur most often in children four to seven years of age. Symptoms are usually associated with the effects of increased intracranial pressure and expanding space occupying lesion. Early signs are fever, headache, nausea, and vomiting. Examples of neurological deficits are hemiparesis, visual disturbances, and ataxia. Residual effects may be seizures, cognitive impairment and hydrocephalus. Kaplan (1985) reports that about one-half of patients have no residuals and about one half have mild to major sequela with one quarter mild and one quarter severe.

Cerebrovascular Disorders

Cerebral vascular disorder (CVD) describes a disruption of brain function arising from a pathological condition related to blood flow in the blood vessels. CVD is relatively rare in children. High end estimates range from 26 to 53 per 100,000 children per year. The most common causes of CVD in children are cardiac disease (cyanotic heart disease), vascular occlusion (arterial and venous occlusive disease), sickle cell anemia, and intracerebral and subarachnoid hemorrhage secondary to arteriovenous malformation. Occlusive conditions or blockages result in cerebral infarction where blood supply to an area of the brain is blocked because of a clot or severe heart failure. Hemorrhage results in disruption of blood flow because of spilling of blood into the cerebral tissue surrounding the compromised blood vessel. The most common time of occurrence of CVD in children is in the first two years of life (Millikan et al., 1987).

Clinical presentation of CVD depends on a number of factors such as cause or pathogenesis, type of lesion (e.g., nonhemorrhagic infarct, hemorrhage), site of lesion, and size of lesion. In the early stages, prognosis is related to the size of the lesion. Signs and symptoms of CVD are of wide diversity and correspond to the artery or arteries sustaining abnormal or disrupted blood flow. Examples of symptoms are homonymous (corresponding) visual field deficits, contralateral impairment of sensation and motor function, constructional apraxia, neglect, denial of symptoms, language deficits including receptive and expressive aphasia, agraphia, alexia, and acalculia, motor disorders of speech, ataxia, diplopia and nystagmus, dysphagia (difficulty swallowing), and mutism.

Childhood Leukemia

Cancer in children is a rare but particularly tragic and devastating disease accounting for about 6,000 cases per year as opposed to about 900,000 for adults (Fernbach, 1990). Of childhood cancer, leukemia accounts for about 2,500 new cases per year. A form of neoplastic (abnormal growth) disease, leukemia is characterized by a proliferation of abnormal white blood cells inhibiting formation of normal blood cells. In order from highest frequency of occurrence to lowest, symptoms are fever, pallor, bleeding, bone and joint pain, abdominal pain, anorexia, and fatigue. While leukemia is primarily a disease of bone marrow and blood, it does have systemic effects that lead to central nervous system (CNS) consequences.

In the past, CNS leukemia was rare since patients usually died before CNS signs became apparent. Weinstein (1986) reports that few children present with CNS leukemia at the time of diagnosis. However, the CNS can become a leukemic focus capable of reseeding other sites after a period of hematologic remission. Menkes (1985) notes this may be related to poor infusion by most cancer toxic drugs across the blood-brain barrier.

As one might anticipate, the psychological consequences of childhood leukemia are overwhelming. The child, faced with a painful, often recurring, and potentially fatal disease, is beset by a cadre of psychological, social, familial, and psychoeducational problems and stressors. However, there are also potential serious neuropsychological consequences that relate to the effects of treatment, especially CNS irradiation. Hynd and Willis (1988) point out possible deleterious effects of chemotherapy and radiation on such variables as intellectual ability, academic performance, attention, and memory.

Childhood Tumors

Intracranial tumor, or neoplasm (abnormal growth), is a mass of cells resembling those cells normally present in the body, but arranged in an atypical fashion which grow unchecked and at the expense of the individual without serving any functional purpose (Walsh, 1987).

Second only to childhood leukemia, brain tumor is one of the most common neoplasms occurring in children under age 15 (Menkes, 1985). While intracranial tumors may be benign or malignant, unfortunately, benign tumors are much less frequent than the malignant type which invade and destroy brain tissue. Benign tumors usually grow from the coverings of the brain and are therefore referred to as meningiomas. They are often slow growing and may become quite large before causing symptoms. They are often successfully treated with surgery since they do not invade brain tissue. Most malignant tumors arise from glial or supporting cells, the most common type being the glioma. Gliomas are termed "primary" since they begin in the brain itself. Tumors are termed "secondary" when their site of origin is in other parts of the body such as the breast or lung. Secondary tumors are also called metastatic tumors.

Immediate effects of tumors are seen as neurological symptoms caused by direct involvement of neural tissues. Secondary effects are seen as the result of tumor interference and disruption of functional systems. Tertiary effects are seen secondary to increase in intracranial pressure.

Signs and Symptoms

In pediatric oncology, the most common tumors are located in the cerebellum and fourth ventricle (Hynd and Willis, 1988). Common symptoms are headache and vomiting secondary to increased intracranial pressure, and cerebellar signs such as unsteady and wide-based gait, postural changes, changes in speech expression and mechanics of writing, and intention tremors (tremors that become worse when a voluntary action is attempted). Since the recurring symptom picture of headache and vomiting often suddenly disappears, it may be mistaken for manifestation of childhood anxiety disorder. Additionally, anorexia and weight loss associated with these tumors may be erroneously associated with a psychiatric eating disorder.

Brainstem tumors, which have a very poor prognosis, are associated with vomiting, cranial nerve deficits, gait abnormalities, and spastic hemiparesis, and progress to expressive language deficits, paralysis, coma, respiratory failure, and death. Visual impairments, abnormalities of the endocrine system, and visual and olfactory hallucinations are symptomatic of brainstem tumors while seizures and psychiatric disturbances are common in cerebral tumors.

ASSESSMENT OF SEVERITY

Measures of Severity (MOS)

Given the relative recency of brain injury research into MOS, clinicians and researchers have been quite prolific in the area of traumatic brain injury (TBI) in providing methods and guidelines to assess severity of brain injury.

Coma and duration of posttraumatic amnesia (PTA) are common MOS. Coma is typically defined as not obeying commands, not uttering recognizable words, and not opening the eyes. To quantify these aspects of coma, and subsequently severity of injury, in a manner that could be objectively used in a variety of settings (scene of injury, emergency room, acute hospital, post acute and outpatient settings), Teasdale and Jennett (1974) developed the Glasgow Coma Scale (GCS).

Coma Scales

The GCS measures the depth of coma obtained by grading eye opening, best motor response, and best verbal response on a scale of 3 to 15. In other words, the total GCS score is equal to the total of the three categories of response. Through the use of the total score, the severity of injury, as measured by loss of consciousness, can be quantified. A score of 3 to 8 indicates severe injury. A score of 9 to 12 indicates moderate injury, and a score of 13 to 15 indicates mild injury. In the acute stages of injury, the GCS is most effective as an index of severity. The lowest score maintained for six continuous hours during the first 24 hours is a useful rule of thumb in making early measurements.

There are some problems with the GCS. First, it does not differentiate well at the milder levels of impairment. Second, it may not be particularly suited for children. Winogron (1984) found that 30 percent of severe injuries were misclassified as mild. Third, the verbal response part of the GCS is clearly not appropriate for young children, and in older children, may reflect fear secondary to hospitalization. However, the use of sounds in place of words for best verbal response may overestimate the child's ability (Lehr, 1990).

For children three and younger, Hanh (1992), with the help of pediatricians and neonatologists at Children's Memorial Hospital, Chicago, developed a children's coma scale. Categories of responsiveness are the same but defined in different terms. For example, best verbal response scores the child's ability to smile, orient to sound, and interact. These behaviors would earn the child full credit or five points. If the child was crying and consolable, but interacting inappropriately, the response would be scored a four.

Inconsistently consolable and interacting with moaning or irritability would earn a score of three and so on. The range of coma scores remained three to 15.

Raimondi and Hirschauer (1984) also developed a children's coma scale. A primary difference in this scale is that it utilizes behaviors and physiological signs that are not dependent on examiner stimulation, but could be passively observed. Categories of responsiveness are ocular response, verbal response, and motor response. For example, for best verbal response, crying receives a score of three, spontaneous respirations receives a score of two, and being apneic receives a score of one. The range of coma scores on this scale is three to 11.

Yet another measure of severity in children is the Neonatal Arousal Scale (NAS) (Duncan, 1981). Categories of responsiveness on the NAS are best response to bell, best response to light, and best motor response. The range of total scores on the NAS is three to 15.

Posttraumatic Amnesia (PTA)

PTA is commonly understood as the period of recovery from coma that extends forward in time until memory for ongoing events becomes reliable and accurate. In other words, once the patient "wakes up," PTA is present until the patient can remember today what happened yesterday. Yet this may be difficult to assess, as criteria may vary and may not be as objective as needed.

Length of PTA correlates with severity of brain injury and has value in predicting degree of disability. PTA's less than one hour indicate mild severity of injury. PTA's of one to 24 hours suggest moderate severity of injury. One to seven days indicates severe injury, and PTA's greater than seven days indicates very severe injury (Jennett, 1976). In adults, return to work (RTW) and PTA are related. For example, patients with mild PTA returned to work within one month, moderate PTA within 2 months, severe PTA within four months, PTA greater than one week within one year, and PTA greater than 2 weeks, never.

Annegers (1983) developed an MOS combining loss of consciousness (LOC), PTA, and extent of injury. From least severe to most severe, his classification system is as follows. A rating of mild was given if LOC and PTA were less than 1/2 hour and there was no skull fracture. A moderate rating was divided into moderate with fracture and moderate without fracture. Moderate with fracture was defined as linear or basal skull fracture with or without documentation of loss of consciousness. Moderate without skull fracture was defined as LOC or PTA greater than 1/2 hour. A severe rating was defined as intracranial hematoma, brain contusion, or LOC or PTA greater than 24 hours. The last rating was "fatal" if death was within 28 days of injury.

As with the GCS, the measurement and meaning of PTA in children is problematic. Children do not remember day-to-day events as adults do. In younger children, memory development may not have progressed to the point to allow for retrospective and prospective thinking. Children tend to be very "here and now" and not very good historians. Even with older children, PTA can be problematic, particularly in mild brain injuries since the period of amnesia is too short or unmemorable. Effects of sedatives and CNS depressants may further complicate measurement of PTA.

At the 1989 meeting of the International Neuropsychological Society, Ewing-Cobbs, Levin, Fletcher, Miner, and Eisenberg presented the Children's Orientation and Amnesia Test (COAT) as an indicator of PTA in children, (Ewing-Cobbs et al., 1989). The COAT is composed of 16 items evaluating general orientation, temporal orientation, and memory. Ewing-Cobbs and her coworkers found that COAT scores provided an objective means for monitoring PTA. They also found that the duration of PTA, as defined by serial COAT scores, related to neurological indices of severity of injury and degree of memory impairment at one year post injury. Both PTA and the GCS were found to be significant predictors of memory performance at one year post injury.

Classifications of Severity

Mild Brain Injury

Collectively, the GCS and duration of PTA are widely accepted as fairly accurate MOS of brain injury. GCS of 13 to 15 and PTA of five to 60 minutes indicate mild severity and are related to good outcome with return to prior activity in about 30 days or less. About 75 percent of adult traumatic brain injury (TBI) cases fall into this category, while for children, up to 88 percent are classified as mild (Langfitt and Gennarelli, 1982; Kraus et al., 1986).

In adults, mild brain injury can produce deficits in attention, memory, language, and judgement with variable but short duration of less than six months. However, in some cases, cognitive and behavioral changes may be more resistant, enduring, and disabling. A three-year study at the University of Virginia (Takayama, 1988) found that at one year post mild head injury, 58.8 percent of patients continued to have at least one cognitive, perceptual, or physical complaint. Often misleading inexperienced clinicians, IQ scores can rather quickly return to preinjury levels, while measures of sustained and divided attention and processing speed show impairment. There are also present associated symptoms of no recall of impact, headache, restlessness, irritability, lethargy, decreased stress tolerance, personality changes, and inability to function normally at work or in every day living. Poorly diagnosed and frequently mismanaged, mild brain injury can produce long-term and intractable disability, in part related to the emergence of secondary psychiatric sequelae.

However, in children, methodological problems have produced research that is conflicting regarding the aftermath of mild brain injury (Levin et al., 1989). The definition of mild brain injury has been inconsistent. There have been problems controlling for preinjury and demographic factors and the availability of comparison groups. However, it appears that during initial hospitalization and shortly after discharge, children present with deficits in language, visual/spatial ability, memory, and motor speed. Graphic ability also seems vulnerable to effects of mild brain injury. Of clinical importance, but experimentally confounding, are findings suggesting children with mild brain injury have a higher frequency of preinjury psychological difficulties.

Long-term neuropsychological sequelae have been demonstrated in complex sensory integration, lowered mathematics, and posttraumatic behavior changes. However, it appears that overall, even though some children may have lasting deficits, children with mild brain injury may recover with minimal residual effect, and that recovery can be influenced by parental anxiety regarding injury.

Of major concern to Levin and his co-investigators is the finding that there exists markedly increased risk of a second brain injury in children sustaining brain injury, and that there may be a cumulative detrimental effect. It was also considered that mild brain injury may be the result of decreased attention and psychomotor retardation.

Physiologically, mild brain injury causes diffuse disruptions and stretching on the nerve fibers throughout the brain. The changes in the brain are microscopic and are not readily visualized on CT (computed tomography) or MRI (magnetic resonance imaging). The stretching and disruption of nerve fibers is often referred to as diffuse axonal injury or DAI.

Moderate Brain Injury

Moderate severity of brain injury is defined as a GCS of nine to 12 and a PTA of one to 24 hours. In these cases, there is CT and MRI evidence of injury, increased incidence of brain edema and hematoma, neurosurgical intervention, and other associated injuries. Outcomes are of moderate impairment as indicated by problems in ADL's and other activities out to 120 days post onset. There are often long-term persistent problems in attention, concentration, memory, problem solving, and behavior.

Severe Brain Injury

Severe brain injury is classified as exhibiting a GCS of 3 to 8 and duration of PTA greater than 24 hours. These patients usually require extensive medical support and suffer persistent intellectual impairment, personality changes, and psychiatric disorders. Symptoms include deficits in attention, memory, spoken and written language, sensory and motor skills, planning and judgement, and marked personality changes such as anxiety, irritability, fatiguability, emotional lability, and poor impulse control.

MECHANISMS OF RECOVERY

Mechanisms of recovery may be based on physiological processes, behavioral compensation, and environmental factors.

Physiological Factors

From a biological viewpoint, recovery is directly affected by the nature and size of the lesion as well as the patient's response to medical and surgical intervention. However, at the neuronal level, there are a number of proposed processes that may account for some degree of recovery following brain damage (Kolb and Whishaw, 1985). Examples of these processes are regeneration, rerouting, sprouting, and nerve growth factor. Regeneration is a process in which damaged neurons and axons regrow and establish previous connections. Rerouting in a process by which axons seek out new targets when their normal destination has been damaged or lost. Sprouting refers to growth of nerve fibers to innervate new targets. Nerve growth factor is a protein secreted by glial cells that promotes growth in damaged neurons and facilitates regeneration and reinnervation of cut axons.

Another physiologically based process, already discussed, is plasticity. In essence, plasticity refers to the theory that in the young, the brain can shift functions from damaged to nondamaged areas. In fact, it appears that large focal lesions occurring before age two compensate rather well. A commonly cited example of this is language localizing to a patient's right hemisphere from a damaged left hemisphere. However, the concept comes into greater question in the presence of diffuse injuries.

In older patients, the process of plasticity seems to be one of reorganization/ substitution. This process operates on the premise that not all functions of the brain are forever linked to particular areas of the brain, and that damage to one part of the brain may cause another part of the brain to compensate. Kolb and Whishaw (1985) summarize issues related to reorganization and recovery as follows: (1) Recovery is likely in complex behaviors that are comprised of many components through a process known as behavioral compensation. (2) Recovery is most pronounced with incomplete lesions, such as those commonly following concussion or penetrating wounds. (3) Recovery is unlikely for specific functions controlled by localized brain areas if all of the area is removed, such as in aphasia following cerebrovascular accident.

Behavioral Compensation

Behavioral compensation refers to the learning and use of a new or different behavioral strategy, or the combination of new strategies and old, less impaired, or spared strategies, to compensate for a lost ability or skill complex. For example, the ability to successfully attend school and perform age appropriate activities of daily living is dependent on many behavioral abilities and configurations of those abilities. Brain damage may affect some behaviors more than others but there are many possibilities for compensation.

In the area of cognition, for example, the easily confused child may learn to avoid unstructured and unsupervised situations and closely follow schedules and routines. Existence of memory problems may require the use of a memory log or memory notebook, mnemonics, and unaffected visual abilities such as imagery. Problems in reasoning and thinking may require learning to adhere to formal external problem solving rules and use of psychological techniques such as "What should I do if . . . ; what might happen if . . . ;" and learning to respond to feedback. Reality orientation exercises may need to be practiced and learned. Lists, diaries, notebooks, computer discs, timers, calculators, and special education materials may need to become as common in the child's experience as his/her backpack, pogs, and action figures. Treatment plans that address academic concerns and problems in adaptive behavior need to carefully assess patterns of strengths and weaknesses so that strengths can be used to support improvement of weaknesses.

In the area of socialization, children and adolescents are frequently plagued by difficulties in accurately picking up on social cues, understanding cause and effect relationships, generalizing from one situation to the next, controlling frustration and impulses, and considering past learning and experience. These problems are enhanced and magnified in children who have sustained brain injuries. Learning of behavioral compensation techniques needs to be designed so that the child has an opportunity to: (1) be repeatedly exposed to the consequences of his/her behavior so he/she will remember them, (2) be given clear, direct, and repeated instruction on rules and conventions of age appropriate behavior, and (3) emphasize those positive skills the child does possess to help build self-esteem and compliance with treatment.

The learning of behavioral compensation in children can be especially challenging. Children have fewer ready to use learning skills and strategies, and have fewer old well established skills to draw on. By nature they act on their feelings rather than rationally or practically. They tend to be more irritable and resistant when stressed or tired. Complicating the picture is anxiety brought about by new education placements, unfamiliar settings and routines, difficulty in competing with and keeping up with friends, loss of peers, social isolation, and both overprotection as well as resentment from different family members. Multimodal treatment in the development of behavioral compensation is critical in the recovery process and underpins the child's availability, or unavailability, to other recovery processes.

Environmental Factors

Knippe (1993) identifies environmental factors as a mechanism of recovery and defines these factors from the standpoint of effects of medical management and oversight, appropriate stimulation, and social and educational influences.

Medical

In the last 15 years, there have been significant advances in time of injury on site paramedical emergency services and development of comprehensive trauma center networks for early medical management of brain injuries. Control of medical complications such as shock, edema, bleeding, infection, gastrointestinal and urologic-renal dysfunction, respiratory distress, hydrocephalus, diabetes insipidus, and pain, are obvious factors in recovery. Advances in reconstructive surgery after severe trauma, brain tumor surgery, and surgical and pharmacological management of epileptic seizures now result in improved functional prognosis (Goodrich, 1993) as well as reduction in mortality and morbidity. Advanced diagnostics, such as magnetic resonance imaging (MRI; snaps detailed image of the brain), positron emission tomography (PET; tracks blood flow, a proxy for brain activity), single photon emission computerized tomography (SPECT; tracks blood flow), superconducting quantum interference device (SQUID; picks up magnetic fields, a mark of brain action), and electro-encephalogram mapping (EEG; brain monitoring technique that detects electrical activity), provide indications for medical management, plotting and recording changes related to injury and recovery, and correlation of static structure and dynamic brain function to external measurement of brain-behavioral relationships (Begley et al., 1992).

Appropriate Stimulation

There is a relationship between severity of brain injury and impairment of cognitive functioning (Lehr, 1990). The more severe the injury, the greater the cognitive impairment. While all brain injuries do not necessarily cause cognitive deficits, some degree of impairment will likely be seen in children who are in coma longer than 24 hours. Cognitive abilities commonly disrupted in children with brain injury are control of attention, memory, language, and visual perceptual and visual motor skills. Intervention through appropriate stimulation may affect the courses of cognitive recovery by taking advantage of changes occurring at the neuronal level.

Appropriate stimulation refers to the systematic application of cognitive and behavioral tasks and physical and social activities that: (1) maintain and maximize weak but present cognitive abilities, (2) decrease cognitive excesses (inappropriate behaviors), and (3) compensate for deficient skills by teaching new skills required to function adequately. To be effective, stimulation must be appropriately timed and delivered at the correct complexity and intensity specific to level of consciousness and developmental stage. Overstimulation produces confusion, disorganization, frustration, anxiety, and decreased responsiveness. Understimulation allows for development of behavioral dyscontrol and learning of maladaptive, and oftentimes intractable, patterns of thinking, reasoning, and acting.

Social Influences

It has been said, "the patient is the family, . . . the family is the patient" (Jackson, 1957). Another cornerstone belief of many pioneering family therapists is "the health of the child relates most directly to the health of the parents" (Satir, 1967). In brain injury, these beliefs certainly hold. There are few who would argue against the notion that family functioning is a critical factor in normal growth and development in any child, disabled or not. Research by Rutter (1981), Shaffer (1975), Brown (1981), Brooks and McKinlay (1983), Gerring (1986), and Knippe (1993) shows that psychiatric disorder is more common in brain-injured children coming from divorced homes and in those with emotionally disturbed mothers. Similarly, social disadvantage and parental discord increase risk for child psychiatric problems following brain injury. Premorbid problems increase the likelihood of postinjury emotional disorders.

At the birth of a neurologically-impaired infant, receiving confirmation from the psychologist that the fear of mental deficiency in their child is true, hearing from the neurologist the CT scan shows a tumor, or pacing the emergency room after traumatic brain injury, parents and family are plunged into a series of emotional responses, the final outcome of which are often determined by preinjury family strengths, weaknesses, and conflicts. Shock, anxiety, anticipation, denial, bargaining, anger, and mourning are typical reactions. Families feel helpless, process information poorly, don't sleep well, and suffer disruption of routines and cycles. They blame themselves, blame staff, look for miracles in small and sometimes insignificant or imagined changes in the patient, minimize the extent of damage, and search for the meaning behind the tragedy. They go through periods of elation over change, often to be crushed when the rate of change is not sustained or stops. The parents struggle with mourning the lost promise of a normal healthy child.

Siblings will often hide their anxiety to spare their parents worry. They may fantasize they were responsible through innocently spoken thoughts such as "I hope you get hurt," or "I wish you were gone." Seeing their ill or injured brother or sister may initially frighten them. Absence of parents and new demands of responsibility may cause resentment and anger. Siblings may develop psychosomatic symptoms and fear the same could happen to them. They may also feel the pressure to "fill in" for the injured or ill brother or sister.

As indicated earlier, the preinjury strengths and weakness of the family affect its ability to successfully cope with their child's brain injury. As with individuals, preinjury factors to consider are level of psychological stress and vulnerability, family rules and expectations, division of labor, tolerance for separation and differences, nature of family coalitions and alliances, means of expressing love and affection, community integration and social support, leisure pursuits, economic stability, and presence of psychiatric illness and substance abuse. A knowledge of the family's coping history (1) gives an indication for the development of behavior and emotional problems in the patient, (2) guides effective treatment planning and an opportunity to alter faulty family rules, and (3) serves as one of many prognostic indicators for the patient's recovery.

Education

The immediate months and years following brain injury are critical since this is a period of greatest potential for recovery, as well as a period for the development of maladjusted behaviors and dysfunctional or inefficient cognitive skills and compensatory strategies. Recovery from brain injury is most rapid immediately subsequent to the injury, with recovery slowing after several months time. Continued recovery may take place over a period of many months and even years post injury. The vast majority of school-age children are often back in some kind of educational program within two to three months from date of onset. This is, of course, during the critical and fast-paced period of neurological recovery. While the more severely impaired children do find their way into programs with varying degrees of special education supports, those with mild brain injury (who make up the majority of children with brain injury), may go undiagnosed and be inappropriately placed. For those children returning to school in the immediate weeks and months following discharge from acute rehabilitation, their programs may mistakenly focus on content acquisition (assistance at new learning), rather than continued remediation of processing deficits (addressing problems in attention, concentration, memory, thought organization, and mastery of previously learned information).

This author recalls when rehabilitation specialists implored school placement teams not to view children challenged by brain injuries as mentally retarded, or worse, place them in a category of severe emotional and behavioral disturbance. Of course, the specialists were not much more sophisticated in methods of assessment, treatment, or placement recommendations. There was little research to identify needs, and a slowness to establish school liaisons, inservice education, or plan for the educational needs of patients from the moment they were admitted to acute rehabilitation programs. "School reintegration" was not a term commonly heard and little was known about the pitfalls in traditional psychoeducational assessment of children challenged by brain injury. Fortunately, this picture is changing for the better. Rehabilitation specialists in the field of brain injury are now reaching out into the community and are actively involved in (1) research into unmet educational needs and availability of resources on a state by state basis, and (2) in education and training of school and rehabilitation personnel in models for school reintegration and consultation protocols (Goldberg, 1993).

Passage of Public Law 94-142, the Education of the Handicapped Act (*Federal Register,* 1975) is a landmark masterpiece of legislation that stands as a major turning point in the process of providing necessary educational and support services to all handicapped children. The appropriate application of the Public Law 94-142, now enhanced by the passage of Public Law 99-457 (*Federal Register,* 1986) and Public Law 101-476, the Individuals With Disabilities Education Act (*Federal Register,* 1991), together with the development of models for school reintegration and consultation protocals, must certainly collectively be viewed as a major environmental mechanism of recovery.

Measurements of Recovery (MOR)

In the late 1960s and early 1970s, Hagan, Malkmus, Durham, and other members of the Rancho Los Amigos Medical Center (RLAMC) adult brain injury team developed a clinically derived and behaviorally-oriented description of the stages of cognitive recovery as observed in the moderate to severe brain injury patients at RLAMC. The Rancho Levels of Cognitive Functioning (Hagan et al., 1981) provided a much needed method of describing a patient's recovery course that went beyond the GCS. Probably of even greater value was: (1) that for the first time, the natural course of recovery in moderate to severe head injury was systematically observed and reported, and (2) the brain injury rehabilitation community was provided a common vocabulary and frame of reference from which to evaluate practical progress in these patients.

To briefly summarize, there are eight Rancho Levels: (I) No response to stimulation; (II) Generalized response to stimulation; (III) Localized response to stimulation; (IV) Confused, agitated behavior; (V) Confused, inappropriate, nonagitated behavior; (VI) Confused, appropriate behavior; (VII) Automatic, appropriate behavior; (VIII) Purposeful, appropriate behavior.

During the 1970s, Brink and other members of the RLAMC pediatric brain injury team developed the Levels of Consciousness (Brink et al., 1980). There are three versions of the scale developmentally geared to ages six months to two years, two to five years, and five years and older. There is a Levels of Consciousness Test Manual that accompanies the scales to insure accurate assessment and interrater reliability.

For each age group there are five levels. The six-month to two-year scale is as follows: (V) No response to stimuli; (IV) Gives generalized response to sensory stimuli; (III) Gives localized response to sensory stimuli; (II) Demonstrates awareness of the environment; (I) Interacts with the environment. For ages two to five, level II changes to "Responsive to environment" and level I changes to "Oriented to self and surroundings." For ages five and older, level I changes to "Oriented to time and place; is recording ongoing events."

It is important to note that the adult and pediatric Rancho scales are not empirically derived, are clinically generated from natural observation, and are not designed or intended to predict outcome. However, they are extremely useful in planning treatment and tracking the course of recovery. The Rancho brain injury teams have developed extensive and comprehensive physical, cognitive, emotional, and social treatment regimens that correspond to the Rancho scales (*Head Trauma Rehabilitation Seminar,* 1977, *Rehabilitation of the Head Injured Adult,* 1979, and *Rehabilitation of the Head Injured Adult and Child,* 1982).

OUTCOME ISSUES

Outcome is primarily a discussion about prediction, asking the question, "Does this brain injury impair function, and if so, over time how much improvement can one expect?" Of equal importance, investigation of outcome allows for evaluation of the effectiveness of medical, rehabilitative, and educational treatment, and development of plans for their revision. Consequently, evaluation of outcome is critical to quality assessment and improvement of programs. However, in today's world of managed care, the issue of outcome takes on a chilling practical significance. Regardless of any clinical argument one wishes to lodge on the necessity for a particular treatment, allocation of increasingly controlled and restricted health care dollars will be based on empirical evidence demonstrating that treatment results in quantitatively measurable functional improvement as indicated by outcome. A discussion of outcome is a complex and multifactorial undertaking. Variables related to outcome are numerous. Quality of medical care, rehabilitative and educational programs, and family functioning have an effect on recovery and outcome. However, there are two broad categories of variables specifically affecting outcome. They are injury-related factors and patient-related factors (Golden, 1981; Begali, 1987).

Injury-Related Factors

Diffuse and generalized brain damage (for example, acceleration/deceleration injury, hypoxic-ischemic insult, severe case of infectious disease such as meningitis, spastic CP) is more likely to produce severe behavioral, cognitive, and motor deficits. Open head injury (e.g., missile penetration of the skull) is more focal in nature. While the latter type of injury may produce less generalized intellectual impairment and show faster recovery rate, there is increased risk for seizures. Children requiring surgical management and demonstrating increased intracranial pressure and early ventricular enlargement may demonstrate a more consistent pattern of cognitive impairment. Though often seen as focal because of actual involvement and loss of a specific area of tissue, a tumor may cause more diffuse cognitive impairment. A tumor can result in serious increase in intracranial pressure, causing impairment of other functional systems. Irradiation of tumor site may also contribute to a more diffuse picture. Abscess and stroke typically produce more focal impairment, although stroke may obliterate entire functional systems.

Site of injury produces differential impairment. For example, verbal impairment is associated with left hemisphere lesions while visuospatial deficits are more typically related to right hemisphere lesions. Affective disorders and behavioral abnormalities seem to be more frequent following right hemisphere and frontal lobe damage. Outcome may also be more in peril when damage involves primary zones as compared to secondary or tertiary projection areas. However, neural shock, direct primary and secondary cell damage, edema, compromised blood flow, altered neurotransmitter release, depressed glucose uptake, and changes in electrical activity are examples that illustrate that there is not one single event that can be solely related to depression of function following brain injury. Consequently, there are many variables other than lesion size or location and mechanism of injury that affect outcome following brain injury.

Patient-Related Factors

Although some of the following information has been discussed earlier, it is important to reemphasize it in this discussion of patient related factors. Age, general health and brain integrity, premorbid personality, intelligence, sex, and handedness are individual-based factors affecting outcome.

Age

Because of the complex process of constantly changing neurodevelopmental maturation and specialization, determining age-related outcome following brain injury is a difficult and complicated task. Consequently, research in this area is incomplete and controversial.

As previously stated, there is a long-standing view that young brains do better after insult than older brains. In fact, children do seem to fare better than adults following brain injury in terms of overall mortality and morbidity. However, in terms of neuropsychological outcomes, this may not be the case. For example, in moderate to severe brain injury, young children appear to perform lower than adolescents on measures of intelligence, visual recognition, memory, and written language (Levin et al., 1982; Ewing-Cobbs et al., 1987). It has also been reported that recovery of memory in children following diffuse injury is slower and less complete than for adults (Gaidolfi and Vignolo, 1980). Consequently, children may be more affected by brain damage than adolescents and adults since the continued acquisition of cognitive skills is dependent on memory (Begali, 1987). Brink and her coworkers (Brink et al., 1970), documented the presence of more severe long-term cognitive deficits in younger children than older children. Of course, the study of children, especially infants and preschoolers, is plagued by methodological problems in assessment and emergence of late onset deficits as different areas of the brain and higher levels of cortical integration come into use. Subsequently, there still remains a strong need for long-term longitudinal follow-up into adulthood to more clearly define neuropsychological outcomes in children who have sustained brain injuries.

General Health

A child's overall health and timely achievement of milestones are significant preinjury factors in recovery and outcome following brain injury.

Equally important is integrity of the brain as evidenced by lack of adverse perinatal and medical history, attention deficit-hyperactivity, and learning disability.

Premorbid Personality

A child's psychological reaction to brain injury is a combination of his emotional response to injury and disability, disruption at the neuronal level that directly affects behavioral control, and preinjury personality characteristics.

It is now well understood that preinjury behavior and personality makeup are critical factors in the occurrence of postinjury psychological disorders. Children who were functioning well prior to injury are less likely to develop new disorders than those previously experiencing psychological difficulty. At one year postinjury, Rutter et al. (1983) found that 25 percent of children with no evidence of preinjury psychological disorder developed psychological disorder, while 50 percent of children with preinjury disorder developed a new disorder. Investigations into the preinjury personality characteristics of children with brain injuries demonstrated a higher incidence of attentional, hyperactive, and antisocial characteristics as well as developmental and learning problems. As reported by Ewing-Cobbs and Miner (1989) and Prigatano (1986), posttraumatic behavioral disturbances seem to reflect exacerbation of children's preinjury personalities.

As reported earlier in this chapter, following brain injury, postinjury psychological disorders were found to be associated with premorbid social disadvantage and parental discord and emotional illness. Lehr (1990) defines the combination of preinjury family and social problems as "psychosocial adversity." Psychosocial disorders were found to be frequent in children when severe injury was combined with psychosocial adversity.

Intellectual Factors

Children with stronger intellectual skills and greater fund of learned information seem to fare better following brain injury than their less gifted counterparts (Ben-Yishay et al., 1970; Rourke et al., 1983). This may be the result of having more cognitive resources available after the injury compared to the child starting with fewer intellectual resources. Well learned and mastered concepts and skills may provide some protection against the disruption of brain damage and form a basis for increased responsiveness to cognitive rehabilitation and behavioral compensation.

Sex and Handedness

For adolescents and adults, sex and handedness may influence outcome of brain damage. There are theories that argue there is less lateralization in female brains (Kolb and Whishaw, 1985). Woods (1980) reported males seem to be more susceptible to verbal/performance IQ discrepancies following one-sided lesions. Familial left-handers are thought by some to be less lateralized in function (Luria, 1970; Smith, 1971; Subirana, 1958). For both factors, it may be that damage in a particular location can be compensated for, to some extent, by the remaining system in the undamaged hemisphere. Following this line of thinking, one might be tempted to conclude, other things being equal, that a left-handed female should fare the best following brain injury. This author is not aware of any research confirming this notion.

Measurement of Outcome (MOO)

In 1975, Jennett and Bond developed the Glasgow Outcome Scale (GOS) which focuses on the level of disability after injury. The five-category scale is as follows:

1. *Good Recovery:* Patients at this level are able to be fully independent in all activities of daily living (ADL's). Although mild neuropsychological impairment persists, they are usually able to resume normal occupational and social activities.
2. *Moderate Disability:* These patients are independent in looking after themselves at home and in performing basic ADL's. They can usually use public transportation and may work, although typically at a lower level or sheltered work shop. There are persistent motor problems, neuropsychological deficits, and personality changes that prohibit the patient from performing previous activities.
3. *Severe Disability:* While these patients are usually alert and awake, they are either totally dependent on others, or require ongoing assistance for completion of ADL's. These patients cannot be left alone and require ongoing supervision because of a combination of physical and mental disability. The worst affected in this category often exhibit marked motor impairment and severely restricted mental and communicative ability. Others may be capable of some mobility, communication, and self care, but with constant supervision.
4. *Vegetative:* Patients in persistent vegetative states (PVS) show no evidence of meaningful response to the environment. The patients may be able to open their eyes and show grasp reflex, but do not speak or respond to commands in a purposeful manner. There is also urinary and fecal incontinence.
5. *Death from Injury.*

Much like the Rancho Levels of Cognitive Functioning, the GOS was intended to provide hospitals and institutions a common language for practically describing the behavioral outcome of brain injury patients. However, also like the Rancho scales, the GOS is relatively crude in that it does not measure fine details contributing to disability, recovery, and improvement. But, unlike the Rancho scales, it is empirically derived. The GOS has high utility in making gross behavioral observations regarding outcome and effects of early intervention and management.

The Functional Independence Measure (FIM) (1993) is a scale developed to document severity of patient disability and measure the outcome of acute medical rehabilitation. It is not disability specific and can be used for all patients over age six regardless of etiology of injury or disability.

By design, the FIM includes only a minimum number of categories: (1) self care composed of eating, grooming, bathing, dressing upper and lower body, and toileting; (2) sphincter control composed of bladder and bowel management; (3) mobility composed of bed, chair, wheelchair, toilet, tub, and shower transfer; (4) locomotion composed of walking or wheelchair locomotion and stairs; (5) communication composed of comprehension and expression; and (6) social cognition composed of social interaction, problem solving, and memory. Items in each category are rated on a seven level scale that designates major gradations in behavior from dependence to independence.

The FIM is not intended to incorporate all activities that could be measured, or might need to be for clinical purposes. Instead, the FIM is intended to be a basic indicator of severity of disability that can be administered quickly, objectively, and discipline free, that is, appropriate for use by any trained clinician. Today, most major rehabilitation centers use the FIM and feed the data into a uniform national data bank. As noted in the preceding discussion on managed care, the FIM provides a method for quality assessment and improvement, and is also one factor third party payers can employ to determine allocation of health care dollars. Recently completed is the WeeFIM, a downward age extension of the FIM.

THE CONTINUUM OF CARE

The continuum of care for children who have acquired brain injuries is divided into four phases: (1) prevention; (2) pediatric critical care; (3) primary-organic phase; and (4) secondary-reactive phase. Funding issues are also related to the continuum of care, and are briefly discussed.

Prevention

A discussion on continuum of care would be incomplete without addressing the issue of prevention. This holds especially true in the area of accidental and nonaccidental brain injury. It is brain injury, not the high profile afflictions of AIDS, cancer, or muscular dystrophy, that is the largest disabler of children. In light of the fact that each year, one million children are taken to emergency rooms as the result of accidental and nonaccidental brain injury (Savage, 1993), it is disturbing to find a dearth of funds and programs devoted to parental-child education regarding prevention of brain injury.

Taking center stage in our schools are programs dealing with substance abuse, and more recently, gang prevention. Taking center stage on the 6 PM news is controversy over school-based sex education regarding "safe sex" and prevention of STD (sexually transmitted diseases) and pregnancy. Of course, these topics and programs are of critical importance to the welfare of our children. But what about the silent epidemic of brain injury?

Only recently, for example, has the issue of protective helmets for children riding bicycles come to the forefront, lagging years behind attention given to motorcycle riders. Child restraint systems for automobiles have been around a long time, and some local and state ordinances required health care agencies to educate parents regarding their use. However, motor vehicle accidents involving unrestrained children continue to be a leading cause of brain injury in children. It took until 1994, for the state of California to make it a "traffic offense" to travel the highways with people, oftentimes children, riding freely in the back of pick-up trucks. Similar legislation was recently defeated in Arizona. Very little education exists regarding the severe brain damage that can be caused by shaking a child, which is now termed "shaken baby syndrome."

Near drownings, choking, preventable infection, exposure to neurotoxic substances . . . the list goes on. Just recently, in California, there was debate that children may be receiving unacceptable amounts of pesticides in the fruit and vegetables they eat. The economic factor in the debate outweighed the health risk.

While advances are being made in medical, neuropsychological, and educational understanding and treatment of brain injury children, it is also critical to create awareness and funding opportunities to generate development of models for prevention of brain injury. Networking and link-ups with currently established pediatric prevention programs may provide an avenue for getting the pediatric brain injury epidemic squarely before healthcare providers, insurance carriers, educators, and families. Current excellent cable channel programming that addresses developmental issues in children could provide a forum to discuss brain injury prevention as well as caring for the needs of children with brain injury. At this point, the author is reminded of a currently running advertisement on a network station where a physician from an HMO gives tips for adults on development of wellness behaviors (for example, stress reduction and anger control). However, there doesn't seem to be anything on the airways on tips for prevention of pediatric brain injury. While there are a number of educational posters on brain injury prevention published by the National Head Injury Foundation and The Easter Seals Society, this author has not seen anything in over 50 schools visited in a dozen school districts.

Critical Care Systems

When prevention fails, and injury occurs, acute medical and rehabilitation services become the initial focus in the continuum of care. Because of social, economic, demographic, and political factors, carefully thought out and painstakingly constructed trauma networks have found it difficult to operate, and in some areas has resulted in the withdrawal of individual medical centers from the networks. This is disturbing since under the best conditions, the majority of children who might benefit from pediatric critical care services do not receive them (Savage, 1993).

At the level of acute rehabilitation, only about 2 percent of children discharged from trauma centers are transferred to rehabilitation programs despite the persistence of motor, cognitive, and behavioral problems. Of those discharged to rehabilitation programs, few were specialized and dedicated to pediatrics (National Pediatric Trauma Registry, 1993). Where pediatric brain injury rehabilitation often does occur is within a children's hospital or general medical center on a general medical unit with no clearly defined pediatric brain injury team of trained rehabilitation nurses and therapists. The National Association of Rehabilitation Facilities (NARF) has established a subcommittee to address issues related to the education and training of pediatric rehabilitation specialists, and the Commission on Accreditation of Rehabilitation Facilities (CARF) has created program standards for facilities serving children and their families.

Primary-Organic Phase

The primary-organic phase is characterized by a number of behaviors and mental changes that are most directly related to the extent and severity of brain injury. This period usually spans the time from onset of injury through acute medical care into acute medical rehabilitation. This phase encompasses the behavioral spectrum from coma to fully alert (Pasino, 1983).

As discussed earlier, Joyce Brink and associates (1980) have constructed a five-point scale of increasing Levels of Consciousness which describes changes typically seen during this phase. Children who are medically stable and beginning to show signs of consciousness at level IV (generalized response), may be transferred from acute care to rehabilitation for a trial admission. This trial admission may last from two to four weeks and continued stay in rehabilitation is contingent on measurable functional improvement. Within the rehabilitation setting, two basic symptom pictures are observed. They are traumatic delirium and traumatic dementia (DSM IV, 1994).

Traumatic delirium is characterized by disturbance or clouding of consciousness and is found at Levels of Consciousness IV and III. Common behaviors include restlessness, fluctuating level of alertness, disorientation, increased or decreased psychomotor activity, confusion, and sensory misperceptions. As the child improves, delirium yields to traumatic dementia which is a syndrome of behaviors primarily characteristic of impaired cognition within clear consciousness.

Traumatic dementia spans Levels of Consciousness II and I. Impairment is multifaceted and involves loss of intellect sufficient to interfere with focused and sustained attention, ability to shift attention, memory, judgement, reasoning, problem solving, visuo-perceptual skills, and academics. Other disturbances may be manifested such as hemiparesis (weakness on one side of the body), apraxia (loss of ability to plan and execute previously learned motor movements), spasticity (inappropriate sustained muscle contractures), agnosias (loss of ability to recognize an event through a particular sensory system), aphasia (deficits in language comprehension, formulation, and/or use), dysarthria (cerebellar loss of control over automatic oral activities such as speech, chewing, and swallowing), and visual field deficits such as hemianopsia. Secondary features may include impulsiveness, emotional lability, and exaggeration of preinjury characteristics.

Strategies for care of the child during phase II is a volume unto itself. However, a few key points are presented.

Cognition: The early focus of rehabilitation is to develop the ability to attend to stimuli, sustain attention over time, maintain attention under conditions of interference, and develop or regain the ability to shift from one idea to another. Once achieved, the child can progress to organization and sequencing skills, integration of new information and old learning (semantic memory), analysis and synthesis of increasingly complex tasks, and execution of intention in a planned fashion. The child is also taught to assess the outcome of his/her actions and modify the intention based on feedback. Underpinning the entire process is the rekindling of autobiographical and episodic memory (memory for personal information and personally experienced events), and the redevelopment of working memory.

Each of these processes must be geared to the appropriate neurodevelopmental stage and to measures of severity and recovery.

Behavior: There are a number of misconceptions regarding the behavioral care of children who have sustained brain injury. One is that all behavior is organic. Another is that the child acts or functions like that of a child of a younger age. A common misconception on hospital units is that inappropriate behaviors, especially if the child is an adolescent, are intentional and deliberate. Yet another misconception is that behavioral treatment needs to be aimed at the elimination of "bad" behaviors.

For a child to respond "normally" or "appropriately" to the stress of hospitalization, separation, and injury, he would need to have normal age appropriate cognitive functioning. With that in mind, one will be in a better position to view the child's behavior as a part of his/her medical diagnosis, or at least, exacerbated by the medical diagnosis. With this viewpoint, one would not be surprised if behavioral problems presented themselves.

Often behavior disturbances after brain injury represent inadequate personal and self-regulation skills. This may be seen in disinhibited behavior where there is no understanding of the consequences. A spitting, cursing eight year old is very traumatic to a bereaved parent and perplexing and irritating to a busy nurse. If the behavior is a change from preinjury style or personality, it is likely the result of changes in cognition and learning ability. A child who was by nature cooperative before injury, may appear oppositional afterwards because he does not remember what is said when requests are made. Looking at brain injury behavior from this viewpoint exemplifies the complexity of the problem and that "elimination" of behavior through aversive control or withdrawal of reinforcement may not be a very therapeutic approach.

An effective treatment program for the care of children who have sustained brain injury and who have behavior problems is the functional or frequency model (Kanfer and Saslow, 1969). Behaviors are classified in terms of excesses (inappropriate behaviors), deficits (lack of skills needed to function appropriately), and assets (appropriate, task-oriented behaviors). With behavioral excesses, management is concerned with reducing their frequency and intensity. However, with behavioral deficits, the goal is to use assets to strengthen weak behaviors, and teach the patient to acquire and maintain new behaviors needed for appropriate functioning. The latter approach (strengthening and learning) is the most appropriate to the pediatric rehabilitation setting.

Psychological and Environmental Concerns: In the treatment of emotional problems following brain injury, a major concern is anxiety reduction. Within the rehabilitation setting, a sense of security is fostered by providing a familiar, friendly, and relaxed environment. Liberal visiting hours, wearing of one's own clothes, group activities, favorite toys, pictures, transitional objects, and open space for families to gather with their children are essential in promoting a sense of belonging and comfort. Relaxation of traditional patient-staff boundaries encourages children to venture out onto the unit and test and practice their recovering abilities.

To further reduce anxiety and establish a trusting, less bewildering atmosphere, the child must be regularly assured, regardless of cognitive level, that the stay in the hospital is according to the doctor's plan to get better and that the parents know about it and agree with it. Always introduce the child to whomever will be taking care of him/her. Changes in staff, program, and physical location must be kept to a minimum. Structure, consistency, and predictability reduce anxiety and support cognitive recovery.

Honesty with the child is encouraged. Hospitals are not fun and children should not be told that they are. One should avoid telling a child he/she is going one place when the destination is another. Don't restrain a child's cries of fear or pain, but support him/her and let him/her have these emotions. Don't tell a child you'll be gone a moment, and then not return. Visiting is one of the most important events in a hospitalized child's experience. Ending a visit causes anxiety for both parent and child and parents will go through any number of maneuvers to avoid the pain of parting. It is better to simply reassure the child that he/she will be missed and that you are looking forward to coming back, stating the day and time of return.

Assessment: Assessment of a child is challenging. Developmental differences vary greatly along lines of language, concept formation, previous learning, and ability to cooperate and understand the demands of the testing situation. While older children may be astute and respond well to testing, the egocentric preschooler may show little regard for correct answers and his/her performance.

With children who have acquired brain injuries, administration and evaluation of assessment procedures must take into account neurologic variables, language disability, memory impairment, sensory and motor dysfunction, personality, and cultural factors. Most formal assessment tools were not developed or normed on populations such as individuals with brain injuries, and results may have quite a different meaning for different groups of children. For example, an IQ of 60 in a youngster with mental retardation does not hold the same qualitative or quantitative value as an IQ of 60 in a child with acquired brain injury. Qualitative factors must be taken into account.

Developmental Stage: Knowledge of the developmental level of the child, and what may constitute age-expected behaviors, leads to a fuller understanding of the effects of brain injury. Poor judgement, distractibility, high motor activity, tantrums, regression, and impulsiveness are not only signs of organic disturbance. Twenty-four to forty-eight-month-old children may normally exhibit such behaviors. Five- to seven-year-old children are often oversensitive, occasionally of somber mood, and prone to temper outbursts and excessive reveries. Eight- to ten-year-old children become more aggressive, secretive, and moody. The 11 to 15 year old may show increased irritability, lack of flexibility, and academic slow down.

Postacute Care: As discharge from acute medical rehabilitation approaches, the child is faced with anxiety over separation from therapists and roommates, and stress related to re-evaluations, school planning, and the excitement and anticipation of family and friends. Today, there may be an intermediate step between the acute rehabilitation hospital and home. This is the transitional living center program. This type of program is being used in an effort to move treatment from the sterile clinic site into community settings. By moving children into transitional living settings earlier, there are cost savings, and treatment may be more relevant and appropriate in leading toward full community reintegration. Often, clients will move from residential programming to day treatment (with increased participation in community activities including school), to outpatient services for continued medically necessary therapies.

Secondary-Reactive Phase

The Secondary-Reactive phase spans the time from full community reintegration through the child's remaining years to adulthood. This period is characterized by the child's long-term reaction and adjustment to the cognitive, psychological, motor, social, and academic consequences of head injury. Three aspects discussed are postacute care, educational placement, and postdischarge adjustment (Pasino, 1983).

Educational Placement: This is a topic discussed at great length in subsequent chapters of this text. However, a few comments are in order. Of critical importance, although often taken for granted, is the question of medical diagnosis. As noted earlier, many brain-injured children do not have the benefit of specialized pediatric rehabilitation services. Consequently, one must be alert to whether the medical diagnosis was rendered by the appropriate specialist. Those not routinely familiar with pediatric brain injury may tend to diagnose the presence of motor and orthopaedic problems or obvious behavioral deficits at the expense of more subtle cognitive and psychological disabilities.

Along this same line of thinking, there are potential pitfalls in psychological testing of brain injury children by psychologists and educators not specialized in pediatric brain injury (Ewing-Cobbs and Fletcher, 1987). Here are the main points to keep in mind.

1. State mandated discrepancy scores for special education placement do not hold up when examining children who have sustained brain injuries.
2. Time at testing as measured from date of onset may adversely affect appropriateness of placement.
3. Well learned and acquired knowledge returns more quickly than ability to learn new skills and novel problem solving. Consequently, measures of basic academic skills may not be immediately affected and may present inflated estimates of ability to function.
4. IQ tests tap acquired knowledge and give limited assessment of attention, memory, and new learning skills, and therefore underestimate deficits following brain injury.
5. Especially in younger children, learning problems may be of late onset and subtle.
6. Typical state mandated or state paid assessments are not of sufficient breath and depth to adequately diagnose the psychological status of the child challenged by brain injury.

From a psychoeducational standpoint, the following procedures are recommended in assessment of children who have sustained brain injuries.

1. Take a developmental history.
2. Review the child's health and medical history.
3. Review family, social, and environmental factors.
4. Secure a detailed educational/school history.
5. Review the child's premorbid personality status.
6. Note the results of any previous testing or evaluations.
7. Record the child's test behavior in terms of:
   a. attention span;
   b. ability to follow directions;
   c. goal directedness;
   d. frustration tolerance;
   e. response latency;
   f. ability to shift from topic to topic;
   g. motivation;
   h. need for structure and cuing;
   i. self-monitoring;
   j. handling of failure.
8. Formally assess psychological functioning in terms of:
   a. general intelligence;
   b. attentional skills;

c. memory and learning;
d. language skills;
e. achievement;
f. sensory and motor skills;
g. perceptual and visuo-constructional skills;
h. sequencing and planning;
i. reasoning, problems solving, and abstraction;
j. adaptive functioning;
k. personality and behavior.

Postdischarge Adjustment: As the child challenged by brain injury re-enters home and community, he/she is faced with a myriad of factors that may potentially lead to adjustment problems and psychological dysfunction. While there are many, some of the more significant stresses the child faces are residual problems in thinking and memory, personality and behavioral changes, motor deficits, difficulty in performing self-care activities and preinjury leisure time and social pursuits.

In school, children who are challenged by brain injuries are sometimes not able to return to their former school settings. Confrontation with new teachers, unfamiliar classrooms, loss of friends, new classmates who are often disabled, and school curriculum, schedules, and physical layouts that are not adjusted to meet the particular needs of the child with a brain injury, may result in adjustment difficulties. Friendships are lost as the child challenged by brain injury finds himself/herself unable to compete and remain on an equal footing with peers in academics, social, and recreational endeavors. The child becomes isolated as relationships dwindle to those available within immediate family or adult caretakers.

Parent-child relationships often become confused and strained. Attachment with anxiety seems to replace normal parental responses. Because the parents were faced with serious illness and sometimes near death in their child, they may adopt a response style that stems from anxiety that their child may be hurt or become ill in the future. This leads them to assume overindulgent and overprotective roles to insulate their child against foreseeable or unforeseeable threat. Unfortunately, resentment and conflict often builds in other family members as the child challenged by brain injury becomes the center of attention.

The community may also contribute to adjustment problems. Brain damage continues to inspire discomfort and anxiety in many segments of the population. Individuals with brain injuries are often stigmatized with stereotypical beliefs of mental retardation, irrational and incorrigible behavior, laziness, and dangerousness.

Faced with cognitive, physical, family, school, peer, and community stressors, the ability of the child with brain injury to function is severely taxed and may give rise to abnormal and maladjusted behavior. However, when a child challenged by brain injury exhibits behavioral and social problems, he is often narrowly viewed as manifesting organicity and not appropriate for counseling and psychotherapy. If the problem is severe, sedation may be the treatment. In the school setting, organic diagnoses are particularly difficult for staff, and they often refer children to specialists out of frustration.

However, in the child with brain injury, behavior has psychological as well as neuronal meaning. Keep in mind that perseveration, attention deficits, inflexibility and inability to shift and remain stimulus bound, and problems with oppositional and defiant behavioral are often ways that children express their anxiety and depression.

In the first year following injury, physical and cognitive status often show improvement sometimes giving rise to undue optimism. However, as the child's cognitive ability improves, the psychological condition often worsens with increased risk of development of psychological disorder. The onset of personality and behavioral changes following even minor brain injury is reported by a number of authors (Telzrow, 1978; Costeff et al., 1985; Deaton, 1987; and Gerring, 1986). In younger children, hyperactivity, attention deficit, and aggressiveness may be seen. Older children tend to manifest problems in poor impulse control and difficulty in self-monitoring. Other signs and symptoms observed are learning deficits and academic failure, fatigability, poor motivation, reduced drive, apathy (which is sometimes mistaken as laziness), resistant behavior, heightened irritability, and low frustration tolerance. Onset of affective disorders, secondary to chronic loss in self-esteem and environmental stress, raise the specter further disability.

The phenomena of "competitive regression" (Klonoff et al., 1977), further emphasizes the long-term care required by children with brain injuries. IQ may show good recovery in such children. However, when other measures are studied, an interesting phenomena occurs. On measures of adaptive behavior, not only are brain injured children found to be delayed when compared to peers, but as time goes on, the rate of improvement drops off, causing them to fall further behind. Knippe (1993) reports an example of competitive regression in an eight-year-old girl with a diffuse brain injury sustained at birth. At age six, IQ was measured at 90, and at age eight, a score of 91 was obtained. Measures of adaptive behavior at age six were at about the four-year level. However, in the 24-month period between ages six and eight, adaptive behavior gained only about 15 months instead of 24 months. Thus, while improving, the child was becoming progressively behind her peers. In Klonoff's study examining children with mild head injury, it was found that while neuropsychological measures improved over a one to five year interval, at the five-year point, 25 percent of those children had failed one or more grades or required remedial placement. This finding was in light of the fact that of the 25 percent failing, 70 percent had no premorbid history of school problems.

Systems of Care: The damage postdischarge adjustment problems bring down on the lives of our children poignantly illustrates the need for careful and long-term outpatient follow-up after discharge from acute rehabilitation. Too often, children with brain injuries are discharged from the general children's hospital or medical center back to the care of private physicians. If problems are picked up, the child is sent to a variety of different specialists for assessment and treatment. However, the needs of such children and their families are far too complex to be handled in this piecemeal fashion.

Once behavioral and social problems are identified, the child may be referred to the county or state mental health system, HMO provider network, or private psychologist or psychiatrist, systems which, typically, are poorly equipped to handle the needs of brain-injured children. The existence of resource materials and directories of individual- and organization-based brain injury providers, obtainable through state and national brain injury organizations, may be unknown to parents and general practitioners. Educationally, if the child is referred to a child study team for special education placement, the full spectrum of services provided for by IDEA (Individuals with Disabilities Education Act) may not be understood, available, or fully utilized, especially in terms of writing into the IEP (Individual Education Plan), treatment goals and objectives for remediation of processing, behavioral, and social disorders. However, for children challenged by brain injuries who have physical residuals, physical and occupational therapists, through MTU's (medical treatment units located on the school site), can provide valuable resources in addressing problems in adaptive behavior especially in daily living, social, and behavioral-emotional domains.

In California, Regional Centers provide central points for individuals with developmental disabilities and their families, to obtain or be referred to needed services. Regional Centers provide diagnosis and coordination of resources such as education, health, welfare, rehabilitation, and recreation for California residents. Individual program plans can include educational planning, speech therapy, day care, behavior modification, sensory motor training, state hospitalization, and residential care. Case management and coordination of services is a valuable service of the Regional Center and includes case review at specified intervals. The Regional Center may purchase needed services if there is not alternative source of funding.

A Regional Center is an important resource in the continuum of care underutilized in many brain injury cases. However, children with brain injury, especially those with mild brain injury, may have difficulty qualifying for services because of the oftentimes subtle disabilities and seemingly normal psychometric profiles they exhibit.

As with acute medical rehabilitation, the totality of the child's outpatient care needs are best addressed in the outpatient clinic of an established pediatric brain injury program. Such a program will have a designated team of interdisciplinary rehabilitation specialists who, by nature of their definition as "pediatric," have established liaisons with local school districts, MTU's, Regional Centers, mental health providers, and state and national brain injury organizations. Such a program will also employ a systematic program for school and community reintegration and long term follow-up.

Funding: From experience, pediatric rehabilitation programs will also be better able to advise parents and families regarding the availability of long-term funding sources such as (1) Regional Center in California (or equivalent), (2) CCS (California Children's Services or equivalent), (3) Social Security Disability Income (SSDI), Supplemental Security Income (SSI), and associated medicaid and medicare health insurance programs, (4) independent living and vocational plans through the Department of Vocational Rehabilitation, (5) independent living centers, (6) Victims of Violent Crimes Program, and (7) national organizations such as United Cerebral Palsy Association and Association for Retarded Citizens. The pediatric team can advise the family on each potential funding resource in terms of purpose, eligibility, services provided, how services are obtained, and what mental and physical conditions are accepted.

REFERENCES

Adler, S. and Toor, S. (1984). Central nervous infection. In J. Pellock and E. Myer (Eds.), *Neurological Emergencies in Infancy and Childhood* (pp. 237–256). New York: Harper and Row.

Allison, M. (1992, October/November). The effects of neurological injury on the maturing brain. *Headlines.*

Annegers, J. (1983). The epidemiology of head trauma in children. In K. Shapiro (Ed.), *Pediatric Head Trauma.* Mt. Kisco, New York: Futura.

Begali, V. (1987). *Head Injury in Children and Adolescents: A Resource and Review for School and Allied Health Professionals.* Charlottesville, Virginia: Clinical Psychology Press.

Begley, S., Wright, L., Church, V., and Hager, M. (1992, April 20). Mapping the brain. *Newsweek.*

Ben-Yishay, Y., Diller, L., Gerstman, L., and Gordon, W. (1970). Relationship between initial competence and ability to profit from cues in brain-damaged individuals. *Journal of Abnormal Psychology, 75,* 248–259.

Brink, J., Garrett, A., Hale, W., Woo-Sam, J., and Nickel, V. (1970). Recovery of motor and intellectual function in children sustaining severe head injuries. *Developmental Medicine and Child Neurology, 12,* 565–571.

Brink, J., Imbus, C., and Woo-Sam, J. (1980). Physical recovery after severe closed head injury in children and adolescents. *Journal of Pediatrics, 97,* 721–727.

Brooks, G., and McKinlay, W. (1983). Personality and Behavioral changes after severe blunt injury—A relative's perspective. *Journal of Neurology, Neurosurgery, and Psychiatry, 46,* 336–344.

Brown, G., Chadwick, O., Shaffer, D., Rutter, M., and Traub, M. (1981). A prospective study of children with head injuries: III. Psychiatric sequelae. *Psychological Medicine, 11,* 63–78.

Costeff, H., Groswasser, Z., and Goldstein, R. (1990). Long term follow-up review of 31 children with severe closed head trauma. *Journal of Neurosurgery, 73,* 684–687.

Costeff, H., Groswasser, Z., Landman, Y., and Brenner, T. (1985). Survivors of severe traumatic brain injury in childhood: late residual disability. *Scandinavian Journal of Rehabilitation Medical Suppliers, 12,* 10–15.

Crothers, B., and Paine, R. (1959). *The Natural History of Cerebral Palsy.* Cambridge: Harvard University Press.

Das, J., Kirby, J., and Jarman, R. (1979). *Simultaneous and Successive Cognitive Processes.* New York: Academic Press.

Deaton, A. (1987). Behavioral change strategies for children and adolescent with severe brain injury. *Journal of Learning Disabilities, 20,* 581–589.

Diagnostic and Statistical Manual of Mental Disorder, Fourth Edition—Revised. 1994. Washington, D.C.: American Psychiatric Association.

Di Scala, C. (1991, Summer/Fall). National pediatric trauma registry. *Rehab Update,* 4–5.

Di Scala, C. (1992, Spring). National pediatric trauma registry. *Rehab Update,* 4–5.

Dodge, P., and Swartz, M. (1965). Bacterial meningitis: A review of selected aspects—II. Special neurological problems, post-meningitic complications and clinicopathological correlations. *New England Journal of Medicine, 272,* 954, 1003.

Duncan, C. (1981). The neonatal arousal scale. *Child's Brain, 8,* 299.

Ehrenkranz, R. (1990). The newborn intensive care unit. In F. Oski (Ed.), *Principles and Practice of Pediatrics* (pp. 286). Philadelphia: Lippincott.

Emory, E. (1991). Neuropsychological perspective on perinatal complications and the law. *The Clinical Neuropsychologist, 5,* 297–321.

Ewing-Cobbs, L., and Fletcher, J. (1987). Neuropsychological assessment of head injury children. *Journal of Learning Disabilities, 20,* 526–535.

Ewing-Cobbs, L., Levin, H., Eisenberg, H., and Fletcher, J. (1987). Language functions following closed head injury in children and adolescents. *Journal of Clinical and Experimental Neuropsychology, 9,* 575–592.

Ewing-Cobbs, L., Levin, H., Fletcher, J., Miner, M., and Eisenberg, H. (1989). Posttraumatic amnesia in head injured children: Assessment and outcome. *Journal of Clinical and Experimental Neuropsychology, 11,* 58.

Ewing-Cobbs, L., and Miner, M. (1989). *Traumatic brain injury in infants and children.* Unpublished manuscript developed for the Pediatric Research Group, National Head Injury Foundation.

Federal Register (1975, November). Public law 94-142: Education for all handicapped children act. Department of Education.

Federal Register (1986, October). Public law 99-457: Handicapped infants and toddlers amendment to the handicapped children's act. Department of Education.

Federal Register (1991, August). Public law 101-476: Individual's with disabilities education act: IDEA. Department of Education.

Fernbach, D. (1990). Neoplastic diseases. In F. Oski (Ed.) *Principles and Practice of Pediatrics* (pp. 1564–1565). Philadelphia: Lippincott.

Fletcher, J. (1987). In H. Levin, J. Gratman, and H. Eisenberg (Eds.), *Neurobehavioral Recovery from Head Injury* (pp. 279–291).

Functional Independence Measure (FIM). (1993, January). Uniform Data Set for Medical Rehabilitation Version 4.0. UB Foundation Activities, Inc.

Gaidolfi, E., and Vignolo, L. (1980). Closed head injuries of school aged children: Neuropsychological sequelae in early adulthood. *Italian Journal of Neurological Science, 1,* 65–73.

Gerring, J. (1986). Psychiatric sequelae of severe closed head injury. *Pediatrics in Review, 8,* 115–121.

Goldberg, A. (1993, January). Pediatric rehabilitation and school reintegration. Unpublished address presented at the *Sheldon Berrol M.D. 11th Annual Southwest Brain Injury Symposium.* Santa Barbara, CA.

Golden, C. (1981). *Diagnosis and Rehabilitation in Clinical Neuropsychology* (p. 221). Springfield, IL: Charles C Thomas.

Goodrich, J. (1993, September/October). Advances in pediatric neurosurgery. *Headlines.*

Granger, C., Hamilton, B., and Kayton, R. (1987). *Guide for use of the Functional Independence Measure for Children (WeeFim) of the Uniform Data Set for Medical Rehabilitation.* Buffalo: State University of New York Research Foundation.

Green, S., and George, R. (1979). Bacterial meningitis. In F. Rose (Ed.), *Pediatric Neurology* (pp. 569–581). Oxford: Blackwell Scientific.

Gurdjian, E. (1971). Mechanisms of impact injury to the head. In *Head Injuries: Proceedings of an International Symposium* (pp. 17–21). Edinburgh: Churchill Livingston.

Hagan, C., Malkmus, D., Durham, P. (1981). *Rancho Las Amigos Levels of Cognitive Functioning.* Downey, CA: Professional Staff Association.

Hanh, Y. (1992, October/November). The right fit: Tailoring diagnostic measures to the young patient. *Headlines, 8.*

Head Trauma Rehabilitation Seminar. (1977). Professional Staff Association of Rancho Los Amigos Hospital, Inc., June 10–11.

Ho, D., and Hirsch, M. (1985). Acute viral encephalitis. *Medical Clinics of North America, 69,* 415–429.

Hudspeth, W. (1992, October/November). An interview by M. Allison. The effects of neurologic injury on the maturing brain. *Headlines, 5.*

Hynd, G., and Willis, W. (1988). *Pediatric Neuropsychology,* (pp. 71–103). New York: Grune and Stratton.

Ingram, T. (1964). *Pediatric Aspects of Cerebral Palsy.* Edinburgh: Livingston.

Jackson, D. (1957). The study of the family. In N. Ackerman (Ed.) *Family Processes.* New York: Basic Books.

James, W. (1890). *The Principles of Psychology.* Vol. 1. New York: Dover, 1950 (orig. pub. 1890).

Jennett, B. (1976). Assessment of the severity of head injury. *Journal of Neurology, Neurosurgery, and Psychiatry, 39,* 647–655.

Jennett, B., and Bond, M. (1975). Assessment of outcome after severe brain injury. *Lancet, 1,* 480–487.

Johnson, R. (1982). Eastern encephalitis virus. In *Viral Infections of the Nervous System.* New York: Raven Press, p. 109.

Kanfer, F., and Saslow, G. (1969). In C.M. Franks (Ed.) *Behavioral Therapy: Appraisal and Status,* (pp. 417–444). New York: McGraw-Hill.

Kaplan, K. (1985). Brain abscess. *Medical Clinics of North America, 69,* 345–360.

Kennard, M. (1942). Cortical reorganization of motor functions: Studies on a series of monkeys of various ages from infancy to maturity. *Archives of Neurology and Psychiatry, 48,* 227–240.

Klonoff, H., Low, M., and Clark, C. (1977). Head injuries in children: A prospective five year follow-up. *Journal of Neurology, Neurosurgery, and Psychiatry, 40,* 1211–1219.

Knippe, J. (1993, June). Mechanisms of Function and Recovery Following Brain Injury. Unpublished Address. Long Beach, CA: Coast Psychiatric Associates.

Kolb, B., and Whishaw, I. (1985). *Fundamentals of Human Neuropsychology.* New York: W.H. Freeman and Company.

Kraus, K., Fife, D., and Conroy, C. (1987). Pediatric brain injuries: the nature, clinical course, and early outcome in a defined United States population. *Pediatrics, 79,* 501–507.

Kraus, K., Fife, D., Cox, P., Ramstein, K., and Conroy, C. (1986). Incidence, severity, and external causes of pediatric brain injury. *American Journal of Diseases of Childhood, 140,* 687–693.

Kyllerman, M. (1982). Dyskinetic cerebral palsy: Clinical categories associated with neurological abnormalities and incidences. *Acta Pediatrics Scandinavia, 71,* 543.

Langfitt, T., and Gennerelli, T. (1982). Can the outcome of head injury be improved? *Journal of Neurosurgery, 56,* 19–25.

Lauerman, J. (1992, May/June). Neurological impairment: Understanding the effects on learning. *Headlines.*

Lehr, E. (1990). *Psychological Management of Traumatic Brain Injuries in Children and Adolescents.* Rockville, MD: Aspen Publishers.

Levin, H., Ewing-Cobbs, L., and Fletcher, J. (1989). Neurobehavior outcome of mild head injury in children. In H. Levin, A. Eisenberg, and L. Benton (Eds.). *Mild Head Injury* (pp. 189–213). New York: Oxford University Press.

Levin, H., Eisenberg, H., and Benton, L. (Eds.) (1989). *Mild Head Injury.* New York: Oxford University Press.

Levin, M., Carey, W., Crocker, A., and Gross, A. (1983). *Developmental Behavioral Pediatrics,* (p. 397). Philadelphia: W.B. Saunders.

Levin, H.S., Eisenberg, H.M., Wigg, N., and Kobayashi, K. (1982). Memory and intellectual ability after head injury in children and adolescents. *Neurosurgery,* *11,* 668–673.

Locke, J. (1690). An essay concerning human understanding. Collated and annotated by A.C. Frasier. Oxford: Calredon Press, 1894 (orig. publ 1690).

Luria, A. (1970). The functional organization of the brain. *Scientific American, 222,* 66–78.

Luria, A. (1973). *The Working Brain.* New York: Basic Books.

Menkes, J. (1985). *Textbook of Child Neurology* (3rd ed.). Philadelphia: Lea and Febiger.

Menkes, J. (1990). *Textbook of Child Neurology* (4th Ed.) (pp. 284–316). New York: Lea and Febiger.

Miller, E. (1984). *Recovery and Management of Neuropsychological Impairments* (pp. 247–252). Philadelphia: Lea and Febiger.

Millikan, C., McDowell, F., and Easton, J. (1987). *Stroke,* (pp. 247–252). Philadelphia: Lea and Febiger.

National Pediatric Trauma Registry (1993). *Pediatric Trauma Registry biannual report:* Boston, MA.

Parke, J. (1990). Acute encephalopathies. In Oski (Ed.), *Principles and Practice of Pediatrics,* (pp. 1842–1844). Philadelphia: J.B. Lippincott.

Pasino, J. (1983). Three phase model for the psychological assessment and treatment of pediatric head injury. *Archives of Physical Medicine and Rehabilitation, 64,* 520.

Piaget, J., and Inhelder, B. (1969). *The Psychology of the Child,* Boston: Routledge and Kegan Paul.

Pipitone, P. (1992, October/November). Acquired pediatric brain damage: Diverse causes. *Headlines, 5.*

Prigatano, G. (1986). *Neuropsychological Rehabilitation after Brain Injury.* Baltimore: Johns Hopkins University Press.

Raimondi, A., and Hirschauer, J. (1984). Head injury in the infant and toddler. *Child's Brain, 11,* 12–35.

Rehabilitation of the Head Injured Adult, (1979, August). Professional Staff Association of Rancho Los Amigos Hospital, Inc.

Rehabilitation of the Head Injured Adult and Child, (1982, November). Professional Staff Association of Rancho Los Amigos Medical Center, Inc.

Rourke, B., Bakker, D., Fisk, J., and Strang, J. (1983). *Child Neuropsychology: An Introduction to Theory, Research, and Clinical Practice.* New York: Guilford Press.

Rutter, M. (1981). Psychological sequelae of brain damage in children. *American Journal of Psychiatry, 138,* 1533–1544.

Rutter, M., Chadwick, O., and Shaffer, D. (1983). Head injury. In M. Rutter (Ed.), *Developmental Neuropsychiatry* (pp. 83–111). New York: Guilford Press.

Satir, V. (1967). *Conjoint Family Therapy.* Palo Alto, CA: Science and Behavior Books.

Savage, R. (1993). Children with traumatic brain injuries. Unpublished report developed for the National Head Injury Pediatric Task Force.

Sell, S. (1983). Long term sequelae of bacterial meningitis in children. *Pediatric Infectious Disease, 2,* 90–93.

Shaffer, D., Chadwick, O., and Rutter, M. (1975). Psychiatric outcome of localized head injury in children. *Ciba Foundation Symposium.*

Shapiro, K. (1985). Head injury in children. In D. Becker and J.T. Povlishock (Eds.). *Central Nervous System Trauma; Status Report,* (pp. 243–255). Bethesda, MD: National Institutes of Health and Neurological and Communicative Disorders and Stroke.

Simpson, D., and Reilly, P. Pediatric coma scale. *Lancet, 2,* 245.

Singer, W. (1992, October/November). An interview by M. Allison. The effects of neurological injury on the maturing brain. *Headlines,* 2–3.

Smith, A. (1971). Objective indices of severity of chronic aphasis. *Journal of Speech and Hearing Disorders, 36,* 167.

Smith, A. (1988). Neurological sequelae of meningitis. *New England Journal of Medicine, 319,* 1012.

Snoek, J. (1989). Mild head injury in children. In H. Levin, H. Eisenberg, and A. Benton (Eds.). *Mild Head Injury,* (pp. 102–132). New York: Oxford University Press.

Subirana, A. (1958). The prognosis in aphasia in relation of cerebral dominance and handedness. *Brain, 81,* 415.

Takayama, E. (1988). Minor head injury: Major adjustments. *Wellbeing.* Huntington Beach: College Health Enterprises.

Teasdale, G., and Jennett, B. (1974). Assessment of coma and impaired consciousness: A practical scale. *Lancet, 2,* 81–84.

Telzrow, C. (1987). Management of academic and educational problems in head injury. *Journal of Learning Disabilities, 20,* 536–545.

Tsai, T. (1990). Viral infections. In F. Oski (Ed.), *Principles and Practice of Pediatrics,* (pp. 1159–1179). Philadelphia: J.B. Lippincott.

Veelken, N. (1983). Diplegic cerebral palsy in Swedish term and preterm infants. *Neuropediatrics, 14,* 20.

Volpe, J. (1987). *Neurology of the Newborn.* Second Edition. Philadelphia: W.B. Saunders.

Walsh, K. (1987). *Neuropsychology: A Clinical Approach.* New York: Churchill Livingston.

Weil, M. (1990). Infections of the nervous system. In J. Menkes (Ed.), *Test Book of Child Neurology,* (pp. 327–423). Lea and Febiger: Philadelphia.

Weinstein, H. (1986). The childhood leukemias. In A. Moosa (Ed.), *Comprehensive Textbook of Oncology,* (pp. 1149–1160). Baltimore: Williams and Wilkins.

Wilson, M. (1992). Injury control. In F. Oski (Ed.), *Principles and Practice of Pediatrics,* (p. 578). Philadelphia: J.B. Lippincott.

Winogron, H. (1984). Neuropsychological deficits following head injury in children. *Journal of Clinical Neuropsychology, 6,* 269–286.

Woods, B.T. (1980). The restricted effects of right-hemisphere lesions after age one: Wechsler test data. *Neuropsychologia, 18,* 65–70.

Zimmerman, R., and Bilaniuk, L. (1981). Computed tomography in pediatric head trauma. *Journal of Neuroradiology, 6,* 257–271.

Chapter 2

SPECIAL EDUCATION LAW

RICHARD E. EKSTRAND, ESQUIRE AND ERIC C. BROUSAIDES, ESQUIRE

INTRODUCTION

The primary federal law regarding the education of children with disabilities is currently known as the Individuals with Disabilities Education Act (IDEA). The IDEA has undergone several name changes over time and was previously known as Public Law 94-142, the Education of the Handicapped Act (EHA), and the Education for All Handicapped Children Act (EAHCA). The IDEA requires that all eligible children with disabilities be afforded a free appropriate public education (FAPE) which includes special education and related services as appropriate. To be eligible for these services, a child must, among other requirements, have a disability that is designated in the IDEA. Prior to the enactment of the IDEA in 1990, the EHA identified the following disabilities (then called handicapping conditions):

> mentally retarded, hard of hearing, deaf, speech or language impaired, visually handicapped, seriously emotionally disturbed, orthopedically impaired, other health impaired, children with specific learning disabilities, deaf-blind and multihandicapped.

20 U.S.C. §1401(a)(1); 34 C.F.R. §300.5(a).

As reflected above, neither brain injury nor traumatic brain injury was a separately defined disability category under the EHA. Thus, students with brain injury or traumatic brain injury who sought special education services under the EHA were required to qualify under one of the categories listed above. Although not designated as a separate disability category, however, the term "brain injury" was referenced as a condition which could lead to special education service eligibility under the category of "specific learning disability." Additionally, the federal Department of Education had indicated that a student with "traumatic brain injury" may qualify for special education services under the category of "other health impaired" (and presumably any other specifically defined category).

With the enactment of the IDEA in October 1990, the law was amended to add "traumatic brain injury" as a separate and distinct disability category.

At the same time, it would also appear that students with a brain injury which does not meet the definition of "traumatic brain injury" may continue to qualify for services by meeting the criteria under one of the other disability categories, such as specific learning disability or other health impaired. It is therefore clear that a student with a brain injury is entitled to services under IDEA if the student meets the criteria for "traumatic brain injury," or if the student meets the criteria for some other disability category identified in the IDEA. This point is significant because, as discussed later in this chapter, some commentators believe that the IDEA's definition of "traumatic brain injury" is drawn too narrowly.

The current trend in the law is to ensure that even the most severely disabled children are provided a FAPE. At least one court has held that the law contains a "zero reject" policy regarding the entitlement to special education services. Furthermore, in addition to special education services, courts have ruled that school systems may be required to provide a wide array of health services if such are necessary to assist a student with disabilities to benefit from special education. Accordingly, school systems must now be prepared to respond to the needs of an increasingly wide spectrum of students with disabilities.

This chapter will review the origins of special education law under the IDEA, its major substantive requirements, and key judicial decisions regarding the education of children with disabilities. Additionally, another federal statute, Section 504 of the Rehabilitation Act of 1973, which is less detailed than the IDEA, will be briefly discussed. This chapter emphasizes the major federal requirements of special education law. State law may expand on these minimum federal requirements. It should also be noted that the federal special education law applies equally to all eligible children with disabilities. Thus, an eligible student with a brain injury has all the rights identified in special education law.

THE ORIGINS OF SPECIAL EDUCATION LAW

The legislative history of the IDEA attributes its genesis to, among other factors, two federal court cases decided in 1971 and 1972. These cases were discussed at length by Congress in its deliberations and thus provide guidance in determining the intent of the law. The first case was *Pennsylvania Assn. for Retarded Children v. Commonwealth,* 334 F.Supp 1257 (E.D. Pa. 1971) and 343 F.Supp 279 (1972) (*PARC*). *PARC* involved a challenge to the constitutionality of a Pennsylvania law which operated to exclude children with disabilities from public education and training. The dispute in *PARC* was resolved when the parties entered into a consent decree which prohibited Pennsylvania from "deny[ing] to any mentally retarded child access to a free public program of education and training." *PARC* at 1258. The second case was *Mills v. Board of Education of District of Columbia,* 348 F.Supp 866 (D. D.C. 1972). In *Mills,* the children with disabilities had likewise been excluded from the public schools. The court in *Mills* held that "no child eligible for a publicly supported education in the District of Columbia Public Schools shall be excluded from a regular school assignment by a Rule, policy or practice of the Board of Education of the District of Columbia or its agents unless such child is provided (a) adequate alternative educational services suited to the child's needs, which may include special education or tuition grants, and (b) a constitutionally adequate prior hearing and periodic review of the child's status, progress, and the adequacy of any educational alternative." *Mills* at 878.

Ten years later in 1982, the United States Supreme Court reviewed the *PARC* and *Mills* decisions in the case of *Board of Education of the Hendrick Hudson Central School District v. Rowley,* 102 S.Ct. 3034 (1982). The Court in *Rowley* found that "*Mills* and *PARC* both held that [children with disabilities][1] must be given *access* to an adequate, publicly supported education." (Emphasis in original) *Rowley* at 3044. The Supreme Court also reviewed the legislative history of special education law and noted that as of 1975, the "most recent statistics provided by the Bureau of Education for the Handicapped estimate that of the more than 8 million children . . . with [disabling] conditions requiring special education and related services, only 3.9 million such children are receiving an appropriate education." S.Rep., at 8, U.S. Code Cong. & Admin. News 1975, p. 1432.

In response to the *PARC* and *Mills* decisions, and the finding that approximately four million children with disabilities were not receiving an appropriate education, Congress enacted what is now known as the IDEA. The contours of this significant federal legislation are reviewed hereafter.

THE INDIVIDUALS WITH DISABILITIES EDUCATION ACT

Purpose

The stated purpose of the IDEA is:

. . . to assure that all children with disabilities have available to them . . . a free appropriate public education which emphasizes special education and related

---

1. Many of the cases, opinions, and other materials referenced in this chapter were written prior to the 1990 enactment of the IDEA and, accordingly, use the former term "handicapped children" instead of the current term "children with disabilities." Where possible, without impacting on context, the term "children with disabilities" has been inserted into these references in recognition of the new term and for purposes of consistency.

services designed to meet their unique needs, to assure that the rights of children with disabilities and their parents or guardians are protected, to assist States and localities to provide for the education of all children with disabilities, and to assess and assure the effectiveness of efforts to educate children with disabilities.

20 U.S.C. §1400(c)

As this provision indicates, the IDEA is designed to provide all eligible children with disabilities special education and related services that are individually tailored to meet their unique needs. Additionally, the IDEA contains detailed procedural safeguards designed to protect these students' right to a FAPE. Accordingly, all eligible children with disabilities, including eligible children with a brain injury, are entitled to a FAPE.

Definitions and Requirements

Children with Disabilities

Prior to the 1990 enactment of the IDEA, the term "handicapped children" (redesignated in 1990 as "children with disabilities") was defined as children evaluated as being:

mentally retarded, hard of hearing, deaf, speech or language impaired, visually handicapped, seriously emotionally disturbed, orthopedically impaired, or other health impaired children, or children with specific learning disabilities, who by reason thereof require special education and related services. [The implementing regulations added the categories of deaf-blind and multi-handicapped.]

20 U.S.C. §1401(a)(1); 34 C.F.R. §300.5(a).

As can be seen, this definition did not specifically include children with brain injury as a separate category. However, as noted above, the definition of the term "specific learning disability" did provide that brain injury was a condition which may lead to eligibility under the specific learning disability category. The law defines a "specific learning disability" as:

a disorder in one or more of the basic psychological processes involved in understanding or in using language, spoken or written, that may manifest itself in an imperfect ability to listen, think, speak, read, write, spell, or to do mathematical calculations. The term includes such conditions as perceptual disabilities, *brain injury,* minimal brain disfunction, dyslexia, and developmental aphasia.

34 C.F.R. §300.7(b)(10) (Emphasis supplied)

Additionally, the Federal Department of Education's Office of Special Education and Rehabilitative Services (OSERS) had stated that a child with traumatic brain injury might fall within the definition of "other health impaired" and thus be eligible for special education services. In a policy letter dated February 26, 1990, before the enactment of IDEA, OSERS responded to an inquiry expressing concern that traumatic brain injury was not a specified disabling condition under the EHA. OSERS stated that:

> Under EHA–B, a "handicapped child" must be evaluated as having one or more of eleven specified physical or mental impairments causing the child to need special education and related services.... One of the eleven specified handicapping conditions listed in EHA–B is "other health impaired."... EHA–B defines children who are "other health impaired" as including those children with "chronic or acute health problems such as a heart condition, tuberculosis, rheumatic fever, nephritis, asthma, sickle cell anemia, hemophilia, epilepsy, lead poisoning, leukemia, or diabetes, which adversely affects a child's educational performance."... *The list of health problems in the definition of "other health impaired" is not exhaustive and could include other health-related impairments, such as traumatic brain injury, if it is determined that such impairments adversely affect educational performance.* ... If the educational evaluation of your daughter determines that her traumatic brain injury "adversely affects educational performance," your daughter would be a "handicapped child" and thus eligible for educational services under EHA–B.

Department of Education Policy Letter, 2/26/90, 16 EHLR 552 (Emphasis supplied)

Thus, while brain injury was not specifically designated as a disabling condition prior to the enactment of IDEA, a student with a brain injury would nonetheless be eligible for special education services under the law if the student met the criteria under any of the specified disability categories such as "other health impaired."

In 1990, with the enactment of the IDEA, the term "handicapped children" was changed to "children with disabilities." The term "children with disabilities" is defined as children evaluated as having:

> mental retardation, hearing impairments including deafness, speech or language impairments, visual impairments including blindness, serious emotional disturbance, orthopedic impairments, *autism, traumatic brain injury,* other health impairments, specific learning disabilities, deaf-blindness, or multiple disabilities, and who because of those impairments need special education and related services.

34 C.F.R. §300.7(a)(1) (Emphasis supplied)

Thus, the 1990 amendments added traumatic brain injury, as well as autism, as a specific disability category which may provide the basis for special education service eligibility.

Traumatic Brain Injury

The IDEA's implementing regulation at 34 C.F.R. 300.7(b)(12) defines the term "traumatic brain injury" as follows:

> "Traumatic brain injury" means an acquired injury to the brain caused by an external physical force, resulting in total or partial functional disability or psychosocial impairment, or both, that adversely affects a child's educational performance. The term applies to open or closed head injuries resulting in impairments in one or more areas, such as cognition; language; memory; attention; reasoning; abstract thinking; judgment; problem-solving; sensory, perceptual and motor abilities; psychosocial behavior; physical functions; information processing; and speech. The term does not apply to brain injuries that are congenital or degenerative, or brain injuries induced by birth trauma.

While the IDEA now includes the specific category of traumatic brain injury, the term "brain injury" has not been deleted from the definition of specific learning disability, nor is it expected that the prior OSERS opinion concerning a brain injured student's eligibility under the category of other health impaired will be negated. As such, it appears that a student who suffers from a brain injury may qualify for services under the IDEA categories of traumatic brain injury, specific learning disability, other health impaired, or any other specifically defined category. This distinction is significant because, as discussed below, some commentators believe that the IDEA's definition of the term traumatic brain injury is too restrictive.

When the proposed definition of traumatic brain injury was first published in August 1991, the term was defined as follows:

> Traumatic brain injury means an injury to the brain caused by an external physical force *or by an internal occurrence such as stroke or aneurysm,* resulting in total or partial functional disability or psychosocial maladjustment that adversely affects educational performance. The term includes open or closed head injuries resulting in mild, moderate, or severe impairments in one or more areas, including cognition; language; memory; attention; reasoning; abstract thinking; judgment; problem-solving; sensory, perceptual and motor abilities; psychosocial behavior; physical functions; information processing; and speech. The term does not include brain injuries that are congenital or degenerative, or brain injuries induced by birth trauma. (Emphasis supplied)
>
> Federal Register, Vol. 56, No. 160, August 19, 1991, p. 41271.

When this initial definition of the term traumatic brain injury was proposed, the Department of Education solicited comments regarding its appropriateness. The Department of Education's responses to these comments, set forth below, help clarify the contours of the definition of traumatic brain injury.

Comment: A commenter suggested that the first sentence of the proposed definition of "traumatic brain injury" be amended by adding "acquired" before "injury," and substituting "impairment" for "maladjustment." The commenter also pointed out that "functional disability" and "psychosocial impairment" resulting from an injury to the brain are not always mutually exclusive, and recommended that the definition be amended to allow for both. One commenter requested the inclusion of adverse effects on social-emotional development, not just academic performance.

Discussion: The Secretary [of the Department of Education] agrees that the definition of "traumatic brain injury" should clarify that the injury (1) occurs after birth, and (2) results in total or partial functional disability, or psychosocial impairment, or both, to provide a more accurate and comprehensive description of children in this disability category. It is not necessary to include a statement of adverse effects on social-emotional development in the definition because social-emotional developmental consequences may be reflected in adverse effects on educational performance.

Changes: The definition has been revised to incorporate the commenter's suggestions, to the extent indicated in the above discussion.

Comment: Some commenters requested clarification as to whether medical verification or physician documentation would be required. In addition, a few commenters requested that specific assessment procedures be developed and required. One commenter stated that LEAs [local educational agencies] do not have individuals skilled in assessing children with traumatic brain injury and expressed concern about assessment costs.

Discussion: The definition of "children with disabilities" in § 300.7(a)(1) states that the term means "those children evaluated in accordance with §§ 300.530–300.534. . . . " The required procedures in those sections are broad enough to ensure that diagnostic and placement decisions are based on comprehensive information about the child, including medical information if it is needed to determine whether the child has a disability and is in need of special education and related services. There should not be a significant increase in the cost of assessing children with traumatic brain injury, since these children are currently being assessed and are receiving special education, although they are identified as having other disabling conditions. The establishment of a separate category should facilitate the development of improved assessment and program planning efforts. These efforts, together with improved personnel training, should help to ensure that required personnel in LEAs are appropriately skilled in the identification, evaluation, and placement of children with traumatic brain injury.

Changes: None.

Comment: Several commenters requested clarification as to whether there is any overlap between the definitions of "traumatic brain injury" and "other health impaired." The commenters asked if an injury resulting from infection, tumor, fever, exposure to a toxic substance, or near-drowning would be considered a traumatic brain injury. A commenter also requested that the definition not exclude other acquired brain injuries when the resulting functional areas of disability are similar to the disabilities resulting from traumatic brain injury.

Discussion: The term "traumatic brain injury," as used in professional practice, applies only to children with acquired brain injuries caused by an external physical force. It does not apply to injuries caused by internal occurrences, such as infections, tumors, fever, and exposure to toxic substances. Children whose educational performance is affected as a result of acquired injuries to the brain caused by internal occurrences may meet the criteria of one of the other disability categories, such as "other health impaired," "specific learning disabilities," or "multiple disabilities." The definition of "traumatic brain injury" does include an acquired injury to the brain caused by the external physical force of near-drowning.

Changes: The phrase "or by an internal occurrence such as a stroke or aneurysm" has been deleted from the first sentence of the definition.

Comment: A commenter suggested that the word "mild" be deleted from the second sentence of the definition of "traumatic brain injury." Another commenter asked that descriptions of the degree of a child's impairment be eliminated from the definition.

Discussion: The Secretary believes that the degree of impairment is not a factor in determining whether a child has a "traumatic brain injury." Therefore, the terms "mild," "moderate," and "severe" should be deleted from this definition. The factors for determining whether a child is eligible under this disability category for services under part B [of the IDEA] are (1) an acquired injury to the brain caused by an external physical force resulting in total or partial functional disability or psychosocial impairment that adversely affects educational performance, and (2) a need for special education and related services because of that disability or impairment. The particular services provided to the child are determined on an individual basis. Thus, as long as the factors described above are met, children are eligible whether or not they have mild, moderate, or severe impairments.

Changes: The descriptions of degree of impairment (mild, moderate, and severe) have been deleted from the definition.

Federal Register, Vol. 57, No. 189, September 29, 1992, pp. 44842–44843.

Following publication of the final regulatory definition of the term "traumatic brain injury," some commentators expressed concern that the definition operated to exclude certain brain injured children. In a March 7, 1993 letter to the United States Department of Education, one commentator stated that:

In the final rule published in the Federal Register in September, 1992, the definition was modified to include only children having brain injury from "external physical force." For some reason, children sustaining brain injury from "internal occurrences" (such as cerebral vascular accidents, tumors, anoxic/ischemic events, or infectious encephalopathy) have now been excluded from the definition. . . . It appears that the Department of Education's decision to exclude children who sustain brain damage from "internal occurrences" leaves many neurologically disabled children in a state of limbo. The exclusion of children who sustain brain damage from "internal occurrences" may present significant legal problems and precipitate fair hearings which will be quite costly in this time of financial restraint.

In a July 13, 1993 response to these concerns, the Department of Education issued a policy letter stating that:

> the Department determined that including the phrase "internal occurrence such as a stroke or aneurysm," would expand the category "traumatic brain injury" beyond its use in professional practice. . . . *The deletion of this phrase was not intended to limit eligibility of children with acquired internal injuries to the brain for services under Part B. Children whose educational performance is adversely affected as a result of acquired injuries to the brain caused by internal occurrences may meet the criteria of one of the other disability categories, such as "other health impairment," "specific learning disability," or "multiple disability."*
> Department of Education Policy Letter, 7/13/93, 20 IDELR 623 (Emphasis Supplied).

Thus, children with brain injury caused by an internal occurrence who meet the definitional criteria of an IDEA disability category other than traumatic brain injury will still be entitled to special education services under the IDEA. In this regard, the Department of Education has issued a policy letter stating that:

> Once a decision has been made that a child is a child with a disability, an individualized educational program (IEP) must be developed and implemented. Under Part B, the IEP must be developed solely on the basis of the individual child's educational needs, not on the basis of the category of the child's disability. Therefore, the decision not to categorize [a] child as a child having a traumatic brain injury should not affect the services that are provided to [that child.]
> Department of Education Policy Letter, 12/18/92, 19 IDELR 928.

Traumatic brain injury (or any other disabling condition) standing alone does not automatically result in an entitlement to special education services. A student with a recognized disability must also meet the IDEA's other eligibility requirements.

Eligibility

In a policy letter dated May 25, 1990, OSERS stated that:

> . . . States and local school districts must make available to eligible children with [disabilities] a free appropriate public education (FAPE), which includes

the provision of special education and related services at no cost to parents. To be eligible, a child must be evaluated as having one or more physical or mental impairments defined [in special education law] that adversely affect educational performance and cause the child to need special education and related services.

Department of Education Policy Letter, 5/25/90, 16 EHLR 961.

Therefore to be eligible for special education services under the IDEA, the following conditions must be met:

1) The student must meet the criteria of one or more of the specified disability categories (e.g. specific learning disability, other health impaired, traumatic brain injury);

2) The impairment(s) must adversely affect the child's educational performance; and

3) The impairment(s) must result in the need for special education.

Evaluations and Reevaluations

In order to determine if a student is eligible for special education services as a child with disabilities, and also for purposes of developing an appropriate educational program, there must first be "a full and individual evaluation of the child's educational needs." 34 C.F.R. §300.531 (20 U.S.C. §1412(5)(C)). Special education law contains specific procedures regarding how these evaluations are to be conducted. 34 C.F.R. §§300.530–300.543.

Because the needs of children with disabilities change over time, which may be especially true for a child with a brain injury, there are specific time lines for reevaluating students with disabilities. Special education law provides that students with disabilities must be reevaluated "every three years, or more frequently if conditions warrant, or if the child's parent or teacher requests an evaluation." 34 C.F.R. §300.534 (20 U.S.C. §1412(5)(C)). It is important to note that the three-year period is the minimum time period for reevaluations. If a child with a brain injury warrants more frequent evaluations due to the changing nature of the condition, the law would require that reevaluations be completed more frequently.

Accordingly, special education law sets forth specific procedures for ensuring that all eligible students with disabilities, including eligible students who have suffered a brain injury, are evaluated and reevaluated so that an appropriate individualized educational program can be developed to meet the student's unique educational needs.

Individualized Education Program

Every child who meets the IDEA's eligibility requirements must be provided an individualized education program (IEP). The United States Supreme Court has described the IEP as the "centerpiece" of the education delivery system for disabled children. *Honig v. Doe,* 108 S.Ct. 592 (1988).

The IDEA's implementing regulation regarding the content of IEP's is as follows:

(a) *General.* The IEP for each child must include—

(1) A statement of the child's present levels of educational performance;

(2) A statement of annual goals, including short-term instructional objectives;

(3) A statement of the specific special education and related services to be provided to the child and the extent that the child will be able to participate in regular educational programs;

(4) The projected dates for initiation of services and the anticipated duration of the services; and

(5) Appropriate objective criteria and evaluation procedures and schedules for determining, on at least an annual basis, whether the short-term instructional objectives are being achieved.

(b) *Transition services.*

(1) The IEP for each student, beginning no later than age 16 (and at a younger age, if determined appropriate), must include a statement of the needed transition services as defined in Sec. 300.18, including, if appropriate, a statement of each public agency's and each participating agency's responsibilities or linkages, or both, before the student leaves the school setting.

(2) If the IEP team determines that services are not needed in one or more of the areas specified in Sec. 300.18(b)(2)(i) through (b)(2)(iii), the IEP must include a statement to that effect and the basis upon which the determination was made.

34 C.F.R. 300.346

Obviously, the IEP is a critical component of the educational program for a child with disabilities and is necessary for the student to receive a free appropriate public education. The United States Supreme Court in *Rowley*, stated that full parental participation in the development of the IEP is especially important.

Thus, all children with disabilities receiving special education services, including children with brain injury, must receive such services pursuant to an IEP. An IEP which does not contain all of the required elements or which was not developed in consultation with the student's parents may be deemed inappropriate.

Continuum of Alternative Placements

After the student's IEP has been developed, a determination is made as to where the student should be placed to receive the identified services. Because of the wide spectrum of educational needs of students with disabilities, the IDEA requires that school systems have available a broad continuum of placements. The law provides that:

(a) Each public agency shall ensure that a continuum of alternative placements is available to meet the needs of children with disabilities for special education and related services.

(b) The continuum required in paragraph (a) of this section must—

(1) Include the alternative placements listed in the definition of special education under Sec. 300.17 (instruction in regular classes, special classes, special schools, home instruction, and instruction in hospitals and institutions); and

(2) Make provision for supplementary services (such as resource room or itinerant instruction) to be provided in conjunction with regular class placement.

34 C.F.R. §300.551

Accordingly, school systems must have available a continuum of alternative placements to ensure that the needs of all eligible children with disabilities, including eligible children with brain injury, can be met.

Free Appropriate Public Education

a) Definition

Students who meet the IDEA's eligibility requirements are entitled to a free appropriate public education. The term "free appropriate public education" means special education and related services which:

(a) Are provided at public expense, under public supervision and direction and without charge;

(b) Meet the standards of the SEA [State Education Agency], including the requirements of this part;

(c) Include preschool, elementary school, or secondary school education in the State involved; and

(d) Are provided in conformity with an IEP which meets the requirements of Secs. 300.340–300.350.

34 C.F.R. §300.8 (20 U.S.C. §1401(a)(18))

A "free" appropriate public education means "at no cost," which is defined to mean that "all specially designed instruction is provided without charge, but does not preclude incidental fees that are normally charged to nondisabled students or their parents as part of the regular education program." 34 C.F.R. §300.17(b)(1).

b) *Board of Education of the Hendrick Hudson Central School District v. Rowley*

The rather skeletal regulatory definition of a free appropriate public education (FAPE) has prompted much litigation regarding its precise boundaries. In a landmark special education decision, the United States Supreme Court in *Board of Education of the Hendrick Hudson Central School District v. Rowley,* 102 S.Ct. 3034 (1982) sought to provide substance to this definition. While the case involved a deaf student, the Court's decision is generally equally applicable to all children with disabilities.

Amy Rowley was a deaf student who was an excellent lip reader. Amy was placed in a regular kindergarten class "with an FM hearing aid which would amplify words spoken into a wireless receiver by the teacher or fellow students during certain classroom activities. Amy successfully completed her kindergarten year." *Rowley* at 3039.

For the following school year, Amy's individualized education program provided that:

> Amy should be educated in a regular classroom . . . , should continue to use the FM hearing aid, and should receive instruction from a tutor for the deaf for one hour each day and from a speech therapist for three hours each week. The Rowleys agreed with parts of the IEP, but insisted that Amy also be provided a qualified sign-language interpreter in all her academic classes in lieu of the assistance proposed in other parts of the IEP.
>
> Such an interpreter had been placed in Amy's kindergarten class for a 2-week experimental period, but the interpreter had reported that Amy did not need his services at that time.

Rowley at 3039–3040

As a result of the parents' disagreement with the school system's proposed educational plan, the parents requested a due process hearing. (As will be discussed below, parents of children with disabilities have numerous due process rights, including the right to administrative and judicial review of the IEP proposed for the student.) The question presented was whether Amy must be provided a qualified sign language interpreter in order to receive a FAPE. At two administrative hearings, it was decided that the interpreter was not required for Amy to be afforded a FAPE. Thereafter, the parents sought judicial review in federal district court. The district court found that Amy was not receiving a FAPE, which the court defined as "an opportunity to achieve [her] full potential commensurate with the opportunity provided to other children." The district court thus defined FAPE under a "full potential" standard and decided that the interpreter was needed for Amy to have a FAPE. *Rowley* at 3040. The school system appealed the case to the United States Court of Appeals for the Second Circuit which affirmed the district court's judgment.

The school system obtained a further review by the United States Supreme Court which reversed the Court of Appeals' judgment. The Supreme Court concluded that the FAPE requirement does not mean that school systems are required to provide the best possible education for children with disabilities. In this regard, the Court noted that "the requirement that a State provide specialized educational services . . . generates no additional requirement that the services so provided be sufficient to maximize each child's potential 'commensurate with the opportunity provided other children.' " *Rowley* at 3046. The Court concluded that "the 'basic floor of opportunity' provided by the Act consists of access to specialized instruction and related services which are individually designed to provide educational benefit . . . " *Rowley* at 3048. While the Court did not attempt to "establish any one test for determining the adequacy of educational benefits (i.e., FAPE) conferred upon all children covered by the Act," the Court stated that:

> Insofar as a State is required to provide a . . . "free appropriate public education," we hold that it satisfies this requirement by providing personalized instruction with sufficient support services to permit the child to benefit educationally from that instruction. Such instruction and services must be provided at public expense, must meet the State's educational standards, must approximate the grade levels used in the State's regular education, and must comport with the child's IEP. In addition, the IEP, and therefore the personalized instruction, should be formulated in accordance with the requirements of the Act and, if the child is being educated in the regular classrooms of the public education system, should be reasonably calculated to enable the child to achieve passing marks and advance from grade to grade.

Rowley at 3049

Thus, the Supreme Court found that a free appropriate public education is an individualized education program, developed pursuant to applicable procedures, which is "reasonably calculated to enable the child to receive educational benefits." *Rowley* at 3051.

Special Education

The definition of a "free appropriate public education" (FAPE) includes the terms "special education" and "related services." Accordingly, the definitions of these terms play an important part in determining the scope of the FAPE obligation.

The federal regulations define the term "special education" as follows:

> (a)(1) As used in this part, the term "special education" means specially designed instruction, at no cost to the parents, to meet the unique needs of a child with a disability, including—
> (i) Instruction conducted in the classroom, in the home, in hospitals and institutions, and in other settings; and
> (ii) Instruction in physical education.
> (2) The term includes speech pathology, or any other related service, if the service consists of specially designed instruction, at no cost to the parents, to meet the unique needs of a child with a disability, and is considered special education rather than a related service under State standards.
> (3) The term also includes vocational education if it consists of specially

designed instruction, at no cost to the parents, to meet the unique needs of a child with a disability.

34 C.F.R. §300.17 (20 U.S.C. §1401(a)(16))

The official Note to the definition of special education is instructive. It provides that:

> The definition of special education is a particularly important one under these regulations, since a child does not have a disability under this part unless he or she needs special education. (See the definition of children with disabilities in Sec. 300.7.) The definition of related services (Sec. 300.16) also depends on this definition, since a related service must be necessary for a child to benefit from special education. Therefore, if a child does not need special education, there can be no related services, and the child is not a child with a disability and is therefore not covered under the Act.

Thus, as the official Note indicates, the term "special education" is closely tied with the definition of "children with disabilities" in that students who do not require special education services will not meet the definition of "children with disabilities" and, thus, will not be eligible for services under the IDEA.

Related Services

While all eligible children with disabilities will receive special education services, not all such children will necessarily receive related services. Whether a particular student is eligible for related services depends on whether the student requires a particular related service in order to assist the student to benefit from special education. However, if a student does require related services in order to assist the student to benefit from special education, then the student is entitled to receive related services.

The term "related services" means:

> ... transportation, and such developmental, corrective, and other supportive services (including speech pathology and audiology, psychological services, physical and occupational therapy, recreation, including therapeutic recreation, social work services, counseling services, including rehabilitation counseling [which was added by the enactment of IDEA], and medical services, except that such medical services shall be for diagnostic and evaluation purposes only) *as may be required to assist a child with a disability to benefit from special education,* and includes the early identification and assessment of disabling conditions in children.

20 U.S.C. §1401(a)(17) (Emphasis supplied)

As illustrated by the following official Note to this definition, the listing of related services is not meant to be complete. The official Note provides, in part, that:

The list of related services is not exhaustive and may include other developmental, corrective, or supportive services (such as artistic and cultural programs, and art, music, and dance therapy), if they are required to assist a child with a disability to benefit from special education.

Thus, the official Note to the definition of the term special education and the definition and official Note to the term related services provides important clarification in two ways. First, if students do not require special education services, they do not qualify as "children with disabilities." Second, those children with disabilities who require related services to assist them to benefit from special education are entitled to related services under the law and the listing of related services is not meant to be exhaustive.

A significant United States Supreme Court decision regarding a student's entitlement to related services is *Irving Independent School District v. Tatro,* 104 S.Ct. 3371 (1984). In *Tatro,* the Court was called upon to determine whether clean intermittent catheterization (CIC) was a related service which the school system was obligated to provide to students with disabilities.

The Court determined that the student was entitled to receive CIC as a related service from the school system and provided the following guidance for determining when the entitlement to related services arises:

First, to be entitled to related services, a child must be [disabled] so as to require special education. . . . In the absence of a [disability] that requires special education, the need for what otherwise might qualify as a related service does not create an obligation under the Act. . . . Second, only those services necessary to aid [children with disabilities] to benefit from special education must be provided, regardless how easily a school nurse or lay person could furnish them. For example, if a particular medication or treatment may appropriately be administered to a [child with disabilities] other than during the school day, a school is not required to provide nursing services to administer it. Third, the [special education laws] state that school nursing services must be provided only if they can be performed by a nurse or other qualified person, not if they must be performed by a physician.

Tatro at 3378

Thus, under the facts of this case, the Court determined that the provision of CIC was a related service which the school system was obligated to provide. Additionally, in accordance with the above referenced regulations, the Court further held that a prerequisite to the entitlement to related services is a finding that the student qualifies as a child with disabilities in need of special education. However, if the eligible student requires a particular related service in order to assist the student to benefit from special education, the school system is obligated to provide the related service.

Assistive Technology

The 1990 enactment of IDEA added the terms "assistive technology device" and "assistive technology service" to special education law. These terms are defined as follows:

The term "assistive technology device" means:

any item, piece of equipment, or product system, whether acquired commercially off the shelf, modified, or customized, that is used to increase, maintain, or improve functional capabilities of individuals with disabilities.

20 U.S.C. §1401(a)(25)

The term "assistive technology service" means:

any service that directly assists an individual with a disability in the selection, acquisition, or use of an assistive technology device. Such term includes—

(A) the evaluation of the needs of an individual with a disability, including a functional evaluation of the individual in the individual's customary environment;

(B) purchasing, leasing, or otherwise providing for the acquisition of assistive technology devices by individuals with disabilities;

(C) selecting, designing, fitting, customizing, adapting, applying, maintaining, repairing, or replacing of assistive technology devices;

(D) coordinating and using other therapies, interventions, or services with assistive technology devices, such as those associated with existing education and rehabilitation plans and programs;

(E) training or technical assistance for an individual with disabilities, or, where appropriate, the family of an individual with disabilities; and

(F) training or technical assistance for professionals (including individuals providing education and rehabilitation services), employers, or other individuals who provide services to, employ, or are otherwise substantially involved in the major life functions of individuals with disabilities.

20 U.S.C. §1401(a)(26)

Prior to the 1990 enactment of IDEA, which incorporated the terms "assistive technology device" and "assistive technology service" into the law, the Federal Department of Education's Office of Special Education Programs issued a policy letter regarding the provision of assistive technology to children with disabilities. This policy letter stated that:

It is *impermissible* . . . for public agencies (including school districts) "to presumptively deny assistive technology" to a child with [disabilities] before a determination is made as to whether such technology is an element of a free appropriate public education (FAPE) for that child. Thus, consideration of a child's need for assistive technology must occur on a case-by-case basis in connection with the development of a child's individualized education program (IEP). . . .

[The] least restrictive environment (LRE) provisions require each agency to ensure "[t]hat special classes, separate schooling or other removal of [children with disabilities] from the regular educational environment occurs only when the nature or severity of the [disability] is such that education in regular classes with the use of supplementary aids and services cannot be achieved satisfactorily." . . . Assistive technology can be a form of supplementary aid or service utilized to facilitate a child's education in a regular educational environment. Such supplementary aids and services, or modifications to the regular education program, must be included in a child's IEP. . . .

In sum, a child's need for assistive technology must be determined on a case-by-case basis and could be special education, related services or supplementary aids and services for children with [disabilities] who are educated in regular classes.

Department of Education Policy Letter, *Goodman,* 8/10/90, 16 EHLR 1317 (Emphasis in original)

The specific addition of the terms "assistive technology device" and "assistive technology service," along with their detailed definitions, clearly establish the entitlement to such services for children with disabilities if such are required in order to receive a free appropriate public education.

Transition Services

With the enactment of IDEA, the IEPs for children with disabilities of a particular age must now include a statement of needed transition services. The term "transition services" is defined as:

a coordinated set of activities for a student, designed within an outcome-oriented process, which promotes movement from school to post-school activities, including post-secondary education, vocational training, integrated employment (including supported employment), continuing and adult education, adult services, independent living, or community participation. The coordinated set of activities shall be based upon the individual student's needs, taking into account the student's preferences and interests, and shall include instruction, community experiences, the development of employment and other post-school adult living objectives, and, when appropriate, acquisition of daily living skills and functional vocational evaluation.

20 U.S.C. §1401(a)(19)

The IDEA requires that once a student reaches the age of sixteen, and annually thereafter, the student's IEP must contain a statement of the needed transition services. 20 U.S.C. §1401(a)(20). With regard to students under the age of sixteen, the inclusion of transition services should be stated in the IEP as appropriate. However, state law may require that transition services be included on the IEP for students under the age of sixteen.

One court has already wrestled with the issue of transition services. In *Todd D. v. Andrews*, (11th Cir. 1991), 17 EHLR 986, the Court of Appeals for the Eleventh Circuit found that a student with disabilities must be "placed at a facility close enough to his home community to allow implementation of his transition goals." While the court's decision in *Todd D.* did not directly interpret the transition services requirement contained in the IDEA, it did note that in "establishing transition goals in Todd's IEP, his IEP team . . . anticipated the current statutory requirements" of the IDEA. *Todd D.* at 989, n.2. Accordingly, the decision in *Todd D.* provides some insight on one court's view regarding a school system's obligation to provide transition services to a student with disabilities.

The facts in the case indicate that Todd D.'s parents were residents of DeKalb County, Georgia. Although Todd required a residential placement, an appropriate residential placement could not be located in the state of Georgia. Accordingly, Todd was residentially placed in the San Marcos Treatment Center ("San Marcos") in Texas. Todd's parents requested a due process hearing, contending that Todd must be provided services "in his home community or at least in the state of Georgia." *Todd D.* at 986.

Realizing that due to Todd's age he soon would be outside of the age range for services in the state, Todd's IEP team developed an IEP which addressed his transition back into his home community.

With regard to the transition goals in Todd's IEP, the court found that:

> The impediment to making progress toward these transition goals was the fact that a facility in Todd's home community, or even the state of Georgia to which he might transfer and at which he might obtain aid in meeting the goals, could not be identified.

Todd D. at 987

As a result, the district court ordered that Todd's IEP be rewritten to allow the transition goals to be implemented at San Marcos.

On appeal, the Court of Appeals for the Eleventh Circuit found that the "district court essentially concluded that Georgia's obligations . . . should be met by altering the transition goals of the IEP rather than altering Todd's placement. In this way, the transition goals as stated in the altered version of the IEP could be achieved at San Marcos." *Todd D.* at 987. The Court of Appeals reversed the district court's decision and stated that:

> This approach is clearly not in line with the . . . requirement that each . . . child's IEP be crafted to meet that child's individual needs. Consequently, we hold that the district court erred in finding that Todd's current IEP need not be implemented as written. *Todd must therefore be placed at a facility close enough to his home community to allow implementation of his transition goals.*

Todd D. at 988 (Emphasis supplied)

While the IDEA's definition of "transition services" does not specifically require that transition services be provided in the student's home community, the definition does provide that such services "shall be based upon the individual student's needs, taking into account the student's preferences and interests." 20 U.S.C. §1401(a)(19). In the case of *Todd D.,* the student's IEP specifically required transition into the home community. Thus, the Court of Appeals determined that it was improper for the district court to rewrite the student's IEP to allow these transition services to be implemented out-of-state. It is interesting to note, however, that the Court of Appeals did not require that the student be placed in his home community. Rather, the court required that the student be "placed at a facility close enough to his home community to allow implementation of his transition goals." *Todd D.* at 988.

Least Restrictive Environment

One of the IDEA's major educational mandates is that children with disabilities be educated with nondisabled students to the maximum extent appropriate to meet their unique needs. This philosophy is embodied in the law's least restrictive environment provisions, often referred to as the "mainstreaming" provisions.

The IDEA provides:

(1) That to the maximum extent appropriate, children with disabilities, including children in public or private institutions or other care facilities, are educated with children who are nondisabled; and

(2) That special classes, separate schooling or other removal of children with disabilities from the regular educational environment occurs only when the nature or severity of the disability is such that education in regular classes with the use of supplementary aids and services cannot be achieved satisfactorily.

34 C.F.R. §300.550(b)

The least restrictive environment regulations also apply to the provision of nonacademic and extracurricular services activities. 34 C.F.R. §300.553. The Federal Department of Education has issued a policy letter regarding the least restrictive environment requirements. The Department of Education has stated that school systems:

must have procedures that ensure that such children are removed from the regular educational environment only when the nature or severity of the [disability] is such that education in regular classes with the use of supplementary aids and services cannot be achieved satisfactorily. If a [child with disabilities] is removed from the regular educational environment, our view is that the removal must not be based on the (1) category of [disability], (2) configuration of the service delivery system, (3) availability of educational or related services, (4) availability of space, or (5) curriculum content or method of service delivery.

Department of Education Policy Letter, *Boschwitz,* 12/5/88, EHLR 213:215

The Department of Education has also stated that in many cases even the most severely disabled students can be mainstreamed for a portion of the school day. The Department of Education has stated that:

There are many models that have convincingly demonstrated that, at a minimum, even the most severely disabled students can participate in lunch room activities, recess, and a variety of nonacademic and extracurricular activities. These same students, with appropriate instructional modifications, are with increasing frequency being served in regular classrooms and in separate classes in regular school buildings. Indeed, many school districts, including Madison, Wisconsin; Takoma, Washington; Albuquerque, New Mexico; Birmingham, Alabama; and Philadelphia, Pennsylvania, have closed their segregated schools for students with severe and profound [disabilities].

Our experience is that both students with disabilities and their [nondisabled] peers benefit from integrated education. Only through frequent and prolonged contact with students with disabilities can nondisabled children begin to focus on the individual strengths, determination, and independence exhibited by individuals with disabilities. Integrated education and community-based programming establishes the expectation that individuals with disabilities are an important and typical part of community and neighborhood activities.

Id. at 213:216

This policy letter clearly confirms a strong emphasis on compliance with the least restrictive environment provisions of special education law.

There are many judicial interpretations of the IDEA's least restrictive environment provisions. Two cases are widely cited. These are *Roncker v. Walter,* 700 F.2d 1058 (6th Cir. 1983) and *Daniel R.R. v. State Board of Education,* 874 F.2d 1036 (5th Cir. 1989). The *Roncker* analysis has been cited with approval by the Court of Appeals for the Fourth Circuit in *DeVries v. Fairfax County School Board,* 882 F.2d 876 (4th Cir.1989) and by the Court of Appeals for the Eighth Circuit in *A.W. v. Northwest R-1 School District,* 813 F.2d 158 (8th Cir.1987). In expressing its view regarding the least restrictive environment requirements, the Court of Appeals for the Sixth Circuit in *Roncker* stated:

In some cases, a placement which may be considered better for academic reasons may not be appropriate because of the failure to provide for mainstreaming. The perception that a segregated institution is academically superior for a [child with disabilities] may reflect no more than a basic disagreement with the mainstreaming concept.

Such a disagreement is not, of course, any basis for not following the Act's mandate. . . . In a case where the segregated facility is considered superior, the court should determine whether the services which make that placement superior could be feasibly provided in a non-segregated setting.

If they can, the placement in the segregated school would be inappropriate under the Act. *Roncker* at 1063

The *Roncker* case identified a number of factors to be considered when determining compliance with the least restrictive environment requirements. The factors articulated by the *Roncker* court are: the extent to which the disabled student would benefit from mainstreaming; whether the benefits gained from mainstreaming would be outweighed by the benefits gained from services which the school system could not feasibly provide in a nonsegregated setting; whether the disabled student would be unduly disruptive in the nonsegregated setting; and the cost of providing the necessary services in the non-segregated setting.

In *Daniel R.R. v. State Board of Education,* 874 F.2d 1036 (5th Cir.1989), the Court of Appeals for the Fifth Circuit articulated a two-part test for determining compliance with the least restrictive environment provisions. The *Daniel R.R.* test has been cited with approval by the Court of Appeals for the Third Circuit in *Oberti v. Board of Education,* 995 F.2d 1204 (3rd Cir.1993) and by the Court of Appeals for the Eleventh Circuit in *Greer v. Rome City School District,* 950 F.2d 688 (11th Cir.1991). The test provided by the Court in *Daniel R.R.* is as follows:

First, we ask whether education in the regular classroom, with the use of supplemental aids and services, can be achieved satisfactorily for a given child.... If it cannot and the school intends to provide special education or to remove the child from regular education, we ask, second, whether the school has mainstreamed the child to the maximum extent appropriate.... A variety of factors will inform each stage of our inquiry; the factors that we consider today do not constitute an exhaustive list of factors relevant to the mainstreaming issue. Moreover, no single factor is dispositive in all cases.

Daniel R.R. at 1048.

With regard to the first prong of this test, the factors the Court in *Daniel R.R.* considered included "(1) the steps the school district has taken in accommodating the child in a regular classroom; (2) whether the child will receive an educational benefit from regular education; (3) the child's overall educational experience in regular education; and (4) the effect the disabled child's presence has on the regular classroom." *Sacremento Unified School District v. Holland,* 20 IDELR 812, n.5 (9th Cir.1994).

With regard to the second prong of the *Daniel R.R.* test, the court stated that:

If we determine that education in the regular classroom cannot be achieved satisfactorily, we next ask whether the child has been mainstreamed to the maximum extent appropriate. The EHA and its regulations do not contemplate an all-or-nothing educational system in which [children with disabilities] attend either regular or special education. Rather, the Act and its regulations require schools to offer a continuum of services. . . . Thus, the school must take intermediate steps where appropriate, such as placing the child in regular education for some academic classes and in special education for others, mainstreaming the child for nonacademic classes only, or providing interaction with [nondisabled] children during lunch and recess.

Daniel R.R. at 1050.

While different courts have articulated different tests for determining compliance with the IDEA's least restrictive environment requirements, it is clear that the IDEA requires that children with disabilities be educated with their nondisabled peers to the maximum extent appropriate. This does not mean, however, that every disabled child must be placed in a regular education setting for all, or even part, of their school day. Rather, the IDEA requires that decisions regarding the appropriateness of a particular program must be individually tailored to meet the unique needs of the disabled child on a case-by-case basis.

Due Process Safeguards

The IDEA mandates that school systems provide children with disabilities proper evaluations, reevaluations, special education and related services as appropriate, and placement in the least restrictive environment, among other requirements. At the same time, the IDEA also gives parents of children with disabilities the right to challenge the school system's actions in both administrative due process hearings and in court. Specifically, a parent may request an administrative due process hearing to contest a school system's proposal or refusal to "initiate or change the identification, evaluation, or educational placement of the child or the provision of FAPE." 34 C.F.R. §§300.504 and 506.

In an administrative due process hearing, the parents and school system have the right to:

(1) Be accompanied and advised by counsel and by individuals with special knowledge or training with respect to the problems of children with disabilities.

(2) Present evidence and confront, cross-examine, and compel the attendance of witnesses.

(3) Prohibit the introduction of any evidence at the hearing that has not been disclosed to that party at least five days before the hearing.

(4) Obtain a written or electronic verbatim record of the hearing.

(5) Obtain written findings of fact and decisions. . . .

(b) Parents involved in hearings must be given the right to—

(1) Have the child who is the subject of the hearing present; and

(2) Open the hearing to the public.

34 C.F.R. §300.508 (20 U.S.C. §1415(d))

Furthermore, after all administrative due process hearing procedures have been exhausted, the parents or school system may appeal the final administrative due process hearing decision to court. 34 C.F.R. §300.511. Thus, children with disabilities have both an administrative and judicial mechanism for ensuring the fulfillment of their rights as delineated in special education law.

ZERO REJECT POLICY

As with all disabled students, the degree of disability suffered by a child who has incurred a brain injury can range from the mild to the severe or profound. A question which has arisen is whether a student can be so impaired as to not be entitled to special education services.

In *Timothy W. v. Rochester, New Hampshire School District*, 875 F.2d 954 (1st Cir. 1989), the Court of Appeals for the First Circuit held that federal law requires that a free appropriate public education be made available to *all* eligible students with disabilities regardless of the severity of their disability. The court, finding that the law embraced a "zero reject" policy, held that school systems may not deny special education services to children with disabilities on the basis that they are "uneducable" due to the severity of their condition.

The student in *Timothy W.* was described as follows:

Timothy W. was born two months prematurely on December 8, 1975 with severe respiratory problems and shortly thereafter experienced an intracranial hemorrhage, subdural effusions, seizures, hydrocephalus, and meningitis. As a result, Timothy is multiply [disabled] and profoundly mentally retarded. He suffers from complex developmental disabilities, spastic quadriplegia, cerebral palsy, seizure disorder and cortical blindness.

Timothy W. at 955–56

The school district rejected the parent's request that the student be provided with special education services, contending that the student was not capable of benefitting from such services and was therefore not entitled to such services. The parents appealed this decision. The federal district court held that "an initial decision must be made concerning the ability of a [child with disabilities] to benefit from special education before an entitlement to the education can exist. . . . Timothy W. is not capable of benefitting from special education. . . . As a result, the defendant [school district] is not obligated to provide [Timothy W. with] special education. . . . " *Timothy W.* at 959.

On appeal, the Court of Appeals for the First Circuit reversed the district court's decision. The Court of Appeals reviewed the language of the special education law and found that it required that all children with disabilities be provided with a free appropriate public education. The court stated that "not only are severely [disabled] children not excluded from the Act, but the most severely [disabled] are actually given *priority* under the Act. . . . The language of the Act could not be more unequivocal. The statute is permeated with the words '*all* [disabled] children' whenever it refers to the target population. It never speaks of any exceptions for severely [disabled] children." *Timothy W.* at 960 (Emphasis in original). The court went on to conclude:

> The language of the Act in its entirety makes clear that a "zero-reject" policy is at the core of the Act, and that no child, regardless of the severity of his or her [disability], is ever again to be subjected to the deplorable state of affairs which existed at the time of the Act's passage, in which millions of [disabled] children received inadequate education or none at all. In summary, the Act mandates an appropriate public education for all [disabled] children, regardless of the level of achievement that such children might attain.

Timothy W. at 960–61

The United States Supreme Court refused the school system's request to review the decision.

MEDICALLY FRAGILE CHILDREN WITH DISABILITIES

As discussed in *Timothy W.,* the court concluded that even those students with the most severe impairments are entitled to a free appropriate public education. As a result, for some severely impaired students, the range of needed services will be wide and may encompass services that are traditionally thought of as medical services. This may be particularly true of children with severe brain injury.

Further, as medical technology progresses, so does the ability of the medically fragile student to attend school. In the past, students with complicated medical problems that required extensive supervision and medical attention were confined at home or in a hospital. With advances in medical technology, many of these students, including those with brain injury, are now able to spend part or all of their school day in a school classroom if certain health related services are also provided.

While school systems are required to provide students with disabilities with related services such as "school health services," school systems are not obligated to provide "medical services" except for diagnostic and evaluative purposes. 34 C.F.R. §300.16(a). The related service of "school health services" is defined as "services provided by a qualified school nurse or other qualified person." 34 C.F.R. §300.16(b)(11). A number of judicial decisions provide guidance in determining where the line between required related services and excluded medical services is to be drawn.

In the previously discussed case of *Irving Independent School District v. Tatro*, 104 S.Ct 3371 (1984), the United States Supreme Court held that the provision of clean intermittent catheterization (CIC) service was "not subject to exclusion as a 'medical service,' and . . . CIC is a 'related service' " under special education law. *Tatro* at 3378.

Subsequent to the *Tatro* case, a number of courts have discussed a school system's obligation to provide medical-type services to students with disabilities. In this regard, it appears that there are two schools of judicial thought concerning the difference between exempted medical services and the related service of school health services which school systems are required to provide as appropriate. One school of thought is that if the requested services do not need to be provided by a licensed physician, and otherwise meet the definition of related services, then those services are a related service which the school system is obligated to provide. Other courts have rejected a distinction which is based on the licensed status of the service provider and, instead, appear to consider a number of factors in determining whether a particular medical-type service is a school health service which the school system is obligated to provide or an exempted medical service which the school system is not required to provide. A discussion of these two approaches is provided below.

In *Macomb County Intermediate School District v. Joshua S.*, 715 F.Supp 824 (E.D. Mich. 1989), the Court applied a bright line test in making the school health service/exempted medical service distinction. In *Joshua S.*, the parents of a severely multiply impaired student challenged the school system's denial of transportation for the student due to his "medically fragile nature."

The court held that "the medical services exclusion is limited to services provided by a licensed physician. . . . While disagreement exists as to whether a trained layperson could adequately service the [student's] needs, we believe that *Tatro* supports the use of a medical professional, other than a physician, if necessary to the safe transport of the [student]." *Joshua S.* at 828. Thus, the court ruled that the school system was required to provide the services to the student on the basis that the services were not required to be delivered by a physician.

Using a different approach, the court in *Detsel v. Board of Education of the Auburn Enlarged City School District*, 637 F.Supp 1022 (ND NY 1986), determined that the extensive health services the student required were not related services (or school health services) that must be provided by the school system.

The Court found that, while at school, the student's nurse was required to:

> check Melissa's vital signs and administer medication through a tube to the child's jejunum. Moreover, she must perform a procedure known as a "P, D and C" which calls for the ingestion of saline solution by the child into her lungs; the nurse subsequently strikes her about the lungs for four minutes and then suctions out any mucus collected in her lungs. Also, the individual who accompanies Melissa must be prepared to perform cardio-pulmonary resuscitation because of complications arising from a tracheotomy. Furthermore, Melissa is likely to suffer from respiratory distress which has been described as a life-threatening condition by her doctor. The school physician has testified that the foregoing procedures would require the services of a licensed practical nurse (LPN) or a registered nurse. Melissa's own physician has testified that the services of a school nurse would be inadequate.

Detsel at 1024–25

The Court ruled that the extensive health services required by the student, which the Court held more closely resembled exempted medical services than the related service of school health services, were not required to be provided by the school system. The Court's decision was affirmed upon appeal to the Court of Appeals for the Second Circuit. See *Detsel v. Board of Education of the Auburn Enlarged City School District,* 820 F.2d 587 (2nd Cir. 1987). Thus, although the services did not have to be performed by a licensed physician, the court determined that the requested services were exempted medical services that the school system was not obligated to provide.

In *Bevin H. v. Wright,* 666 F.Supp 71 (W.D. Pa. 1987), the Court, following the same rationale applied in *Detsel,* ruled that the school system was not required to provide the extensive health services required by the student to allow her to attend school. In *Bevin H.,* the court observed that the student suffers from "multiple [disabilities], principally Robinow Syndrome (fetal face syndrome), severe broncho-pulmonary dysplasia, profound mental retardation, spastic quadriplegia, seizure disorder, and hydrocephalus. She is also legally blind. She breathes through a tracheostomy tube and is fed and medicated through a gastrostomy tube." *Bevin H.* at 72.

As the Court noted, "the services Bevin requires at school are extensive. The attending nurse must accompany Bevin to and from school. She is responsible for the care and cleaning of the tracheostomy and gastrostomy tubes, she administers a constant oxygen supply to Bevin. She supervises positioning for physical and occupational therapy. She administers chest physical therapy each day to break up mucous, and must suction the mucous from the lungs. Above all though, the nurse must remain with Bevin at all times because of the constant possibility of a mucous plug in the tracheostomy tube. Such a plug is a common event, occurring several times each day, and must be cleared by the nurse within thirty seconds to prevent injury to Bevin." *Bevin H.* at 73.

The Court rejected the parents' argument that the requested services were related services and concluded that "the nursing services required are so varied, intensive and costly, and more in the nature of 'medical services' that they are not properly includable as 'related services'" which the school system would otherwise be obligated to provide. *Bevin H.* at 76.

The above referenced cases illustrate that there are two schools of thought regarding the distinction between school health services and excluded medical services. At least one court (*Joshua S.*) has held that the medical services exclusion is limited to those health care services which are provided by a licensed physician. Thus, pursuant to the *Joshua S.* rationale, any health care service which otherwise qualifies as a related service and which does not need to be administered by a licensed physician would be the responsibility of the school system. Other courts, however, have adopted a multifactored analysis for making the distinction between school health services and excluded medical services. At this time, it appears that the trend is to follow the latter school of thought, i.e., the multifactored analysis, when making this distinction. However, future court cases, and possibly a second look at this issue by the United States Supreme Court, are expected to clarify the issue.

EDUCATIONAL V. NONEDUCATIONAL PLACEMENTS

Tied closely to the issue of the distinction between related services and excluded medical services is the question of residential placements for educational as compared with noneducational reasons. The IDEA requires school systems to ensure "that a continuum of alterative placements is available to meet the needs of children with disabilities for special education and related services." 34 C.F.R. §300.551(a). Among the various types of placements along this continuum is a residential placement. In this context, the law provides that:

> If placement in a public or private residential program is necessary to provide special education and related services to a child with a disability, the program, including non-medical care and room and board, must be at no cost to the parents of the child.

34 C.F.R. §300.302

While the IDEA envisions that residential placement may be necessary to afford some students, including children with brain injury, an appropriate education, it also recognizes that some children with disabilities may require a residential placement for noneducational reasons. The official Note to the federal regulation regarding residential placements provides that:

> This requirement applies to placements that are made by public agencies *for educational purposes,* and includes placements in State-operated schools for children with disabilities, such as a State school for students with deafness or students with blindness.

Note, 34 C.F.R. §300.302 (Emphasis supplied)

This official Note implies that not all students with disabilities who need a residential placement necessarily require such a placement for educational reasons.

The distinction between educationally-based and noneducationally-based residential placements is an important one because the distinction serves to facilitate a determination regarding who is responsible for funding the placement. It is clear that if a child with disabilities requires a residential placement in order to receive a free appropriate public education, the school system is responsible for funding the costs of the appropriate residential placement. However, if a residential placement is necessitated by noneducational concerns, the residential component of the student's program may not be the responsibility of the school system. The following cases provide guidance in making this distinction.

An oft cited case regarding the distinction between educationally-based and noneducationally-based residential placements is *Kruelle v. New Castle County School District,* 642 F.2d 687 (3rd. Cir. 1981). The Court of Appeals for the Third Circuit described the student as follows:

> Appellant [Paul Kruelle] is profoundly retarded and is also afflicted with cerebral palsy. At age thirteen he has the social skills of a six month old child and his I.Q. is well below thirty.... "he cannot walk, dress himself, or eat unaided. He is not toilet trained. He does not speak, and his receptive communication level is extremely low. In addition to his physical problems, he has had a history of emotional problems which result in choking and self-induced vomiting when experiencing stress."

Kruelle at 688–89

The parents requested that the school system provide a residential placement for Paul and this request was denied. The case proceeded ultimately to the Court of Appeals for the Third Circuit.

The school system argued that the student's residential placement was "required only for reasons of medical and domiciliary care, not for educational purposes." *Kruelle* at 693. In response, the court stated that:

> the concept of education is necessarily broad with respect to persons such as Paul. "Where basic self-help and social skills such as toilet training, dressing,

feeding and communication are lacking, formal education begins at that point."...

Analysis must focus, then, on whether full-time placement may be considered necessary for educational purposes, or whether the residential placement is a response to medical, social or emotional problems that are segregable from the learning process.

Kruelle at 693–94

Applying this analysis, the court found that "consistency of programming and environment is critical to Paul's ability to learn, for the absence of a structured environment contributes to Paul's choking and vomiting which, in turn, interferes fundamentally with his ability to learn.... Indeed, it would be difficult to conceive of a more apt case than Paul's for which the unique needs of a child required residential placement." *Kruelle* at 694.

In determining that residential placement was necessary to meet the student's educational needs, the court also considered the least restrictive environment provisions of the law. The court stated that:

> before ordering residential placement, a court should weigh the mainstreaming policy . . . which encourages placement of the child in the least restrictive environment. The district judge here, however, carefully undertook such a calculation. He noted that in the past attempts to provide in-home care and after-school instruction had been singularly unsuccessful; all had occasioned regression for Paul.

Kruelle at 695

Thus, the court found that the student required a residential placement to address his educational needs and, as such, the school system was required to pay for the placement.

As indicated, the *Kruelle* case is often cited by courts regarding the distinction between educationally-based and noneducationally-based residential placements. A critical passage from *Kruelle* states that the "analysis must focus . . . on whether full-time placement may be considered necessary for educational purposes, or whether the residential placement is a response to medical, social, or emotional problems that are segregable from the learning process." While it is sometimes difficult to apply this test, it appears to be the standard upon which many courts will rely in making a determination as to whether a residential placement is needed for educational or noneducational reasons. For example, the following case applied the *Kruelle* test, but based on the different facts, reached a contrary conclusion.

In *Clovis Unified School District v. Shorey,* 903 F.2d 635 (9th Cir. 1990), the court determined that the student's hospitalization was not educationally based and, thus, was not the responsibility of the local school system. While there was no dispute that the student required a residential placement in order to receive a FAPE, the school system maintained that it was not responsible for funding the student's placement at a hospital.

The school system argued that "placement at the hospital was for medical, rather than educational reasons, and that therefore, the district was not obligated to fund such a placement." *Clovis* at 640. The parents subsequently requested a due process hearing and a hearing officer ruled in their favor ordering the school system to pay for the student's hospitalization. This decision was ultimately upheld by a federal district court.

On appeal, the Court of Appeals for the Ninth Circuit outlined its analytical framework for deciding when a placement is for educational as compared with noneducational reasons. The court stated that:

> . . . our analysis must focus on whether . . . placement may be considered necessary for educational purposes, or whether the placement is a response to medical, social, or emotional problems that is necessary quite apart from the learning process.

Clovis at 643

Adopting the test articulated in *Kruelle* to determine whether the student's hospitalization was a response to medical, social or emotional problems that were separate from the learning process, the court concluded that the student was "hospitalized primarily for medical" reasons and, therefore, the school district was not required to fund this hospitalization. *Clovis* at 645.

As indicated, in this case it was conceded by the school system that the student required a residential placement in order to receive a free appropriate public education. However, the court found that the particular placement in question, a hospital, was in response to a medical crisis. Thus, the *Clovis* decision provides an illustration of a case where a court has determined that a residential placement was in response to medical problems that were separate from the student's educational needs and, thus, the school system was not responsible for funding the residential portion of that placement.

SECTION 504 OF THE REHABILITATION ACT OF 1973

In addition to the IDEA, another statute entitled Section 504 of the Rehabilitation Act of 1973 (Section 504) provides protections for handicapped students. (The Section 504 regulations use the term "handicapped" when referring to students with disabilities.) Some of the most significant elements of this law are summarized for general information.

Section 504 provides that:

> No otherwise qualified individual with handicaps in the United States . . . shall, solely by reason of her or his handicap, be excluded from the participation in,

be denied the benefits of, or be subjected to discrimination under any program or activity receiving Federal financial assistance or under any program or activity conducted by any Executive agency or by the United States Postal Service.

29 U.S.C. §794

As noted, Section 504 prohibits discrimination against "qualified handicapped" persons. A "handicapped person" under the Section 504 regulations means any person who:

(i)   has a physical or mental impairment, which substantially limits one or more major life activities,

(ii) has a record of such an impairment, or

(iii) is regarded as having such an impairment.

34 C.F.R. §104.3(j) (1)

A "physical or mental impairment" means:

(A) any physiological disorder or condition, cosmetic disfigurement, or anatomical loss affecting one or more of the following body systems: neurological; musculoskeletal; special sense organs; respiratory, including speech organs; cardiovascular; reproductive; digestive, genito-urinary; hermic and lymphatic; skin; and endocrine; or

(B) any mental or psychological disorder, such as mental retardation, organic brain syndrome, emotional or mental illness, and specific learning disabilities.

34 C.F.R. §104.3(j) (2) (i)

"Major life activities" means:

functions such as caring for one's self, performing manual tasks, walking, seeing, hearing, speaking, breathing, learning, and working.

34 C.F.R. §104.3(j) (2) (ii)

"Handicap" means:

any condition or characteristic that renders a person a handicapped person as defined [above].

34 C.F.R. §104.3(1)

With respect to public preschool, elementary, secondary or adult educational services, "qualified handicapped persons" means a handicapped person:

(i)   of an age during which nonhandicapped persons are provided such services,

(ii) of an age during which it is mandatory under state law to provide such services to handicapped persons, or

(iii) to whom a state is required to provide a free appropriate public education under Sec. 612 of the Education of the Handicapped Act [now called the IDEA].

34 C.F.R. §104.3(k) (2)

It can be seen that the basic definition of handicapped person under Section 504 is very broad. While both Section 504 and the IDEA require that students who fall within the purview of those statutes be provided a free appropriate public education, the Section 504 protections extend to a larger population of students. For those students who are disabled under Section 504 and also disabled under the IDEA, compliance with the IDEA's requirements will generally constitute compliance with the Section 504 requirements.

CONCLUSION

The enactment of the IDEA in 1990 marks an important milestone in special education law. Although prior federal special education law did provide eligible students with brain injuries the right to a free appropriate public education, there was no separate disability category identified for this population of students. The enactment of the IDEA established a separate disability category entitled "traumatic brain injury." Thus, students who meet the criteria of this disability are no longer required to satisfy the definitional criteria of other specifically recognized disabling conditions in order to receive special education services under the IDEA. At the same time, even if a student with brain injury does not meet the specific definitional criteria of traumatic brain injury, services may still be available if the student qualifies under specific learning disabled, other health impaired, or any other disability category. Most importantly, federal special education law applies equally to eligible children who have brain injuries and as such they are entitled to all of the rights and protections under the law.

NOTE: The reader is cautioned that the court cases referenced in this chapter are provided for general information only and, except for decisions by the United States Supreme Court, are not necessarily binding in all states. Special education law is a rapidly changing area of the law and any court decision or federal opinion is subject to expansion, clarification or reversal in the future. Additionally, it is important to note that this chapter has focused on federal special education law. Individual states have discretion to provide a greater level of protection to children with disabilities than is required by federal law. Finally, the information contained in this chapter is provided for general background information only and does not constitute legal advice. If legal advice is required, the services of a competent professional should be obtained.

---

*This chapter is dedicated to Louis Rosa, M.D. and G. Nicholas Rogentine, M.D. in profound appreciation by Richard E. Ekstrand.

CITATIONS

Individuals with Disabilities Education Act, 20 U.S.C. §1400 *et seq.*

    20 U.S.C. §1400 (c)
    20 U.S.C. §1401 (a) (1)
    20 U.S.C. §1401 (a) (16)
    20 U.S.C. §1401 (a) (17)
    20 U.S.C. §1401 (a) (18)
    20 U.S.C. §1401 (a) (19)
    20 U.S.C. §1401 (a) (20)
    20 U.S.C. §1401 (a) (25)
    20 U.S.C. §1401 (a) (26)
    20 U.S.C. §1412 (5) (C)
    20 U.S.C. §1415 (d)

    34 C.F.R. §300.5
    34 C.F.R. §300.7
    34 C.F.R. §300.8
    34 C.F.R. §300.16
    34 C.F.R. §300.17
    34 C.F.R. §300.302
    34 C.F.R. §300.340
    34 C.F.R. §300.346
    34 C.F.R. §300.504
    34 C.F.R. §300.506
    34 C.F.R. §300.508
    34 C.F.R. §300.511
    34 C.F.R. §300.531
    34 C.F.R. §300.534
    34 C.F.R. §300.550
    34 C.F.R. §300.551
    34 C.F.R. §300.553

Section 504 of the Rehabilitation Act of 1973, 29 U.S.C. §794

    34 C.F.R. §104.3 (j) (1)
    34 C.F.R. §104.3 (j) (2) (i)
    34 C.F.R. §104.3 (j) (2) (ii)
    34 C.F.R. §104.3 (k) (2)
    34 C.F.R. §104.3 (l)

Department of Education Policy Letter, 12/5/88, EHLR 213:215
Department of Education Policy Letter, 5/25/90, 16 EHLR 961
Department of Education Policy Letter, 2/26/90, 16 EHLR 552
Department of Education Policy Letter, 8/10/90, 16 EHLR 1317
Department of Education Policy Letter, 12/18/92, 19 IDELR 928
Department of Education Policy Letter, 7/13/93, 20 IDELR 623

Federal Register, Vol. 56, No. 160, 8/19/91
Federal Register, Vol. 57, No. 189, 9/29/92

Pennsylvania Assn. for Retarded Children v. Commonwealth, 334 F.Supp 1257 (Ed Pa. 1971) and 343 F.Supp 279 (1972)

Mills v. Board of Education of District of Columbia, 348 F.Supp 866 (D D.C. 1972)

Board of Education of the Hendrick Hudson Central School District v. Rowley, 102 S.Ct. 3034 (1982)

Honig v. Doe, 108 S.Ct. 592 (1988)

Irving Independent School District v. Tatro, 104 S.Ct. 3371 (1984)

Todd D. v. Andrews, (11th Cir. 1991), 17 EHLR 986

Roncker v. Walter, 700 F.2d 1058 (6th Cir. 1983)

Daniel R.R. v. State Board of Education, 874 F.2d 1036 (5th Cir.1989)

DeVries v. Fairfax County School Board, 882 F.2d 876 (4th Cir.1989)

A.W. v. Northwest R-1 School District, 813 F.2d 158 (8th Cir.1987)

Oberti v. Board of Education, 995 F.2d 1204 (3rd Cir.1993)

Greer v. Rome City School District, 950 F.2d 688 (11th Cir.1991)

Sacramento Unified School District v. Holland, 20 IDELR 812 (9th Cir.1994)

Timothy W. v. Rochester, New Hampshire School District, 875 F.2d 954 (1st Cir. 1989)

Detsel v. Board of Education of the Auburn Enlarged City School District, 637 F.Supp 1022 (ND NY 1986)

Detsel v. Board of Education of the Auburn Enlarged City School District, 820 F.2d 587 (2nd Cir. 1987)

Bevin H. v. Wright, 666 F.Supp 71 (WD Pa. 1987)

Macomb County Intermediate School District v. Joshua S., 715 F.Supp 824 (ED Mich. 1989)

Kruelle v. New Castle County School District, 642 F.2d 687 (3rd Cir. 1981)

Clovis Unified School District v. Shorey, 903 F.2d 635 (9th Cir. 1990)

Chapter 3

LABELING AND ENTRANCE INTO SPECIAL EDUCATION

LAURIE GRAHAM, DIANA TOGNAZZINI, AND MARTHA LYONS-HOLDEN

HISTORY

To assist in understanding the philosophy and service delivery model of special education, one must return to its roots and growth process over the years. Special education emerged from various fields including medicine, psychology, and public education. By traveling back to special education's beginnings, one can comprehend why the present system of special education exists and, more importantly, where it is heading.

Public Education

The development of public education in the United States began in the 1700s when the leaders from other countries realized the need and importance in establishing an educational system. In 1779, Virginia established the first state school system. Soon after, the United States Constitution gave state jurisdiction over educational policies in the Tenth Amendment. A national movement in education was evidenced in the early 1800s by the establishment of the National Education Association, an organization for teachers, and the United States Office of Education (Meier, 1992).

Although it seems to have been always in existence, it was not until the mid 1800s that public schools initiated an age-grade level structure. Children with special educational needs were either retained or accelerated. Emphasis was placed on homogeneous grouping according to age, and individual differences were placed on the back burner.

The development of the first intelligence test in 1916 by Terman paved the way for categorizing learning ability. The Stanford-Binet Scale of Intelligence introduced the concept of intelligence quotient (IQ) to predict school success (Sattler, 1982). The test was originally designed to assess a child's cognitive ability to determine whether he/she would benefit from a regular education program. Thus, the use of the "IQ" increased the educator's awareness of individual differences.

A more recent wave in public education was the launching of Sputnik in 1958, resulting in a push in the academic areas of math, science, and foreign language. In 1965, the Elementary and Secondary Education Act was passed which provided federal support for new educational programs. In the 1970s and 1980s the government took a closer look at public education. The end product was a document published in 1983 called *A Nation At Risk* which criticized the educational practices in the United States and called for higher standards.

Special Education

The term "special education" brings many connotations to light, one of which most frequently associated is mental retardation. Although special education today covers a wide gamut of disabilities, its earliest history lies in the treatment of mentally retarded individuals.

One of the first documented educational attempts of a mentally retarded individual was conducted by Dr. Jean Itard, a physician. Dr. Itard developed methods to teach Victor, the "wild boy of Aveyron" social and academic skills. In 1799, Victor was found outside the province of Aveyron in France and was diagnosed by the leading psychiatrist, Pinel, as an idiot and incurable. Dr. Itard was able to teach Victor some social skills but was unable to reach the goals of developing his understanding and intelligence (Strauss, Lehtinen, and Kephart, 1989).

Prior to the 1800s, treatment of the mentally retarded was led by superstition and was grossly inhumane. Many children did not live past infancy. Abandonment and deliberate killing of children with severe impairments were common practices (Anderson, Greer, and Rich, 1982). However, the rise in Christianity provided a more humane view of the unfortunates. Institutions or asylums were established to house the "feebleminded and idiots," as they were classified in the 1800s. Conditions in these asylums were far from humane and education and training were but a dream. It was not until 1896 that the first public school special class was held for mentally retarded children (Heward and Orlansky, 1988).

The more apparent handicapping conditions of blindness and deafness also greatly influenced the delivery of services and direction in special education. In 1578, Pedro Ponce de León started a school for deaf children of noble families in Spain. He taught the deaf through speaking, reading, and writing. Due to Ponce de León's success, schools for the deaf were set up throughout Europe during the 18th century. In the United States, the American Asylum for the Education of the Deaf and Dumb opened in Hartford, Connecticut in 1817. At that time it was viewed that the best delivery of services was in residential treatment centers away from public settings (Heward and Orlansky, 1988).

Blind students were also housed and educated in separate residential institutions. The first school for the blind was established in Paris in 1784. Throughout Europe, this trend was continued and institutions were established during the 19th century. The United States followed Europe's lead and the first residential schools for the blind were opened in 1830 in Boston, New York, and Philadelphia. Residential schools were dominant and it was not until 1930 that Chicago opened the first classroom in a public school for the blind.

Special Education services as we see them today have a relatively short history. Meier (1992) identifies the 1960s as the Era of Special Education. The following six events account for this increased awareness and policy making in special education:

1. President John F. Kennedy acknowledged that he had a mentally retarded sister. Hubert Humphrey had a grandchild with Down syndrome.
2. The economic situation was relatively stable.
3. The civil rights movement shed light on equal opportunity of education.
4. Parent organizations such as the National Association for Retarded Citizens and professional organizations such as Council for Exceptional Children combined their strength for advocating education for all children.
5. Sputnik launching made Americans take a serious look at education.
6. The category of "learning disabilities" emerged. These combined events led the nation into actively initiating a federal policy for providing education for handicapped children.

The greatest influence in the government developing laws to guarantee education for handicapped individuals was the Civil Rights case of Brown v. Board of Education of Topeka in 1954. This landmark case challenged the existence of segregated schools according to race. "The U.S. Supreme Court declared that education must be available to all children on equal terms" and stated "In these days, it is doubtful that any child may reasonably be expected to succeed in life if he is denied the opportunity of an education" (Heward and Orlansky, 1988, P. 37).

It is the civil rights movement in addition to the following court cases which outlined the policy and delivery of special education services today.

1. 1967 Hobson v. Hansen in Washington D.C. which declared the track system, using standardized tests as a basis for special education placement, as unconstitutional.
2. Diana v. State Board of Education of California which declared

children could not be placed in special education on the basis of culturally-biased tests or tests not in the child's native language.
3. 1972 Mills v. Board of Education of the District of Columbia which established the right of every child to an equal opportunity for education and lack of funds could not be used for an excuse to not provide education.
4. 1972 Pennsylvania Association for Retarded Citizens v. the Commonwealth of Pennsylvania class action suit to establish the right to a free public education for all retarded children.

A combination of all of these forces, including court cases, professional and parent advocacy organizations, and life work of individuals throughout history, resulted in the writing of Public Law 94-142 which was passed in 1975 and fully implemented in 1977. This law "mandated free, appropriate public education for all handicapped children regardless of degree of severity of handicap; protected rights of handicapped children and parents in educational decision making; required that an individualized education program (IEP) be developed for each handicapped child; and that handicapped students receive educational services in the least restrictive environment" (Heward and Orlansky, 1988, p. 37). In addition, Section 504 of the Vocational Rehabilitation Act of 1973 is a civil rights statute which affirms the rights and protection of handicapped children outlined in P.L. 94-142 (Ballard and Zettel, 1977).

ENTRANCE INTO SPECIAL EDUCATION

P.L. 94-142, The Education for All Handicapped Children Act, was fully implemented in 1977 but may not have begun benefitting children and youth with brain injury in organizing appropriate educational programs until recently (Pimental, 1989). Initially, as many young people began surviving brain injury, they were inappropriately labeled as mentally retarded or seriously emotionally disturbed and their educational programs were designed to follow the characteristics of those labels. As educators are becoming increasingly aware of brain injury and its many unique characteristics, educational programming for ABI students is becoming more appropriate.

This new awareness in brain injury is especially evident in P.L. 101-476 (the IDEA), which includes the traumatic brain injury eligibility category.

P.L. 94-142 and its reauthorization with amendments (IDEA) mandate appropriate education for "all" children regardless of the severity of handicapping conditions. The conditions of the law mandate a step-by-step procedure for identifying children in need of special education and require an individualized educational program to be written for every child receiving special education programming.

FIGURE 3.1
INDIVIDUAL EDUCATION PROGRAM (IEP)

Essential Steps for Successful Programming

1. REFERRAL	Early Identification
2. ASSESSMENT PLAN DEVELOPED	Parent-School Communication
3. ASSESSMENT CONDUCTED	Understanding Student's Needs
4. IEP MEETING	Designing an Educational Program
5. PROGRAM IMPLEMENTED	Developing Awareness to Brain Injury
6. REVIEWS	Ongoing Follow-Up Annually and/or as Scheduled

The flow chart seen in Figure 3.1 outlines the procedural steps for special education placement which are mandated by law. This first step, which is the referral, is especially important for children with brain injury. If a child returns to school from a rehabilitation or hospital setting, then identification is not an issue and the IEP process can continue on to review of assessments and programming. However, many students who sustain brain injuries are treated in emergency facilities and then are returned to home and school without further interventions. If these students return to school without a report of having experienced a brain injury, or if the educational staff is not aware of characteristics relating to brain injury, these students may experience unnecessary difficulties. In many cases, the students are not identified as needing help until they exhibit cognitive, behavioral, or psychosocial problems. Behaviors relating to fatigue and attention problems may be viewed simply as manipulation. Some students exhibiting behaviors relating to aggression or disinhibition may be suspended several times or even expelled before appropriate interventions can be organized. In other cases, a student's emotional stability is affected and identification for intervention does not occur until a suicide attempt or other emergency brings the student to the attention of someone who may recognize the symptoms.

Once a formal referral for special education evaluation is made, an assessment plan must be developed for parents to review. The development of the assessment plan is an excellent point at which to build a working relationship with parents. For many parents of brain-injured students, entering the world of special education is a frightening and confusing experience. This may be because of historical views, or the mass of people and paperwork which can be part of the IEP process. Parents who are part of the process will be much more receptive and agreeable to an assessment plan when treated with sensitivity. Parents should be viewed as being instrumental in providing the assessment team with valuable information regarding behaviors and abilities that have been documented prior to injury. Also, if a cooperative working relationship is established, meetings and programming will generally proceed with ease and flexibility. The end result of providing an appropriate and successful program is much more likely to occur if parents feel in control and understand their child's needs.

The actual assessment must be conducted by a multidisciplinary team that evaluates areas of suspected need. The purpose of the assessment is to evaluate a child's present level of functioning and understanding. Student needs are obviously a critical component of successful educational programming. Areas evaluated may include health, vision, hearing, speech and language abilities, motor skills, academic achievement, cognitive abilities, personal care skills, community integration awareness, social and emotional status, and vocational abilities and interests. The assessment must be completed and a review meeting held to discuss results. State time lines vary as to the amount of time which can pass prior to the review meeting.

IEP Process

The IEP meeting needs to be attended by the student's parents or legal guardian and any individuals they wish to invite. In addition, other members of the team should include the school administrator, the assessment team, appropriate regular and special education teachers, and any outside agency representatives necessary for understanding the child's needs. This would be especially important if a child is returning to school after a rehabilitation or hospitalized placement. The IEP meeting is held to discuss assessment results, eligibility for special education services, as well as placement and program decisions. Important elements that need to be written into the IEP during this meeting include but may not be limited to:

1. Specific placement, instruction, and services required.
2. Extent to which the student can be mainstreamed into regular programs.
3. Date of initiation and anticipated duration of special services.
4. Duration and frequency of services.
5. Student's present level of performance.
6. Goals and short-term objectives.
7. Criteria by which the goals and objectives will be measured.
8. Appropriate evaluation procedures.
9. Schedule of review to measure the student's progress.
10. Transition component (Federal law requires this by age 16).

Least Restrictive Environment: The IEP team must look to place the student in the least restrictive environment. Figure 3.2 presents a continuum of

FIGURE 3.2

Placements: From Most to Least Restrictive.

Hospital or Public Institution
Residential School
Home Instruction
Special School—Day Program
Special Day Class—Public School
Special Day Class—Mainstreaming
Regular Education Class—Resource
Regulation Education Class—Supplementary Instruction (Speech, APE, OT PT, Counseling)
Regular Education Class—Inclusion Program
Regular Education Class—Consultation
Regular Education Class—No Interventions

possible placements moving up from least to most restrictive options for educational programming. While some students with brain injuries may not require any special interventions at all, many students do. Some are able to maintain themselves socially, behaviorally, and academically in a regular class program, but in a regular classroom where the class is "team taught" by both regular and special educators. Here, teachers collaborate and plan instructional strategies for all students. This concept is fairly new and is often referred to as the Inclusion Model. This model is significant to the least restrictive placement concept as it incorporates more severely handicapped children into the mainstream for the entire day and curriculum. Students with less significant needs may be successful in the regular class curriculum but may need to leave the room to receive supplementary instruction in such areas as speech and language, adaptive physical education, occupational therapy, physical therapy, and counseling. Other students may leave the classroom to receive supplemental or direct instruction in academic areas. A special day class program usually provides instruction for a small group of students with various handicapping conditions who are unable to function successfully in a regular program. These students may be mainstreamed into regular programs for part of their day. More restrictive programs may be run by county and private organizations where the schools are in physically separate sites from the public school sites. Some students are provided with tutorial programs at home. This is usually organized for a brief amount of time relating to issues of health. Most restrictive but often necessary for victims of brain injury, especially immediately following injury, are residential schools and hospital or institutional facilities. The continuum of possible services needs to be viewed as just that, a continuum, and students with brain injury may need different placements for different stages of their rehabilitative processes.

The goals and objectives for instruction need to be organized before placement can be determined. These goals and objectives also need to be written with an understanding of characteristics related to brain injury. For example, if an individual gets easily disoriented with environmental auditory stimulation, writing the vocational goal of learning to bowl in a public bowling alley would be inappropriate. Individuals who have sustained head injuries will also require different evaluation procedures. Testing for standard scores or age equivalencies may not be of value. Students with brain injuries may be better evaluated by looking at "how" they do things and not what they do. Also, frequent reviews may be necessary for students with brain injuries as their progress is not as predictable as that of those with other handicapping conditions. Frequent formal reviews allow educators working with these students an opportunity to monitor not only progress toward written goals but also a review of the students' overall reactions to their environments and evaluate social and emotional status. IEP reviews must be conducted at least yearly and overall reevaluation must be done at least every three years for special education students.

The entire IEP process is critical to affect successful academic programming for all children receiving special education. Students with acquired brain injury will require individualized programming that may involve the input and net working of many more outside agencies than what is normally seen today in special education programming. Collaboration and consultation between parents, school, and involved agencies will provide for better awareness and understanding of the student's needs and additionally will educate the other members of the triangle working with the student.

PLACEMENT ISSUES

An examination of the history of special education with its highlights of Federal Law 94-142 and current reauthorization 101-476, known as IDEA (Individuals with Disabilities Education Act), leaves the question, "Where does the ABI student fit in the special education process?".

Labels and Their Implications

The eligibility definitions in P.L. 94-142 list the following children as eligible for services through special education: "... mentally retarded, visually handicapped, seriously emotionally disturbed, orthopedically impaired, or other health impaired children or children with specific learning disabilities, who by reason thereof require special education and related services." Under these guidelines, a variety of labels have been used to qualify ABI students for special services. "Other health impaired" has been used often because of "concomitant traumatically induced orthopedic handicaps or other residual defects" (Bigler, 1987). It was deemed appropriate by the Office of Special Education Policy in California on responding to a parent letter regarding their child traumatically injured in an automobile accident. "Some children with such injuries may be considered 'health impaired', one of the conditions listed in EHA's definition of handicapped," OSEP said, noting that "the list of health problems in the definition is not exhaustive. If a multidisciplinary team determines that the injury adversely affects the child's educational performance, he or she would be eligible for special education" (The Special Educator, 1990). In addition, the label of other health impaired has enabled school districts to work with insurance companies and other third party payers to share escalating medical costs (Savage, 1990).

There have even been cases where mental retardation was used as the qualifying label in addition to learning disability. Specific learning disability included brain injury within its definition under P.L. 94-142. The term "mentally retarded" may be particularly objectionable to parents of a previously normal student who have just experienced the stress and shock of an acquired brain injury in the family. Additionally, lack of appropriate educational programs is cited by Martin as one of the contributing causes of family stress (Martin, 1988).

Chapter I discusses the wide variety of types of brain injury and that each is different with memory loss occurring in a diffuse variety of ways and leaving some long-term memory intact; thus mental retardation would in most cases be inaccurate. A labeling of specific learning disability may be accurate in many closed head injury cases; however, it fails to tell the whole story and places emphasis on specific academic deficiencies when the cognitive disabilities are considerably broader, and include attention, disinhibition, short-term memory, initiation of task, and a wide variety of speech and physical disabilities. Based on behavior and emotional issues, some ABI students are placed in seriously emotionally disturbed programs. In some cases, this "may be the best alternative available to ensure safety and to manage the behavior of these children" (Carney, 1990).

The IDEA (P.L. 101-476) has added two new qualifying categories to the list of eligible disabilities; thus, autism (previously under "other health impaired") and traumatic brain injury (previously under specific Learning Disability) now are separate categories. This addition to the federal law was only accomplished through extensive lobbying by the National Head Injury Foundation and a plethora of concerned parents and rehabilitation professionals. The addition of TBI to the qualifying labels will eliminate for many reentering students and their parents some of the frustration and confusion related to placement that has occurred over the past few years in this relatively new field of education.

Even though qualification may have been simplified, the path to special education placement and services may appear confusing and disjointed to parents and students being introduced to the process for the first time. Although there is a percentage of ABI students who have received previous special education services, the majority are new to the system as a result of their head injuries. Learning about procedures, timeliness, and mandates at an already traumatic time in a family's life can be demanding and overwhelming. Not enough can be said about the stress on the family at this time; a grieving process is taking place with outside pressure to acquire an appropriate next step in a system that may be unfamiliar. There are numerous steps that can be taken by all involved to ease the process, educate others, and prepare the returning student prior to completion of the referral process and placement in special education.

School/Rehab Communication

Since special education service is a public school process, it is essential that the home school be notified as soon as possible that they have a student who has suffered a brain injury. This can be initiated by the parents, hospital, physician, or rehabilitation center; the contacting party may want to notify several school offices or officials depending on the size of the school, as schools, like other systems, are not always efficient in passing information within the system. Elementary schools are generally small in student numbers and a call to the principal and classroom teacher would be a good start; however, in a large high school where a student has several teachers per day, a contact to the main office may not be enough. Suggested other contacts at the high school would include an administrative official, attendance office, guidance office, and special education office. The purpose of the initial contact to the home school is to notify them that the student will be out of school for an extended period of time, to request materials for current courses if appropriate, to request the school make contact either with the current home/hospital instructor or rehabilitation center if the hospital setting is out of the area to coordinate services, and to request information on the special education referral processes as each state has legislated its own process to meet federal guidelines. Of course, written consent from the parent is necessary before any information can be released between agencies.

Ongoing communication between the school and hospital/rehabilitation setting can ease the return to home, community, and school for the returning student. Figure 3.3 illustrates important issues which are useful to address in information gathering/dispersal between schools and hospital or other therapy settings. Videos of the recovering student, neuropsychological testing, and written observations from the hospital/rehabilitation setting will assist the school to prepare for its returning student are important. Visits to the rehab setting by school officials for observation and sharing of unique aspects of the receiving school site that will need to be made to accommodate the returning student. This kind of communication is ideal, but sadly, past history has shown a high percentage of students released from rehab/hospital settings return to schools with no communication or coordination between the two agencies and thus no preparation for the family and student.

Experience has shown the most ideal situation occurs when communication between the hospital/rehabilitation setting and a school psychologist and/or special education coordinator can be established. Other good contacts at the school site would be a counselor or special education teacher. Santa Barbara County in California has established a resource team to assist in educating school personnel about acquired brain injuries, and facilitate communication between public schools and rehabilitation settings. This concept is relatively new but may prove to be an excellent model for other areas and counties to consider.

Parent Participation

Parents can assist school personnel and the reentry process by keeping careful records and copies of pertinent information during the recovery process such as neurological reports, neuropsychological testing reports, team rehabilitation progress reports, and medication records. Since post-accident behavior and attitude characteristics are often an exaggeration of premorbid dispositions, a search of old school report cards and family records for unique or pertinent comments would also be helpful.

School Planning

Schools, by law, bear the responsibility for the referral and placement of special education students. An excellent initiation to the special education process and placement procedures can be accomplished by the school through

FIGURE 3.3
INTAKE FOR SCHOOL RE-ENTRY

Name of student _____ Age _____

Birthdate _____ Grade _____

Name of Parents/Guardian _____

Address _____ Phone _____

Emergency contacts/work phone _____

Date of accident or injury _____ Length of coma _____

Describe hospital and rehabilitation experience _____

Name and location of hospital/rehab _____

Name and title of contact at hospital/rehab _____

Family involvement _____

What was the last school placement—include all special services _____

Where are these records located? _____

Please list any ongoing past educational concerns or problems _____

Premorbid personality and behavior traits
Strengths _____

Weaknesses _____

Health issues:
      Visual ____ _____ Auditory _____

      Speech _____

      Fine motor _____

      Gross motor _____

      Scizure disorder _____

      Medication _____

      Other complications _____

Observations related to:
      Memory _____

      Mobility _____

      Behavior _____

      Socialization _____

      Self-Esteem _____

      Recreation _____

      Vocational interests _____

      Relationships _____

      Other _____

Other Services and agencies currently involved:
    Occupational therapy _____
    Physical therapy _____
    Speech/language pathologist _____
    Insurance C. (Case Manager) _____
    Regional center _____
    Support groups _____
    Counseling _____

a parent interview in which helpful information can be gathered and the referral completed. If the student is physically handicapped as a result of an acquired brain injury, a walk of the campus should be done with the parents to identify any physical barriers. This kind of approach will ease parent concerns and help to set a tone of teamwork and cooperation for the benefit of the returning student.

Concerns addressed early by school personnel and parents will result in a well designed IEP at the initial placement meeting. The length of the school day may need to be shortened for primary return to school and slowly lengthened; some students have lost sufficient long-term memory such that even though they are ambulatory and may have walked to school previously, they may no longer remember the route and require busing. Should memory, physical disability, or disinhibition be a major problem, supervision between classes or at lunch should be considered. The need to take medication at school and the details of that should be addressed. Provisions should be made with parents for emergency phone numbers for pick up at school of their student should their student tire excessively, get despondent, violent, or suicidal. For high school students, it is important to talk early about the possibility of slowing down the school process and extending the length of time required to complete a high school diploma.

Medical issues which could confound the educational process include seizures, feeding problems, and bowel/bladder problems. Often there is a plethora of follow-up medical appointments and it is not always possible to schedule them after school; time will be lost from school and planning early for missed lessons and returned homework will acknowledge this rather than leaving it unmentioned to become a problem.

The most important pre-IEP meeting preparation for school personnel is a staff training related to characteristics and needs of students with acquired brain injuries. The reason this is seen as necessary is that "most teachers receive very little or no training specific to ABI and are thus ill-equipped to adequately assess a program for these students' strengths and needs" (Savage, 1991). Parents of the returning student may wish to attend such an inservice. Enough information should be given regarding brain injury in general and some specifics about the returning student to enable teachers and DIS

(Designated Instructional Service) staff to write quality, specific IEP goals at the initial placement meeting.

SUMMARY

Although special education has been serving a variety of student disabilities over the last fourteen to sixteen years through P.L. 94-142, it has only been recently that TBI has been written into public law (P.L. 101-476) as a separate disability category. The process of placement has included use of a variety of labels, all having their own drawbacks as none specifically address issues unique to traumatic brain injury. As the IDEA is implemented and educators become more familiar with brain injury, delivery of special education services will improve. Educating service providers, including schools and parents, is the main step to accomplishing effective programming.

REFERENCES

Anderson, R.M., Greer, J.G. and Rich, H.L. (1982). An introduction to severely and multiply handicapped persons. In J.G. Greer, R.M. Anderson, and S.J. Odle (Eds.), *Strategies for helping severely and multiply handicapped citizens.* Baltimore, University Park Press.

Ballard, J., and Zettel, J. Public Law 94-142 and Section 504, (1977). What they say about rights and protections. *Exceptional Children, 44,* 177–183.

Bigler, E.D. (1987). Acquired cerebral trauma: An introduction to the special series. *Journal of Learning Disabilities, 20,* 454–457.

Carney, J., and Gerring, J. (1990). Return to school following severe closed head injury: A critical phase in pediatric rehabilitation. *Pediatrician, 17,* 222–229.

Heward, W.L. and Orlansky, M.D. (1988). *Exceptional Children,* An introductory survey of special education. Columbus: Merrill Publishing Co.

Martin, R. (1988). Legal challenges in educating traumatic brain injured students. *Journal of Learning Disabilities, 21,* 471–475.

Meier, F.E. (1992). *Competency-based instruction for teachers of students with special needs.* Boston: Allyn and Bacon.

Pimental, P.A., and Kingsbury, N.A. (1989). *Neuropsychological aspects of right brain injury.* Austin: Pro Ed.

Sattler, J.M. (1982). *Assessment of children's intelligence and special abilities,* Boston: Allyn and Bacon.

Savage, R.C. (1991). Identification, classification, and placement issues for students with traumatic brain injuries. *Journal of Head Trauma Rehabilitation, 6,* 1–9.

Strauss, A.A., Lehtinen, L.E. and Dephart, N.C. (1989). Psychopathology and education of the brain-injured child. Austin: Pro Ed.

Students with brain trauma may qualify for special education (April, 1990). *The Special Educator,* p. 116.

Chapter 4

SERVICE DELIVERY MODELS

Marcia Nordlund

After a full case study has been completed and educational goals determined as part of the IEP process, appropriate educational placement must be determined. The interdisciplinary team which develops the IEP is charged with the responsibility of finding an educational placement which will meet the student's needs in the least restrictive environment.

THE LEAST RESTRICTIVE ENVIRONMENT

P.L. 101-476 (also called the Individuals With Disabilities Education Act) guarantees all students regardless of disability a free and appropriate education in the least restrictive environment. "Restrictive" refers to the amount of time a student with a disability spends with nondisabled peers. Being with nondisabled students is considered less restrictive than being educated in a classroom or building with only students with disabilities. Thus, it is necessary that placement decisions reflect consideration of the least restrictive environment for each student. For some students, restrictive environment, being placed with students of similar needs, is the most appropriate placement. A structured program designed specifically to meet the needs of students with similar disabilities is often the most effective method of remediating deficits. It is important to note that students with acquired brain injury may not have static conditions. Each day the diagnosis and educational needs may be changing; therefore, frequent assessment of the student's educational needs and placement is necessary, particularly if the student has been placed in a restrictive setting.

Regardless of placement, several issues remain consistent as key components to educational planning for students with acquired brain injury.

Academic Skill Acquisition

This part of a program deals with teaching students age-appropriate academic skills utilizing special methods and materials. For many students, reentry into the educational system requires the relearning of pretraumatic academic skills. Many students may be several years behind their nondisabled peers in certain academic areas while on grade level in other academic areas. It is important, therefore, that the academic needs of a student returning to school following head injury are generally not static. Progress may be very rapid in areas of relearning, while extremely slow in areas of new academic acquisition. As improvement is seen in cognitive strength, academic needs will change and so must the focus of the student's educational program.

Metacognition

Metacognition refers to the awareness of one's systematic thinking strategies that are needed for learning (Learner 1990). Secondly, metacognition refers to the student's self-regulation of these strategies (Flavel 1978). Generally, for students in levels one through six on the Rancho-Los Amigos Scale, a highly structured environment is required as skills of metacognition are taught and practiced with the student. Compensatory strategies which determine the most effective way of learning initially must be externally determined for each student. As the student progresses to later phases of cognitive recovery, environmental supports are lessened to increase the student's independence. Good learners know how to approach a learning task utilizing their strengths and weaknesses. A student with acquired brain damage often has difficulty remembering, organizing, and evaluating personal learning strategies. By teaching the student specific skills to aid in deficit areas, the student is able to make adjustments for weaknesses. A student who is taught to carry an assignment notebook used for writing **ANY** important dates will learn to compensate for short-term memory deficits. Students involved in metacognition instruction are made aware of personal learning strengths and weaknesses and are taught methods of remediation for each.

Remediation

The third area of focus of the educational program is that of remediation of core academic skills. Students with acquired brain injury often need special methods of learning (or relearning) reading, math, and writing skills. While students in regular classes may be able to master phonics with a brief overview from the teacher, students with special needs often require intensive phonics instruction for skill acquisition. Additional instruction and practice may be required to master math facts and computational processes. Placement discussions may consider the need for additional time for this instruction.

Behavior Management

Behavior management is often the primary focus of early and middle stages of rehabilitation. As the cognitive status improves, there is often a decrease in compliance behavior (Divack, Herrle, and Scott 1985). In an attempt to gain greater control over the environment, students often demonstrate agitated behavior. A structured behavioral program, initially focusing on planned reinforcement schedules, is necessary. During later stages of recovery, the goal is to generalize behavioral programs from the structure of the classroom to daily living environments such as home, community, or regular education settings.

TYPES OF SERVICE DELIVERY MODELS

In determining the student's needs in relationship to the least restrictive environment, a variety of service delivery models can be considered. Reynolds (1962) first outlined the range of placements that should be available for children with special needs. This "Cascade System of Special Education Service" was later expanded by Deno (1970), Dunn (1978), and Lilly (1970, 1971). All of these authors discussed the need for public school systems to provide a continuum of services ranging from full-time residential placement to inclusion in the regular classroom. The critical factors in this determination include the degree of the handicapping condition and the extent of needed support services.

The models below are presented from most restrictive to least restrictive. Students are generally placed in special classes or programs based on their primary disability (i.e., learning disability, behavior disorder, mental impairment). Each of the placements discussed in this chapter is applicable for each disability. It is important to remember that the placement may change. Initial placement in a more restrictive environment may be most beneficial for the student with continued review of the placement by the transdisciplinary team.

Hospital Program

Many students with acquired brain injury will begin their reentry into the school system in a hospital setting. As soon as the child is medically stable and aware of the surroundings, the educational process can begin. In most states, the local school district is required to provide instruction in the hospital if the student will be absent from school for more than two consecutive weeks. This instruction can be provided by a teacher from the local school district, a district staff member assigned solely to hospital and homebound instruction, or by a hospital teacher who is employed by the hospital and reimbursed by the school district. If an educational component is offered through the hospital, local school districts will generally elect to utilize these services. Depending upon the extent of the injuries and subsequent deficit areas, the tutor should have contact with the student's regular classroom teacher in hopes of working on the same skills taught in the home school. If the injuries and resulting cognitive deficits are extensive, it is necessary to develop a new educational plan to meet the immediate educational needs of the student. These needs may be long-term or short-term and will need updating and adjustment.

Homebound Instruction

After a child with acquired brain injury has been discharged from the hospital to home, homebound instruction often begins. In many states, five hours of direct instruction is the time required although many school districts allow additional time. Some states will also accept a home-school telephone hook-up but will generally require an additional two hours weekly of direct instruction. Homebound instruction will occur only on regular school days; however, if the transdisciplinary team determines that a student would regress academically or behaviorally during the summer, a summer program of homebound instruction may be initiated. Homebound instruction cannot be used to avoid establishing a program for a child in the public schools. Homebound instruction is intended as a temporary method of educating a student whose physical or medical needs preclude attendance at a public school.

Residential

Residential facilities provide placement on a full-time basis. In such a school, the student receives 24-hour care. These placements are generally reserved for children whose medical, cognitive, or behavioral needs are so intense that these needs cannot be met at home and in the public school system. If the child's handicapping condition and the family's emotional well-being are significantly jeopardized, residential placement may be warranted. IEP goals should be determined and educational needs met regardless of the placement. The goals of a student with extremely challenging needs may be very different from other students; however, all children who are medically stable should have appropriate educational goals established and implemented. It is the charge of the transdisciplinary team to determine specific goals and methods of implementation.

Special Day Schools

If the local school is unable to meet the child's educational needs within the school system, a special day school may be required. These schools are generally established for students with a specific disability, such as emotional disturbance, physical limitations, or cognitive deficits. These schools may be either private or public. Certain advantages in the form of specialized staff, equipment, and materials may be gained from such a placement. Intensive physical and occupational therapy may be offered at a special school for students with physical challenges. Intensive psychiatric and psychological services may be available to students enrolled in a special school for students with emotional or behavioral needs. The disadvantages of such a placement include lack of interaction with nonhandicapped peers and often lengthy traveling distance. Again, it is imperative that the progress of a student with acquired brain injury be closely monitored and educational methods and placement adjusted as needed. Self-contained classes are designed for students who need special instructional methods to meet their educational needs. Students placed in a self-contained classroom need a highly specialized curriculum which varies greatly from the curriculum used with nondisabled peers. This curriculum may be different in content, method of instruction, or ability level. Students may require a self-contained classroom for part of the day and be integrated or mainstreamed into regular education classes for specific portions of the school day. The concept of Least Restrictive Environment requires that students placed in self-contained be educated alongside typical peers as much as possible. This may mean that the student will use the self-contained classroom for academic instruction while attending noncore classes (P.E., art, music, lunch, recess) with their nondisabled peers. Many students in self-contained classrooms may be several years behind their nonhandicapped peers in certain academic areas while on grade level in other academic areas. Other students will be deficit in several areas. Each student in the self-contained classroom may have different educational needs and methods of reaching maximum potential; therefore, the teacher/student ratio for self-contained classrooms is greatly reduced from regular classrooms. Academic programs must be specifically designed to meet the individual needs of each student.

Resource Room

Students assigned to a resource classroom spend no more than 50 percent of their school day attending such a class. Wiederholt, Hammill, and Brown

(1978) defined a resource room as "any instructional setting to which a child comes for specific periods of time, usually on a regularly scheduled basis" (p. 13). If the needs are more substantial, a self-contained classroom is warranted. In a resource setting, students spend part of their day attending regular classes while receiving special instruction in the resource room for other subjects. Assessment, remedial instructional, and metacognition strategies are part of a resource placement. The goal of the resource room is to give students specific skills necessary to achieve as close to grade level as possible. Resource teachers must work closely with the regular classroom teacher to insure continuity of instruction. The resource teacher may provide services in three ways. Services may be given directly to the student in the resource classroom. In this method, students go to the resource room to receive direct instruction in subject skills, study skills, or remediation. Secondly, the resource teacher may give the regular classroom teacher direct instruction as to methods of adapting the regular curriculum and instruction to meet the needs of a special students. In this scenario, the resource teacher does not work directly with the student. Instead, instruction is given to the regular classroom teacher, providing the teacher with methods of working with a student with special needs. Finally, a combination of these two methods is often provided. Students are given direct instruction by the resource teacher, either in the resource room or in the regular classroom, while the resource teacher works with the classroom teacher establishing specific methods for the child within the regular classroom instruction.

Regular Classroom

If a student's needs are minimal upon reentry, placement in a regular classroom with or without special supports may be appropriate. The student may need special equipment, materials, or instruction in order to be successful in such a placement. Often the child will be assigned to a special educator on either a resource or consultation basis. If the special educator is working solely with the regular classroom teacher and not providing direct service to the student, a consultation placement on the Individual Education Plan is appropriate. Minor changes in instruction, seating endurance, or materials may be all that is necessary to insure success. Other students may require elaborate changes in the regular program in order to be successful. Close monitoring of the student's progress is required to insure that the student is not frustrated or underachieving. Specific staffing patterns for maintaining students in the regular class will be discussed in the following chapter.

Regular Education Initiative

A relatively new concept in delivery of services is sweeping the nation. As a result of a 1986 report written by Madeleine Will, then Assistant Secretary of the Office of Special Education and Rehabilitative Services, school districts are thoughtfully considering the principles of Least Restrictive Environment in a new light. Regular Education Initiative is a term used to describe the idea that students with special educational needs are the joint responsibility of both regular educators and special educators. Although the pragmatics of equal educational opportunities for both regular education and special education students vary greatly from school to school, the "neighborhood school" concept is changing how special education services are delivered.

An understanding of three terms associated with Regular Education Initiative is necessary to fully conceptualize this movement. *"Mainstreaming"* infers that the student has prerequisite skills necessary to complete the same curriculum as other students enrolled in the class. The student may need adapted assignments, but the student can generally complete the same work as other students. On the other hand, *"Integration"* means that the student does not have the prerequisite skills necessary to complete the same curriculum as other students. The student may have an adapted or parallel curriculum designed to meet specific IEP goals. The purpose of integrating a student into a class with nondisabled peers is not to improve *age-appropriate* academic skills but rather to improve the *student's* level or skill development, either social or academic. *"Inclusion"* is a fully integrated program whereby the student receives all instruction within the regular classroom. The student may follow the standard curriculum in some areas while having adapted curriculum for other areas. All instruction is based upon the needs of the IEP. The responsibility for educating the student placed in an inclusion setting is equally divided between the regular and special educator. Generally the special educator determines the special needs of the student (IEP goals), while the regular educator takes the responsibility for the day-to-day education of the student. The special educator and the regular classroom teacher collaborate to determine curriculum adaptations and modifications. Advocates for Inclusion feel that students with special needs learn best when placed in their home school alongside their neighborhood friends and siblings. Positive peer modeling and neighborhood friendships are noted as strong benefits of inclusion placement.

RELATED SERVICES

Related services may be provided in any of the previously discussed settings. The IDEA mandates related services to be provided, as needed. These services include school health services, transportation, medical services *for diagnostic or evaluation* purposes, speech pathology and audiology services, psychological services, counseling and social work services, physical and occupational therapy, and parent counseling and training. These services are not intended to replace outside medical treatment. The focus of support or related services in the school setting is to consider a child's physical and emotional concerns which *interefere with the child's ability to learn.* A school district is not responsible for long term medical care. Rather the district must provide support services at no cost for conditions which directly affect a child's ability to learn. It is the responsibility of the team to determine which services are necessary for the child to benefit from special education. These services must be listed on the child's Individual Educational Plan and reevaluated annually.

REFERENCES

Cartwright, G.P., Cartwright, C.A., and Ward, M.E. (1989). *Educating special learners* (5th ed.). Belmont: Wadsworth.

Deno, E.N. (1970). Special education as developmental capital. *Exceptional Children, 37,* 229–237.

Divack, J., Herrle, J., Scott, M. (1985). Behavior management. In Ylvisaker, M. (Ed.), *Head injury rehabilitation.* San Diego: College-Hill Press.

Dunn, L.M. (1968). Special education for the mildly retarded: Is much of it justifiable? *Exceptional Children, 35,* 5–22.

Flavell, J. (1978). Metacognitive aspects of problem solving. In L.B. Resnick (Ed.), *The nature of intelligence.* Hillsdale: Erlbraum.

Kirk, S.A. and Gallagher, J.J. (1989). *Educating exceptional children,* Boston: Houghton Mifflin.

Lerner, J.W. *Learning disabilities: Theories, diagnosis, and teaching strategies.* Dallas: Houghton Mifflin.

Lilly, M.S. (1970). Special education: A teapot in a tempest. *Exceptional Children, 37,* 43–49.

Lilly, M.S. (1971). A training based model for special education. *Exceptional Children, 37,* 745–749.

Lynch, E. and Lewis, R. (1988). *Exceptional children and adults: An introduction to special education.* Boston: Foresman.

Mandell, C.J. and Fiscus, E. (1981). *Understanding exceptional people.* New York: West.

Reynolds, M. (1962). A framework for considering some issues in special education. *Exceptional Children, 28,* 367–370.

Wiederholt, J., Hammill, D., Brown, B. (1978). *The resource teacher: A guide to effective practices.* Boston: Allyn and Bacon.

Chapter 5

CONSULTATION MODELS

MARCIA NORDLUND

As discussed in the previous chapter, upon reentry into the school system, students with acquired brain injury may be placed in a variety of education settings based on the student's educational needs. In most cases, the placement determination is based on the student's primary disability. Students with acquired brain injury often do not fit into any category of special education; rather these students exhibit a myriad of special needs. Thus, their education needs to be addressed by a variety of specialists. This transdisciplinary approach to the student's education may be handled in-house through the use of a Teacher Assistance Team already established in school. Another approach may be the use of district staff which float between schools to work with students with special needs. In some cases, the use of an outside consultant may be required.

TEACHER ASSISTANCE TEAMS

Many states now require the establishment of Teacher Assistance Teams within every school district. The purpose of such teams is to provide systematic procedures for solving education problems, either learning or behavioral, before they become pathological. A Teacher Assistance Team is a team of teachers who meet with a referring teacher for a structured process of brainstorming solutions and planning interventions which the referring teacher can use in the classroom. When a child presents a challenging behavior or learning problem, the classroom teacher makes a referral to the Teacher Assistance Team. The Team leader reviews the referral and gives copies of the referral to all team members. The team members then observe the child and the teacher. During the problem-solving meeting which follows, a structured format is generally utilized. The team spends a brief period determining the exact area of concern and defining the problem in objective terms. The team then brainstorms alternative suggestions as possible intervention strategies. The classroom teacher then selects the suggestions which best suit his/her style of teaching. The chosen interventions are then refined, and an evaluation plan is determined. Often, the intervention strategies address a specific intervention which can be utilized with the student in need. Other times, the intervention is classroom strategy which will benefit many, if not all of the students. Many states now require the establishment of Teacher Assistance Teams in every school. The first step in a special education referral is often taking the concern to the Teacher Assistance Team. After several interventions have been tried, the student is then referred for a full case study and possible special education services.

The purpose of the initial establishment of Teacher Assistance Team was to decrease the number of special education referrals. Chalfant, Push, and Moultrie (1979) were among the first researchers to develop the assumption that regular classroom teachers can help a variety of students with special needs within the regular classroom if they have assistance in developing special interventions. Considerable knowledge and talent is available among teachers in any given building which can be utilized to solve many problems.

Many students with acquired brain injury can be serviced in the regular classroom. These students often need special intervention strategies. The regular classroom teacher can turn to the budding Teacher Assistance Team to help gain new insight and brainstorm solutions.

The Teacher Assistance Team model is also used by many special education programs. A group of specialists (teachers, occupational therapist, physical therapist, speech/language therapist, psychologists, nurses, social workers, administrators) may meet on a monthly basis to engage in collaborative problem solving. The special education teacher (or other professional working with the student) will bring an area of concern to the Teacher Assistance Team meeting. Each discipline will analyze the problem and brainstorm solutions to the problem. This method is particularly useful for the student with acquired brain injury because the educational needs are often nonstatic conditions which need continual reevaluation and new program planning. The use of a transdisciplinary team encourages viewing the educational needs form a multi-faceted perspective.

CONSULTING/COLLABORATING TEACHER MODEL

After a student with acquired brain injury has been placed in either a regular or special education setting, the need often arises for another educator to help the primary teacher solve educational concerns. In some schools, the Teacher Assistance Team is not a suitable arena for specific problems associated with acquired brain injury or the team does not exist.

Neal (1991) described three types of consulting teacher models which are often used. In the Purchase Model, short-term direct services are provided to the student by a "specialist." The role of the specialist is to cure the problems without developing new strategies for use by the classroom teacher. At times, this model is appropriate, particularly when a student is in crisis or demonstrates a specific problem which requires minimal interventions (i.e., problem with long-division while other math skills are at grade level). A second model often used is the Doctor/Patient Model in which the consultant diagnosis the problem and prescribes remediation techniques. The problem with this model is that the consultant must give the diagnosis and prescription to the teacher. The classroom teacher may feel no investment as no collaboration has taken place between the classroom teacher and the consultant. The consultant has not worked with the classroom teacher to brainstorm solutions which would be a match with the teacher's style of teaching. Rather, the consultant imposes solutions on the teacher. In comparison, the Process-Consultation Model allows the classroom teacher a voice in defining the problem, developing solutions, and determining evaluation procedures. This model is generally viewed as collaborating effort because both parties have a voice as well as a responsibility in determining options and following through with the suggested program. In the consulting/collaborating teacher model (Miller and Sabatino, 1978) another professional is consulted to convey suggestions to the primary teacher while this teacher accepts the primary responsibility for implementation of suggestions. The consultant generally does not work directly with the student for long periods of time, as in the resource teacher's role (see previous chapter), but rather works with the teacher to determine new methods of dealing with areas of concern. A very special relationship must be present between both professionals for this model to be successful. Both parties must have excellent communication and problem-solving skills. They both must be familiar with the curriculum, large and small group instruction, behavioral interventions, and other resources which are available in the building, the district, and the community. A genuinely collaborative relationship must exist. Both parties must provide knowledge and skills in a non-hierarchical relationship. The consultant's role to provide support or assistance to the consultee who has the primary responsibility for educational of the student. The student is the reason and focus of the interaction which helps to relieve guilt of the consultee. Although the consultant can provide short-term direct services to the student, the primary focus is to help determine alternative strategies which can be employed by the primary teacher. Pugach and Johnson (1988) developed a four-step plan for use in peer collaboration. First, it is necessary for the consultee to describe the educational problem in objective terms and for the consultant to ask clarifying questions. Secondly, both parties summarize the prevailing concern into as concise a statement as possible. Both the consultant and the consultee then determine interventions and predictions regarding the effectiveness of the strategies. Finally, an evaluation plan is determined. If the data reveal that the initial strategies were ineffective, a second intervention plan must then be determined.

In order for Peer Collaboration to be effective, a climate of true collegiality must exist. The main premise must be peers helping peers which is carried out in a safe environment encouraging professionals to question themselves and their current strategies. No advice is given; rather professionals brainstorm suggestions together.

USE OF OUTSIDE CONSULTANTS

Often the very special needs of a student with acquired brain injury require the use of outside consultants. Some smaller or rural school districts may not have an abundant supply of educational specialists who can best determine specialized strategies to help the student with acquired brain injury. Additionally, medical and rehabilitation needs of the students may be as great as educational needs, thus requiring the collaboration of all professionals to ensure a successful reentry for the student. As soon as it is determined that the student will be released shortly from rehabilitation and returning to school, all professionals, educational, medical, and rehabilitation, should meet to determine the short-term and long-term needs of the child. The teacher from the child's home school district may be a valuable resource to the rehabilitation facility in determining the educational direction of rehabilitation. The teacher can help the rehabilitation team to understand the role of classroom and school schedules, academic loads, and curriculum content which will become part of the child's schooling once released from rehabilitation. An abbreviated "mock school" may be followed in the rehabilitation facility to familiarize the student with expectations of the public school setting. Specialized strategies may be developed in rehabilitation to help memory problems associated with assignments, note taking, and test taking. Strategies may also be developed to help the student adjust to physical demands if fatigue and physical maneuvering are concerns. Because a positive relationship often develops between the rehabilitation staff and the patient, this wealth of information should be shared with the educator before the student is released from rehabilitation and enters the public school system. Learning problems and behavioral concerns may have been addressed by the rehabilitation team. This team can offer suggestions and strategies for use by the classroom teacher. Having the rehabilitation team observe the classroom setting to which the child will return and having the classroom teacher observe the rehabilitation setting in which the student currently resides, produces collaboration which will ensure a smooth transition.

After the student is released from rehabilitation and returns to the public school, continued meeting between professionals from both agencies can help alleviate minor problems often associated with transition. The rehabilitation team may offer explanations for learning and behavioral concerns which may help the educator to determine new strategies. Again, it is important that a true feeling of collegiality exist. It is easy to fall into the trap of casting blame on another agency for difficulties which arise. The rehabilitation team should be careful not to infer the problems with the student did not exist in the rehabilitation facility. Conversely, the educational team should be careful not to cast blame on the rehabilitation facility for problems which now exist in the school setting. The purpose of an outside consultant is to offer another vantage point of expertise. By combining many fields of expertise, the child's educational program can be a culmination of the work and suggestions of many different professionals. Each professional group, whether medical, rehabilitation, or educational should seek and respect suggestions offered by other disciplines. It is important to note that each professional group must also respect the limitations and focus on other groups. Although the educational professional may see the child's education as a primary focus, the rehabilitation facility may consider the child's physical needs to be a focus on their program. Conversely, the rehabilitation specialist must understand the limitations of the school setting which may preclude certain therapeutic interventions.

SUMMARY

Many consultation models have been developed for a variety of uses. Because students with acquired brain injuries often require a variety of educational, rehabilitational, and medical procedures, several different collaboration models may be utilized in harmony. Mutual respect and understanding are the keys to successful collaboration between professions.

REFERENCES

Carter, J. and Sugal, G. (1989). Survey on pre-referral practices: Responses from state departments of education. *Exceptional Children 55*, 298–302.

Chalfant, J., Push, M., Moultrie, R. (1979). Teacher assistance teams: A model for within-building problem-solving. *Learning Disability Quarterly, 2*, 85–91.

Huefner, D. (1988). The consulting teacher model: Risks and opportunities. *Exceptional Children, 54*, 403–414.

Knight, M., Meyers, H., Paolucci-Whitcomb, P., Hasazi, S., Nevin, A. (1981). A four-year evaluation of consulting teacher service. *Behavioral Disorders, 6*, 62–72.

Miller, T. and Sabatino, D. (1978). An evaluation of the teacher consultant model as an approach to mainstreaming. *Exceptional Children, 45*, 86–91.

Neal, R. (1981). How to put the consultant to work in consulting teaching. *Behavior Disorders, 6,* 78–81.

Pugach, M. and Johnson, L. (1988). Peer collaboration. *Teaching Exceptional Children, 20,* 75–77.

Pugach, M. and Johnson, L. (1988). Rethinking the relationship between consultation and collaborative problem solving. *Focus on Exceptional Children, 21,* 1–8.

Pugach, M. and Johnson, L. (1989). Prereferral interventions: Progress, problems, and challenges. *Exceptional Children, 56,* 217–226.

Wixson, S. (1980). Two resource room models for serving learning and behavior disordered pupils. *Behavior Disorders, 5,* 116–125.

Chapter 6

ORGANIZING A CONSULTATION SYSTEM FOR BRAIN INJURED STUDENTS

Laurie E. Graham and Alan L. Goldberg

Advancements in medical technology have paved the way for children with health impairments, including those with brain injuries to participate in public education (Caplan, 1987). It is clear that alternatives to home/hospital instruction are needed due to the nature of long-standing health impairments. Children with brain impairments and their parents are no longer satisfied with home/hospital instruction for extended periods, which may cause social isolation (Kleinberg, 1982). Home/hospital instruction frequently does not meet criteria for placement in educational programming which represents the least restrictive environment for the student.

The Education for All Handicapped Children Act, Public Law 94-142 was passed in 1975. It was amended and reauthorized in 1990 as P.L. 101-476, and is now known as the Individuals with Disabilities Act (IDEA). The purpose of the act is to "guarantee the availability of special educational programming to handicapped children and youth who require it" (Ballard and Zettel, 1977). In addition, Section 504 of the Vocational Rehabilitation Act of 1973 is a civil rights statute that declares that handicapped people cannot be discriminated against on the basis of the handicap, and that federally funded programs must be accessible. These two landmark pieces of legislation have opened public school doors for handicapped children including those born with brain injuries, whose educational performance is adversely affected by their conditions. The aforementioned laws mandate that children receive free and appropriate educational programming.

In order to be eligible for special educational programming, a child must qualify according to one of the conditions listed in P.L. 101-476. These conditions include specific learning disability, mental retardation, visual impairment, deafness, serious emotional disturbance, multihandicap, orthopedic impairment, autism, traumatic brain injury and other health impairment. Historically, the majority of children who have health impairments qualified in one of two categories: other health impairment or orthopedic impairment. P.L. 101-476 defines "other health impairment" as including children with limited strength, vitality, or alertness from the following conditions: heart condition, tuberculosis, rheumatic fever, nephritis, asthma, sickle cell anemia, hemophilia, epilepsy, lead poisoning, leukemia, or diabetes. The category of orthopedic impairment includes congenital anomalies such as clubfoot, impairments caused by disease (poliomyelitis, bone disease) and impairments from other causes (cerebral palsy, amputations, and fractures and burns which result in contracture). Due to the heterogeneity of brain injured students, they have qualified for special educational services under a variety of conditions or categories. Often, the "other health impairment" category has been used—as a broader range of services can be accessed under this category—while a student who has sustained a traumatic brain injury may qualify for services under that category, and additional funding may be available.

Children who have sustained brain injuries are surviving in greater numbers that at any other time in history. The numbers of brain injury survivors is a reflection of improved medical technology. While acute medical problems associated with injury to the brain can be cured or effectively managed, cognitive and/or behavioral sequelae of the injuries may prove to be chronic. If we look at the category of acquired brain injury alone, approximately one million children suffer a blow to the head each year, with one in five hundred hospitalized as a result (Mira, Tyler, and Tucker, 1989). Although children challenged by acquired brain injuries are often served under the "other health impairment" category (Begali, 1987), accurate tracking of the brain injured in school systems is difficult since they may be served in programs for the learning disabled, mentally retarded, socially and emotionally disturbed, or physically impaired. Under P.L. 101-476, children are eligible for special education services if their handicapping conditions adversely affect educational performance. The number of brain injured children is increasing, and both P.L. 101-476 and Section 504 of the Rehabilitation Act of 1973 have guaranteed that these children can attend public schools.

Participation of brain injured students who do not appear to fit into established special educational programs has created numerous questions related to educational needs, physical site adjustments, counseling, assessment, and placement. Back in 1986, educators in Santa Barbara County had few answers to these perplexing questions raised by brain-injured students and their families. In response to recommendations from a local rehabilitation neuropsychologist, three Santa Barbara County Schools staff members attended a workshop entitled "Integrating the traumatically brain-injured student into the mainstream." The workshop was co-sponsored by the National Head Injury Foundation and the Washington State Head Injury Foundation. Subsequent to the conference, the two school psychologists and special education teacher met to gather additional information and began collaborative consultation with the rehabilitation neuropsychologist to enable successful placements and ultimate success of brain-injured clients. The trio of educational professionals have been officially recognized as the county's Brain Injury Resource Team.

The team has worked on a variety of projects to benefit students who have sustained brain injuries and other medically fragile students. They have presented workshops to local educators, school administrators, psychologists, speech/language pathologists, nurses, students, and parents. The workshops have had the ultimate goal of increasing awareness of the needs of the aforementioned student populations. Topics covered have included brain physiology and mechanisms of injury to the brain, eligibility for special education programs, characteristics of brain injury survivors, and educational interventions for use with these special populations. The team is responsible for more than conducting workshops. Team members are also responsible for providing consultative services to school personnel, parents, and students. Cases may be referred from rehabilitation facilities, physicians, parents, or teachers. Team members have been available to conduct observations and attend meetings where individual Educational Plans are developed so as to enable successful, flexible programs.

Through the process of exploring services for students who have sustained brain injuries and collaborating with health care professionals, the team has utilized a variety of consultation models (see the preceding chapter by M. Nordlund in this book). Perhaps the most important issue that has been identified by the team through experiences in providing educational services to youngsters with acquired brain injuries has been that consultation must be individualized. The unique needs of each student necessitates individualization of consultation as well as individualization of the educational plan. Consultants in the form of in-school instructional support teams, identified school system experts who go to schools with a mandate of consulting on brain injury cases, and specialists external to the school system have all been utilized. The latter consultants may be neuropsychologists, speech/language pathologists, or other health care professionals who typically provide time limited services. In some cases, each of the aforementioned types of consultation will be utilized at different times. The model which may lead to the finest service delivery is one in which there is development of an integrated, coordinated system between health care agencies and the school, which involves ongoing contact and follow-up to ensure appropriate delivery of educational services.

Experience with interagency collaboration and cross-training has led t' the identification of six essential steps needed to guide and develop succr ful educational programs for students with acquired brain injuries. Alth' characteristics of each injury are different, and each student has unique needs and goals, these six steps provide a framework for a systematic integrative approach to meet the needs of brain-injured students.

The first step involves early identification of the students. The school must be aware of the need for special services before such services can be designed and implemented. Schools may gain awareness of potential need through contact with hospital personnel, other health care professionals, or parents. Data from a survey conducted in Maryland indicates that numerous students who sustain brain injuries are never identified by their schools. This may be due to the fact that many youngsters who sustain injuries receive emergency care but are never admitted to hospitals (Janus, 1991). Such individuals may be identified by the schools only when academic, behavioral, social, or emotional sequelae of injuries become disruptive to routine classroom functioning.

The second step is to establish early contact between the school system and the parents of a brain-injured child (Van Eys, 1982). Before such a child enters school, it is helpful for the school to collect background information regarding the medical history and current condition of the student. It is essential that a case manager/contact be identified in the school. This may be the school psychologist, nurse, special education teacher, or principal. The collection of background information should involve obtaining data on services which have already been provided (i.e., home/hospital instruction), test results, and reports from health care settings. Contacts with parents at this time affords the opportunity for explanation of special education services and eligibility requirements. Parents may not be prepared for the scenario of assessment, Individual Educational Plan (IEP) procedures, and labeling (Martin, 1988). Early inclusion of parents helps to increase their investment in goal setting and service planning while decreasing opportunities for parent/professional polarization.

The third step is to assess the child's needs and develop specific goals. School districts must obtain written permission from parents before any initial evaluation can be conducted under the auspices of the school. Review of pertinent data from health care professionals working with the child can help in avoiding unnecessary duplication of evaluations. Observations of the child in the home or hospital setting can prove the invaluable. The following issues are important ones to address during the course of evaluation:

1. Nature and severity of the brain injury
2. Cognitive and academic functioning levels
3. Gross and fine motor skills
4. Receptive and expressive language skills
5. Adaptive behavior including social and daily living levels

6. Behavioral deficits and/or excesses
7. Fatigue and frustration tolerance levels
8. Vision and hearing status
9. Need for special equipment (including high technology assistive devices)
10. Seizure activity
11. Medication use and possible side effects of medications
12. Potential for additional hospitalizations that may interrupt educational programming

The fourth step involves meeting to develop an educational program. Such a meeting may involve school personnel, health care professionals, and parents. In addition to direct educational services, the student may also be eligible for related services as adaptive physical education, speech/language therapy, occupational therapy, physical therapy, and/or counseling services. Special considerations such as shortened day, visits to the school prior to placement, and combination of shortened day with home instruction should be discussed at this meeting. Transportation, medication use, and physical accessibility must all be taken into account. When working with individuals who have sustained brain injuries, it is important to review the Individual Educational Plan regularly (perhaps as often as every thirty to sixty days) so that changes can be made to keep programming in line with abilities and progress.

The fifth step is to develop and implement programming to build teacher, staff, and peer awareness and education to specific problems of the brain-injured. Savage and Allen (1987) suggest that an in-service be given to teachers, counselors, the school nurse, and the school administrators prior to commencement of school programming. All personnel who may have contact with the student (including secretarial and custodial staffs, school librarian, and aides) should be included. This is particularly important in cases where sequelae of injury involve behavioral and/or cognitive disturbances. A school-based resource team which has been extensively trained in issues concerning schooling of brain-injured youngsters can prove invaluable in conducting these sessions. Health care professionals who are working in tandem with schools to enable successful programming can participate in in-servicing as appropriate. Parents can be included to help answer questions. Specific issues such as restrictions during recess or physical education, special equipment use, medication usage and possible side effects, potential behavior problems and techniques for dealing with them, and emergency contacts should be addressed. During in-servicing of the child's teachers, a plan should be developed with them to provide classmates with an explanation of the handicapping condition (Ross, 1984). This can be achieved through classroom discussion led by the teacher, parent, and/or member of the in-service training team. Children are naturally curious, and will ask questions. Do not hesitate to bring pictures or address topics such as further hospitalizations, fatality of condition, and contagiousness (Kleinberg, 1982).

The final step in the process involves regular follow-up and program modification as necessary. This step is frequently overlooked, and yet is the key to on-going success of the child in the school setting. An Individual Educational Plan meeting can be convened at any time at the parents' request, to discuss possible program modification. In cases where the child's condition is changing as opposed to static, it may be necessary to convene IEP meetings more frequently than is customary. Observations of the child in the classroom and with peers also provides valuable information concerning appropriateness of programming and need for fine tuning.

The process of guiding and developing successful educational programs for students with acquired brain injuries is challenging and complex. In response to the needs of increasing numbers of brain-injured students with neurocognitive deficits, Santa Barbara County's schools have successfully implemented a Brain Injury Resource Team composed of specially trained educators from within their own school districts. The team has been involved in helping to secure with appropriate placements and services for a variety of brain-injured students, including those with traumatic head injuries, vascular disorders of the brain, and brain tumors. Elements from the team's model of service delivery/consultation have been utilized in providing services to medically fragile children with other special education qualifying conditions as well.

Our public school systems are being faced with increasingly complex service delivery needs in order to provide programming for students who have sustained brain injuries. Cooperative, interdisciplinary problem solving involving educators and health care professionals will help to ensure that the needs of these unique students are met in an appropriate manner in the least restrictive environment.

REFERENCES

Ballard, J. and Zettel, J. (1977). Public Law 94-142 and Section 504: What they say about rights and protections. *Exceptional Children, 44,* 177–184.

Begali, V. (1987). *Head injury in children and adolescents.* Brandon, Vermont: Clinical Psychology Publishing.

Caplan, S. (1987). Annotation: The fetal alcohol syndrome. *Journal of Child Psychology and Psychiatry, 28,* 223–227.

Janus, P. (1991). Personal communication.

Kleinberg, S. (1982). *Educating the chronically ill child.* Rockville: Aspen Publications.

Martin, R. (1988). Legal challenges in educating traumatically brain injured students. *Journal of Learning Disabilities, 21,* 471–476.

Mira, M., Tyler, J. and Tucker, B. (1989). *Traumatic head injury in children: A guide for schools.* Kansas City, Kansas: University of Kansas Medical Center.

Ross, J. (1984). The child with cancer in school. In J. Fithian (Ed.) *Understanding the child with chronic illness in the classroom* (pp. 152–164). Phoenix: Oryx Press.

Savage, R. and Allen, M. (1987). Educational issues for the traumatically brain injured early adolescent. *The Early Adolescent, 1,* 23–27.

Van Eys, J. (1982). Reintegration of the medically exceptional child. In J. Van Eys (Ed.), *Children with cancer: Mainstreaming and reintegration.* New York: F.P. Medical and Scientific Books.

Chapter 7

PRACTICAL GUIDELINES FOR TEACHERS

SALLY B. COHEN

INTRODUCTION

Educational systems are equipped to handle the learning capabilities of a variety of students. Yet, many authors here and elsewhere (Begali, 1987; Cohen, 1991; Cohen, Joyce, Rhoades & Welks, 1985; DePompei & Blosser, 1987; Fuld & Fisher, 1977; Lehr, Lantz & Doranzo, 1990; Rosen & Gerring, 1986; Telzrow, 1987) state that school programs that meet the needs of students with acquired brain injuries (ABI) often must differ from those that are already in place. Although professionals in medical and rehabilitation facilities provide assessment reports describing the impact these students' impairments can have on school functioning, and some present examples of tasks that help these students learn more effectively, it often is difficult for educators to relate this information to programs the students should have in school.

School staff need help in translating reports they receive about students with ABI into functional educational goals. They need assistance in developing appropriate teaching tasks. They need to determine both when students can fit into existing educational formats and how to implement program adaptations that students may need in order to perform successfully.

Program planners should develop a process to identify the educational needs of each student with ABI. For example, planning teams can use the following strategy (which happens to help individuals with ABI organize their thinking) and gather information about: the *WHO* (the student, education staff, family); the *WHAT* (program components); the *WHERE* (program location: school and classrooms); the *WHEN* (time of reentry, time for program changes, scheduling issues); the *WHY* (clarification of program adaptations); and the *HOW* (development of techniques to implement the adaptations).

Although the authors of previous chapters target factors to consider when integrating students with ABI into community schools, brief comments about a few factors are warranted here.

It is important to note that the law now mandates that appropriate educa-

126

tional programs be developed for students with traumatic brain injuries (TBI). In P.L. 101-476 (EDLAW, 1991), the Individuals with Disabilities Education Act, which amends P.L. 94-142 (Congressional Record 1975), the Education of All Handicapped Children's Act, traumatic brain injury is included for the first time as a disability which educators must address. At this point, the law defines TBI narrowly, and it does not describe placements or programs for students with TBI. However, it is an important first step in assuring that appropriate programs are planned for these students. Some states, such as Colorado (Colorado State Board of Education, 1991), already have regulations which delineate program components for this population; but educators in most states are devoid of this information. Therefore, in order to develop suitable programs for students when they first return to school after sustaining brain injuries, professionals who have worked with them in hospitals and rehabilitation centers and educational program planners and direct service staff in school systems must share information about: students' current learning capabilities; teaching and treatment techniques and performance expectations in various settings; and how different settings meet students' needs in different ways (Cohen, 1986; DePompei & Blosser, 1987; Ylvisaker, Chorazy, Cohen et al., 1990). This process of linking information among medical, rehabilitation and educational systems will help the professionals involved better understand ABI and its impact on educational programming.

Once the students are back in school, their programs may need to change fairly often (Cohen, 1991; Ylvisaker, 1991), reflecting changes in their abilities as they move through the recovery process. School staff must continue to share information, relating students' program adjustments to performance expectations in present and potential classrooms or in community transition placements that may be part of programs at the high school level (Baumeister & Morris, 1992; Chadsey-Rusch, Rusch & O'Reilly, 1991; Meers, 1992; Sailor, 1991; White & Bond, 1992).

In order to accommodate the span of ability levels that students with ABI may present, many educators have used a noncategorical approach to programming. They have bypassed regulations regarding student qualifications for specific categorical programs in order to match students' needs in subject or skill areas with teaching groups in different settings. It is becoming easier for educators to develop appropriate programs for these students, since school systems are: implementing noncategorical programs more routinely; following the Regular Education Initiative and evaluating the effectiveness of integrating students with different capabilities into mainstream programs (McDonnell, McDonnell, Hardman & McCune, 1991; Osborne, 1992; Semmel, Abernathy, Butera & Lesar, 1991; Zigmond, 1990); and providing special education services both in and out of the main classroom. Although most students with ABI can be integrated into existing school programs, they should be mainstreamed with caution (Cohen, 1985, 1986, 1991). Educators must assess whether classrooms provide the degrees of individualization that meet students' rehabilitation and education needs. Professionals such as Silver (1991), Zigmond & Baker (1990), and members of the National Joint Committee on Learning Disabilities (1992) advocating for students with learning disabilities, express concerns about totally embracing the new educational formats and disregarding more restrictive programs that have been available to students. School staff should heed these concerns when working with students with ABI who also have learning problems. The above authors caution that some students still require more structured learning environments such as LD settings have traditionally provided, and they recognize that if teachers in integrated mainstream settings are to be effective, they must expand their teaching skills to meet the educational needs of students with a broad variety of learning styles. This should, of course, include developing an understanding of the impact ABI can have on students' academic and social functioning.

STUDENTS WITH COGNITIVE PROBLEMS

Adequate school performance requires students to have the more general cognitive skills intact. That is, they must be able to: *attend* to significant information and *understand* and *remember* it correctly; *concentrate* for periods of time; *think* and express themselves in an organized and flexible manner; *problem solve; plan and monitor performance; make appropriate judgments; have some degree of self-control;* and *have some awareness* (relative to their level of maturity) *of both their abilities and of the skills that are needed to do tasks.*

Although students with ABI may have residual physical impairments, authors cited previously who have addressed these students' needs emphasize that cognitive impairments have a significant effect on the way they function in school. These impairments influence how students think, learn, communicate and respond emotionally and behaviorally. For instance, students with ABI may have lost some of the fund of knowledge they previously had and may not be able to use materials they once did. Their impulsive behavior may cause them to: interrupt a lot and disturb the class; blurt out incorrect answers without taking time to think about content; be unable to wait their turn or participate effectively in groups; and be undiplomatic or unthinking, saying whatever comes to mind and often making comments that disturb others.

Because of difficulties with task organization and comprehension, they may not be able to follow directions to complete school tasks correctly; and those with poor expressive organization skills may not be able to take part in discussions or give clear and correct answers even though they understand the content. Severe memory or retrieval problems can prevent students from learning day-to-day and are distressing for them and for school staff. Furthermore, deficits in any of the cognitive areas can result in these individuals having difficulty learning new information or understanding and responding to the subtle nuances that are typically a part of social interactions.

Investigators have written about the similarities and differences between students with ABI and those in mainstream or special education programs (Arffa, Fitzhugh-Bell & Black, 1989; Begali, 1987; Cohen, 1986, 1991; Cohen, Joyce, Rhoades & Welks, 1985; Lehr, Lantz & Doranzo, 1990; Rosen & Gerring, 1986; Savage & Wolcott, 1988; Williams, Gridley & Fitzhugh-Bell, 1992; & Ylvisaker, 1991). Many students have some degree of cognitive or processing difficulties, but the difficulties students with ABI have often are more extreme. They have *more* problems attending, remembering, organizing, and manipulating information; their impulsivity, as described earlier, interferes greatly with thinking requirements in academic and social situations; they have *more* strategies to help them compensate for lost or recovering skills in order to interact appropriately and to continue learning; and they need *more* teacher assistance to participate in school activities. Those who deny having problems (adolescents especially) are difficult to work with, as they insist on using premorbid learning styles (e.g., reading rapidly with comprehension at age-appropriate levels) which are no longer effective and resist new placements, materials, or teaching techniques which accommodate their present abilities.

All students have a range of skill levels. However, that range can be much broader for students with ABI who have retained some premorbid abilities but also have lost skills as a result of their traumas. Gaps in their knowledge base and aptitude can be dramatic, making it difficult for them to participate in classroom activities. In addition, when these students demonstrate good comprehension, it may only be for limited amounts of information; as they get overloaded easily and their comprehension breaks down when content becomes too lengthy or too complex.

It is important to acknowledge that students with cognitive problems may struggle to meet performance expectations in school and that they may feel uncomfortable and incompetent in many situations. For example:

A. Students who attend poorly often have an unclear understanding of what they should do and become embarrassed or confused when they are reprimanded for not completing tasks appropriately.

B. Students who have trouble retaining or retrieving information may feel uncertain about what they know and unsure whether they can answer questions or participate in activities.

C. Impulsive students do not take the time to think and can get into unsafe predicaments unknowingly. Also, their spontaneous, often peculiar remarks may result in either unsuccessful responses to academic tasks or in social rejection causing them to feel isolated.

D. Students with dramatically short overload limits may become confused or stressed because they cannot work with the same amount of information as their peers.

E. Those who have trouble organizing thoughts or tasks become anxious when they cannot meet teacher expectations for planning and carrying out activities.

F. Students who lack initiation skills (they know what to do but cannot get started) as well as those who have trouble with flexible thinking, generalization and rate of processing and performing have trouble keeping up with the class, and many cannot work independently. They become frustrated when their nonparticipation or poor performance are viewed as resistance or as reflecting a negative attitude; and, as a result, they feel they are unsuccessful participants in activities.

Implications For Educators

Professionals state that students with ABI are unusually challenging to work with because: (a) their proficiency levels can be extremely uneven and (b) the changes that occur in their abilities due to the recovery process are unpredictable. In addition, these students may *look* competent (be physically adept and communicate meaningfully) and, yet, have trouble in school; and educators must probe to find the source of their problems. Some students may demonstrate isolated skills but may not be able to integrate the skills that are needed to complete tasks. For instance, their visual perception or language skills may be age appropriate, so that they can select words from a list and fill in the blanks of a printed story; but they may have trouble listening to and remembering directions that instruct them to do this. There may be significant differences between what students are able to say and what they are able to do. That is, they may tell you how to get from the classroom to the lunchroom, but become completely disoriented when they proceed to actually traverse the route. Or, they may gather together and appropriately manipulate materials in order to make a project and not be able to tell you what the materials are or describe how to construct the project.

Moreover, students' rigid, perseverative thinking patterns can prevent them from using more flexible, divergent or convergent thinking processes that are needed for problem solving. Inflexibility and failure to recognize problems that have occurred since their brain injuries also may cause some not to see the need to develop or use strategies. However, others may use strategies ineffectively, because they are unable to evaluate task requirements. In general, these students are dependent learners, and they need a great deal of teacher attention to assist them in thinking about and proceeding through tasks.

Returning to school after sustaining a brain injury is a major event for students with ABI. Students at various levels of recovery, including those who can only attend school for short periods of time, usually feel comfortable in the familiar classroom setting. They have a sense of the importance of school work and of the teacher-student relationship. Consequently, teachers take on valuable roles in the rehabilitation process.

Aside from creating learning tasks which are meaningful for students and which students can complete successfully, teachers can help students: recognize their present levels of functioning; become aware of improvements they are making; and, thus, develop or maintain a sense of self-esteem. It is often in this supportive environment that the students exhibit their highest quality of performance.

In general, then, to develop appropriate programs for students with acquired brain injuries, educators should use a problem-solving approach and assess the W–H components of the organization strategy described earlier: *WHO, WHAT, WHERE, WHEN, WHY,* and *HOW.*

Program and Placement Decisions

There are some general guidelines that program planners should follow when working with individuals with acquired brain injuries. They are:

1. **Don't misread** these people and their abilities.
2. **Don't assume** anything when working with them.
3. **Do have students demonstrate** their comprehension and knowledge. Have them show you what they know and can do.
4. **Do regard students' performance problems as** *signals* of possible cognitive/ processing impairments and . . .
5. **Do look for and expect change** in their abilities and performance.

Professionals who keep these points in mind and who understand how cognitive impairments of students with ABI can affect school functioning realize that they must use different, and perhaps unique approaches to programming for these students. These approaches will be discussed in the following sections.

THE ASSESSMENT PROCESS

Formal & Informal Procedures

Assessments are administered to students with acquired brain injuries to obtain baseline or comparative information at specific points during the recovery process as well as to determine educational placements. This author and others (Baxter, Cohen & Ylvisaker, 1985; Burns, Cook & Ylvisaker, 1988; Cohen, Joyce, Rhoades & Welks, 1985; DePompei & Blosser, 1987; Ylvisaker, 1991; Ylvisaker, Chorazy, Cohen et al., 1990) have listed assessment instruments and described assessment procedures that are effective to use with these students. It is essential to understand that the assessment *process* may need to be altered for individuals with ABI. The aspects of assessment that will be discussed here deal with this process. They should be considered when students are evaluated for reentry into the school system and whenever their progress and needs are examined subsequently.

It is often necessary to test students with ABI more frequently in order to keep accurate track of their abilities. Testing sessions may need to be shortened to accommodate problems students have with fatigue or with anxiety or overload. Sessions also may need to be scheduled at specific times of day or in locations that are familiar to students in order to capture their highest levels of performance.

Ylvisaker, Chorazy, Cohen et al. (1990) have written about the importance of combining formal and informal assessment information before deciding on program goals for individuals with ABI. Many professionals such as Rispens, van Yperen, & van Duijn (1991) now realize that an individual's intellectual capacity should be measured by more than an I.Q. score. All of the above authors state that formal testing conditions and the use of standardized materials provide important but limited information about students. They explain that data obtained informally over time by working with and observing students in home and school settings is very significant. It reveals, among other things, how cognitive disabilities influence performance in practical, everyday activities.

Students may demonstrate adequate attending and comprehension skills in a quiet, formal testing situation and become distracted by the stimulation and overloaded by the amount of information that is dealt with in a classroom. They may exhibit knowledge and skills in specific contexts when tested formally and not be able to generalize and *apply* skills to new situations in class. The controlled, formal testing conditions often structure an individual's behavior so that impulsive tendencies are not apparent until that person enters the more complex classroom setting.

Additionally, specific teaching techniques or activities that were not a part of the testing experiences may have a positive impact on students' performance. For instance, discussions may clarify information for them and, thus, improve memory skills which were impaired when testing tasks did not include explanations of content. Also, meaningful, functional activities such as setting the table or sorting and putting away tools or groceries may reveal skills in areas such as task organization that were not apparent during formal, assessment sessions.

The Relationship Between Testing and Teaching

When formal and informal assessment approaches are used to complement each other, testing and teaching are linked very closely. In fact, there always should be a direct relationship between these two procedures (Baxter, Cohen & Ylvisaker, 1985; Cohen, Joyce, Rhoades & Welks, 1985). Typically, test results help to determine teaching objectives; and teaching approaches, especially those used for specialized instruction, e.g., prescriptive teaching, integrate the assessment process into all activities that are done with students.

Reuven Feuerstein has developed the Learning Potential Assessment Device, LPAD (Feuerstein, 1980; Lidz, 1991), which is based on adapting and connecting testing and teaching procedures in order to discover the conditions under which students learn. This type of dynamic assessment process emphasizing a test-teach-test continuum and incorporating teaching in the testing process promotes on-going changes in teaching and learning patterns and should be considered when programming for students with ABI. Through its use, educators problem solve to develop effective teaching interventions and, in some cases, students, themselves, can discover strategies and approaches to thinking that are effective to use in school settings and elsewhere.

When evaluating student performance, then, it is important to explore the interactive roles of examiners and students, S-timulus$\longleftrightarrow R$-esponse relationships which are fundamental to most learning experiences. The S = the staff's, assessment/teaching task including the manner of task presentation and expected response; the R = the student's actual response to the task. How does the structure of an examiner's task (the S) influence a student's performance (the R)? And, does a student's response to one task influence the way in which the examiner presents the next task?

Adaptations such as the following may need to be made to the S$\longleftrightarrow$R components of testing or teaching materials in order to accommodate the varied impairments of students with ABI (physical, speech, cognitive/ language, emotional/behavioral) and to determine what students know and what they can do: (a) directions may need to be shortened or demonstrated, and practice items may need to be provided for clarification; (b) directions or test content may need to be presented orally vs. in print; (c) response requirements may need to be written vs. spoken or changed from open-ended questions requiring memory skills to a multiple choice format; and (d) additional performance time should always be provided to compensate for delayed processing or for impaired fine-motor skills.

Assessments can evaluate general cognitive skills (Cohen, 1986; Ylvisaker, Chorazy, Cohen et al., 1990). Although formal tests have not been devised that scrutinize many of the general cognitive skill areas, examiners' detailed notes throughout the testing period can reveal students' cognitive strengths and weaknesses and indicate whether: answers reflected organized, fragmented or flexible thinking; responses were delayed in general or just when specific content or skills were tapped; memory tasks were difficult but students' comprehension was adequate when they were able to refer to material for answers and memory was not required; or students either were overloaded by lengthy directions and could not respond well or they attempted to *control the input* by asking to have information clarified so they could proceed.

School programs are beginning to implement informal assessment procedures that focus on cognitive/processing skills and the thinking and learning process (Rothman and Viadero, 1991; Lidz, 1991). These relatively new formats appraise students' classroom performance over time, reviewing materials filed in their portfolios, and analyzing their abilities to do such things as: answer essay questions, write critiques, describe activities or their thoughts about activities in personal journals, or problem solve to carry-out projects.

At this point in time, it is more difficult for staff to use these particular methods, since neither conditions of task presentation nor criteria for scoring or mastery have been clearly defined. However, since these approaches to testing and teaching are, indeed, worthwhile, researchers should develop standardized guidelines which orient staff to this type of evaluation and to training the thinking and learning process.

Curriculum-Based Assessment (CBA)

Another process which connects testing and teaching procedures is CBA (Mercer & Mercer, 1989; Smith, 1991; Whinnery & Fuchs, 1992). It allows teachers to target competencies and difficulties that students exhibit using materials and activities in actual classroom settings. This process makes it easy for teachers to probe frequently and note what students are learning, where learning breaks down, and which teaching techniques and materials are effective. CBA is becoming more popular in all educational learning environments and is certainly one way to investigate both the capabilities of students with ABI and the appropriateness of their programs.

Interpreting Students' Performance

As professionals learn about students with acquired brain injuries, they realize that assessment data must be interpreted differently for this population and should not be used to predict classroom performance (Baxter, Cohen, & Ylvisaker, 1985; Begali, 1987; Burns, Cook, & Ylvisaker, 1988; Ylvisaker, Chorazy, Cohen et al., 1990). These students may be able to execute short assessment items and achieve scores at age-appropriate levels; however, their problems with overload may prevent them from understanding or completing lengthier classroom assignments at those same levels. Furthermore, their characteristically inconsistent performance resulting from physical fatigue or from weaknesses in areas such as attention, comprehension, memory, and generalization can prohibit them from maintaining abilities they exhibited during testing when working in class. For all these reasons, educators should never assume what these students can do. Rather, further teaching should evaluate whether students are capable of doing new and different work.

Meaningful Reports

Assessment information from a team of professionals in disciplines such as neuropsychology, psychology, speech pathology, occupational therapy, and special education should be combined to decipher the competencies and learning styles of students with ABI (Ylvisaker, Chorazy, Cohen et al., 1990). The examining team should be sure to evaluate how students integrate skills in order to perform, since school activities and interactions outside of school regularly require people to: attend + comprehend + organize and remember + think flexibly and problem solve + express themselves in some way. Then, in order to target impairments that have resulted from the students' brain injuries, staff must compare students' present behaviors with their premorbid learning profiles. It is not unusual to find that previous personality traits or characteristic behaviors are presently intensified. However, in order to determine whether or not students' behaviors are *problems,* staff must also relate these behaviors to normal developmental and educational milestones.

To assure a common understanding of the assessment data and to make the data educationally relevant, all reports must provide *details* about students' performance noting the S$\longleftrightarrow$R conditions. Adaptations made to task procedures document the conditions under which the students performed and must be pointed out. Otherwise, those receiving the information will assume that standardized or curricular assessment tasks were given *as written,* students' skills will be misinterpreted, and inappropriate goals will be developed for their school programs.

Furthermore, therapists' reports must describe and not merely label students' cognitive impairments, because educators and families often are not accustomed to discussing the development of general cognitive skills. For example, when stating that students are *impulsive,* therapists also must specify what this behavior looks like, i.e., the student interrupts a lot or blurts out incorrect answers without thinking. Therapists then should explain how specific strategies help the students perform more appropriately, i.e., when cued to raise his hand and wait to be called on, a student is no longer disruptive or when prompted to *take thinking time* a student can follow directions and complete work sheets. It is essential to report that much questioning and cuing are needed to keep her on track and to clarify information. For instance, a cue sheet is used that tells her to: *Find the directions . . . , Read #1 . . . , Write the answer on the line next to #1.*

Similarly, educators need to provide information about variations in different mainstream and special education learning environments that could influence how students function, such as: the number of students in a class or teaching group, and the length of assignments, independent performance requirements, and staff assistance that is available or given. This helps therapists, families, and teachers who exchange students within school systems recognize that the structure provided in one setting may not be present in another and that adaptations in teaching approaches may need to be made for particular students. Programs in classrooms where lengthy discussions are common, for example, may be inappropriate or may need to be adjusted for students whose thought organization is good for only limited amounts of information.

To conclude, staff must know the important assessment content to report **and** the questions to ask of others if pertinent details have not been provided. When the reporting process is effective, family members and rehabilitation and medical staff realize that schools have different learning environments for students, and educators learn as well that any one of these settings may need to be modified to accommodate particular students with ABI.

The Family: Team Members and Advocates

Sometimes students with ABI perform better with familiar family members and in familiar home settings. Information about $S \longleftrightarrow R$ components of these situations can be helpful to the professional team. On the other hand, when professionals investigate family interactions, they may find that unstructured family activities are problematic for those with ABI. In such cases, therapists can assist families in structuring activities and in adjusting methods of communication and expectations of what their impaired family member can do so that everyone at home is more comfortable. Moreover, therapists and educators may determine that program goals should include developing skills or strategies to improve students' functioning in the family.

In addition to providing information for the team, families serve as advocates (Savage, 1991) for those members who have been injured. As such, they must be informed about ABI and be able to evaluate treatment and educational programs. In most cases, this means they have to learn not only new terminology but also content that is totally foreign to them. Therapists from disciplines mentioned previously all may discuss assessment data with them in areas such as auditory and visual processing, language comprehension and expression, memory and reading. It can be difficult for families to understand the significance of a *delayed language level* or a *visual memory problem* when their child communicates meaningfully with them and seems to recognize, remember, and use items correctly at home. However, because families have a better understanding of the importance of educational tasks, this same information becomes noteworthy when the educational diagnostician reports that the sixteen-year-old student cannot understand fifth grade reading concepts or that the eight-year-old has trouble with written assignments because he cannot remember the letter shapes or letter sequences needed to write answers to questions. Since educational evaluations and tasks connect students' performance to the graded, teaching process and are more meaningful, other professionals should indicate how their assessment findings will influence school functioning.

When family education is incorporated into the total educational plan, professionals can help family members identify students' current and changing abilities and realize that suitable school programs which are different from those the students were in premorbidly (and may be considered undesirable) could be temporary and will be monitored frequently and revised to meet students' needs.

Staff must understand that because these families have a vital need to know what is going on, there usually will be and should be more family contacts in these situations. As a part of their assessment and learning process, family members often want to make first-hand observations of classroom activities, and some like to keep in touch with school staff through the use of log books which carry reports of daily activities and *news* that is significant both in school and outside of school.

Individualized Education Program (I.E.P.) meetings which usually are held annually to plan programs for students who receive special education services should occur at least every three months for students with ABI (Cohen, 1991; Lehr, Lantz, & Doranzo, 1990; Savage & Carter, 1984). This assures that program goals and objectives address students' changing levels. Also, parents of students with ABI have requested additional program updates before the meetings in order to understand meeting content and contribute to the program planning (Cohen, 1991).

CAUTIONS

Evaluating Students With Unidentified or Mild Brain Injuries

It is not uncommon for a school-age person to fall and bump his head or to hit his head on the seat when a car stops suddenly. These situations often are considered to be inconsequential, and they may not even be acknowledged by the individual or by those around him. However, a bump on the head can cause a brain injury which, though mild, results in considerable learning and behavior difficulties (Barth, 1986; Boll, 1983; Segalowitz & Brown, 1991). In such a case, a student may come to school with undiagnosed problems that educators should be addressing.

Students do not have to be diagnosed as having acquired brain injuries for professionals to implement assessment procedures that have been delineated here. It is valuable to analyze aspects of the learning and teaching process when working with every student. However, in cases where students exhibit unexpected, significant performance problems or behaviors that have either changed inexplicably and are hard to manage or require more attention than usual, educators should investigate whether the students have had an ABI of some sort. Identification of an ABI will help people understand and not misread students' behavior. Ultimately, this can substantiate reasons for making adjustments in their educational programs and clarify the type of assessment and teaching approaches they should have.

Evaluating Very Young Students Who Have ABI

Very young children who have sustained brain injuries may achieve maturational milestones in a timely fashion. If their injuries were mild, their parents may not be aware of delays or aberrations in their development.

In fact, it can be difficult to ascertain whether young children have cognitive deficits. Characteristically, they have short attention spans, limited amounts of self-control and limited abilities to organize thoughts and tasks and to problem solve. If they have not been exposed to school programs, their knowledge base and, often, their thinking and communication patterns are directly related to their life experiences which can vary greatly.

Developmental checklists and assessment batteries provide guidelines which help relate their skills to those of other children their age. Some examiners use the dynamic assessment process mentioned earlier to discover how very young people think and learn (Burns, 1991; Lidz, 1991). As with older individuals, however, one should not use formal assessment information to predict what these children will be able to do in a busy classroom. Instead, programmers should evaluate the childrens' performance in the specific settings.

Preschool placements can reveal whether young people can learn, retain and use information, and communicate and interact effectively with others. Moreover, teachers can probe to see if students' poor response in testing sessions were due to lack of knowledge (limited experiences) and if classroom training has a positive impact on their performance.

Even though young children with ABI have performed fairly well at home or in preschool, though, their performance should be monitored closely as they move along the educational continuum. Cognitive/processing problems can emerge when students are faced with the increased structure of school activities and with increasingly more complex thinking requirements of both academic tasks and social interactions.

Placement Considerations

The experience of education staff authoring this text and of others referred to within this context indicate that educators often have to implement more than the customary amount of program adaptations for students with ABI. Teachers in mainstream and special education settings generally are equipped to work with these students, but they need input about the program adjustments the students require.

Inservice Training

Professionals knowledgeable in the areas of brain injury can inform school staff about the needs of students with ABI who are entering school programs. As inservice consultants, they can provide materials (including the content of this volume) that relate students' capabilities with teaching goals and techniques (Blosser & DePompei, 1989 & 1991; Burns, Cook & Ylvisaker, 1988; Cohen, 1986 & 1991; Cohen, Joyce, Rhoades & Welks, 1985; Cook, 1991; DePompei & Blosser, 1987). Their training promotes positive attitudes toward programming by helping school staff alter their expectations for specific students and learn teaching approaches that are currently effective to use with them. This content is crucial for staff to know, because, though they learn that many students' cognitive processes are not intact, they also recognize that teaching manuals may not focus on developing skills in these areas. Joint training of supervisory and direct service staff also creates understanding on the part of educational administrators of the need for program formats that may differ from those described in state regulations, and it establishes the supervisory support that school building staff need to execute unique educational plans.

Some general points that inservice training should include are discussed below:

> When students with ABI first return to school, staff should be cautious about automatically placing them back in their premorbid classrooms, as they may no longer have all the performance skills that are required there. Instead of assuming that students can rapidly review and understand missed curriculum content and catch up with the class, staff must verify students' abilities and identify their current learning needs. As has been stated, the students' needs and programs can change unpredictably, and educators should consider placements to be temporary steps that will accommodate the recovery process (Cohen, 1991). In this way, staff will be able to tolerate the interruptions in program continuity that are likely to occur.

Inappropriate program decisions can be made for students when program planners don't attend to cognitive impairments and don't recognize that strategies can help students function more adequately. For instance, students with initiation problems may *appear* to be slow learners, and impulsive students may *appear* to have behavior problems. Those with poor expressive organization skills may *seem* to have fragmented thought patterns or bizarre responses that reflect disturbed behaviors, while students who get overloaded easily may *look as if* they are working in materials that are too difficult. Educators should not always think that patterns of wrong answers indicate that students are working either in incorrect materials or at incorrect levels. Strategies and teaching approaches such as those presented in this chapter should be tried, as they can improve the performance of students resembling those described above.

Schools should not routinely create classrooms solely for students with ABI. Such settings are likely to bring together young people of very different ages and with very diverse skills who cannot work or socialize together. These situations are difficult for teachers who become individual tutors; and they are not totally beneficial for students, because they lack stimulation and experiences in the socialization area.

As was stated earlier, students with ABI usually can and should be integrated into existing educational formats. However, Cohen et al. (1985) explain that if students with ABI are to profit from classroom experiences, they must be able to: attend to a task for at least five to ten minutes without being unduly distracted; tolerate classroom stimulation for a minimum of twenty to thirty minutes; communicate meaningfully verbally or nonverbally; follow simple rules or directions, perhaps with cues of some sort; retain small amounts of information, i.e., demonstrate they are able to learn and use information; and work in a group of two or more.

In essence, interdisciplinary programming is transferred from the rehabilitation facility to the school setting. There, staff must define their own process for maintaining continuity among the many parts of a student's program and establish efficient methods for program monitoring. Although everyone's input is important, students' teachers are key people for identifying and ranking problem areas.

Since it is not easy to insert additional meeting times into professional schedules, the team should appoint a leader to arrange scheduling and to implement procedures that will maintain program accountability. When appropriate, information from professionals the students are seeing outside of school and from family members should be shared with the group. When procedures are efficient and effective, team members grow to realize the benefits of joint planning and of information sharing.

Currently, classroom teachers gain support and instructional assistance from teacher consultants and school-based instructional support teams (Mercer & Mercer, 1989; Smith, 1991) as well as from other educational programs referred to earlier. These instructional formats require increased communication among school staff. It is this author's experience, nevertheless, that staff who work with students with ABI work more closely together than they ever have.

PLANNING PROGRAM COMPONENTS

Programmers who study the strategy elements *who, what, where, why, when, how* discussed earlier (see page 126) and who assume a noncategorical point of view can attempt to match the range of students' abilities with content in existing classrooms. The above strategy findings will explain *why* unusual decisions need to be made for some individuals, such as planning to place a student who has very uneven scores in a group for students with Learning Disabilities when some performance criteria indicate that programs for students with mental retardation are fitting.

Planning team members must look carefully at the differences in mainstream and special education teaching formats described in Table 7.1. This content, while familiar to educators, often is unfamiliar but very valuable to family members. It indicates clearly that different learning environments benefit students with different capabilities. It points out among other things: that the rate at which students think and perform may determine whether they can meet teaching standards and make progress in particular settings; and that self-control, social competencies and independent functioning are *expected behaviors* in mainstream environments and *goals to work toward* in special education programs. It is important for the team to talk with current teachers who may reveal that present curriculum goals, student profiles, and teaching techniques differ from those typically found in school programs, e.g., a mainstream setting is small and offers more individualized attention, or

TABLE 7.1

Comparing Learning Environments

Mainstream	*Special Education*
1. Larger class size.	1. Smaller class size.
2. Stimulating settings.	2. More structured settings.
3. Relatively fixed range of academic levels and learning styles.	3. Varied range of academic levels and learning styles.
4. Much larger group instruction.	4. Individualized and small group instruction: increased teacher attention; strategy development.
5. Students handle significant amounts of material.	5. Students handle limited amounts of material.
6. Expected performance rates.	6. Students work at their own pace.
7. Expected levels of self-control and social competencies.	7. Goals to increase self-control and social competencies.
8. Expected levels of independent learning and performing.	8. Goals to develop independent learning and performing skills.

Sally B. Cohen, M.Ed.

they may find that Regular Education Initiative programs meet students' needs.

Cohen (1986) developed the form labelled as Figure 7.1 to assist professionals in refining their placement decisions. Used as a checklist, the top section highlights facts team members should report about students' present programs; and the bottom section identifies procedures in potential settings that should be noted, since they directly influence the functioning of those who have cognitive impairments. Classroom observations should yield information related to the checklist items including teaching approaches used with individual students and with groups and details of the way students *and* teachers handle transition times and social interactions.

The team should not assume that students with ABI can move from a one-to-one situation in a specialized rehabilitation or education placement to larger group arrangements where they will have to use increased amounts of information, tolerate more stimulation and exhibit more self-control. Observation notes and reports will indicate whether students have behaviors that are required in more complicated surroundings or whether behaviors have to be trained (see Specific Teaching Techniques).

Group experiences are valuable for most of these individuals, but their group goals may be different from those of other group participants.

FIGURE 7.1

Considerations For Community Placements
When visiting community placement sites and talking to staff about potential student placements, be sure to describe:
   — the *structure* that is provided at the present placement.
   — the *strategies* that are used *by TBI individuals.*
   — *the amount of work* students are able to do (rereading assignments, written work, materials used).
   — the amount of *staff attention* that is required per task/within specific time frames.
   — the *attention span* of the TBI individuals.
   — the *independent work* the TBI individuals can do.
When observing the existing placement, note:
   — structured vs. unstructured situations.
   — flexibility required: schedules, routines, materials.
   — independent work required: amount/type.
   — independent thinking required.
   — amount of work: time allotments/adaptations possible?
   — time available to adapt to individual differences; amount of staff assistance given.
   — how information is presented: rate, technique, memory requirements.
   — academic levels/materials.
   — support services available.
   — physical plant (as it relates to physical and cognitive impairments).
   Sally B. Cohen, M.Ed.

Groups provide avenues for them to work on socialization skills, increase memory abilities, strengthen attention, and learn to follow and contribute to expanding dialogue. Therefore, program planners must investigate group formats to ensure that teachers will be able to individualize for specific students and that students will not get overloaded by the content and will be called upon often to demonstrate whether they are comprehending and learning.

THE INTERDISCIPLINARY TEAM

A variety of school staff may be selected to work with students with ABI. Physical therapists, occupational therapists, speech-language clinicians, psychologists, and counselors can help students counteract impairments that have an impact on school functioning. Their services can be delivered in Push-In and Pull-Out formats (Smith, 1991); each has a purpose. It may also be worthwhile to work with a student *in* class, integrating treatment techniques into actual school activities. The latter format, when feasible, is enriching for teachers and therapists who can share ideas and learn directly from each other. In fact, tasks become more meaningful for students when treatment approaches are applied to actual classroom materials. This also avoids generalization problems students may have, i.e., they oftentimes are unable to recognize when techniques practiced in therapy activities can be used with different but similar activities in class.

Different school staff can assist in carrying-out educational programs when busy schedules prohibit students' classroom teachers from offering students the extra time they need to learn and practice skills or when fatigue limits students' classroom participation. In addition to working on speech and language and communication skills, speech-language clinicians are well qualified to provide cognitive remediation and to treat learning impairments. They also can train social behaviors and develop learning strategies that are needed for classroom activities. Moreover, mainstream or special education staff as well as itinerant teachers and reading or other specialists can work cooperatively with classroom teachers providing extra tutorial services. They also can serve as the primary educators when arrangements cannot be made to include students in classroom programs.

CHALLENGING PLACEMENTS

Kindergarten and primary students may not be able to tolerate the pace, stimulation, and complexity of regular school programs. They may need a more exclusive education setting. Sometimes special education services are scant for young students, and program planners have to call on school staff mentioned above to assist with program delivery.

Similarly, junior high and high school students with ABI can have a vast range of skills which cannot be accommodated in existing classes. Though special education services are more prevalent for this population, special education teachers may not be able to provide students with enough individualized time, and some teachers are not accustomed to the lower level teaching that may be required. Many programs for older students should include functional academics. Prevocational curricula and transitional plans already are stipulated by law for students this age (Edlaw, 1991), but they may need to be custom-made for those with ABI integrating the cognitive approaches discussed here. Again, a variety of school staff may be enlisted to serve these students adequately.

Recovery Levels Influence Program Content

Individuals in *early stages of recovery* (Ylvisaker, 1985) from acquired brain injuries do not participate in community school programs. They usually are in hospitals or rehabilitation centers where doctors and therapists treat their medical and physical problems and interdisciplinary staff work together to stimulate their sensory and cognitive awareness.

School-age persons in the *middle stages of recovery* (Ylvisaker, 1985) generally are in rehabilitation programs; but since they occasionally return to schools, they warrant discussion here. Since the greatest and most rapid recovery strides are seen during the first 18–24 months following a brain injury, rehabilitation and education staff can anticipate that middle level students whose injuries have been fairly recent can demonstrate frequent and perhaps dramatic changes in functioning which require corresponding changes in programming.

These students, too, are challenging for educators. They have very short attention spans, are disoriented, disorganized and confused, and demonstrate fragmented patterns of thinking and expression. Their school programs should emphasize strengthening attending and communication skills. The programs need to be highly individualized, because: (a) teaching tasks must be extremely short, simple and repetitive to hold their attention, decrease their confusion and establish comfortable and predictable learning situations; (b) they may have many significant impairments requiring increased amounts of therapies which decrease time in the classroom; (c) their poor and often distorted perceptions of what is happening around them are due partly to the fact that they no longer understand the concepts that are basic to good thought organization, so program content should focus on assessing cognitive abilities, such as those in Figure 7.2, at very fundamental levels; and (d) they fatigue easily, and this can limit their class participation as well as the length of their school day.

Since these students often cannot tolerate much classroom stimulation, therapists and other school staff may become their primary educators. It can be difficult to coordinate the schedules of the variety of staff involved, and, on occasion, the planning team must identify prerogatives for specific students, deciding which therapy should be a priority or whether it is all right to remove a student from class at times when he or she could benefit from the experiences there. This type of decision-making may be necessary in lesser degrees, as students move along in the recovery process.

FIGURE 7.3

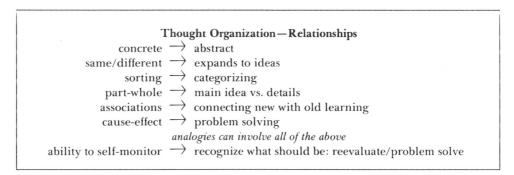

Most students with ABI who return to school are in the *late stages of recovery* (Ylvisaker, 1985). Though they still may demonstrate greater changes in abilities than their peers, they usually can fit into existing programs more easily. Their attending skills have improved; they think and express themselves more clearly and need fewer therapies to support their educational programs; and fatigue does not interrupt program continuity. Educators should focus on expanding thought organization while continuing to probe for gaps. The concept relationships in Figure 7.3 are essential parts of school curricula at all developmental levels, and this can serve as a checklist to assist teachers in determining why students may have difficulty comprehending specific material. Program goals also should include enhancing socialization skills and helping students recognize their present levels of functioning and the value of using compensatory strategies. In addition, teaching should encourage students to handle lengthier and more varied materials and to think and work more rapidly and more independently.

TEACHING TECHNIQUES

Mainstream and special education teachers always are pleased to discover that teaching techniques that are necessary for students with ABI also are beneficial to use with other students. Some of these techniques will be presented in this section. Though teaching content and some teaching styles may differ for younger and older students, this discussion will focus on instruction that promotes successful learning experiences for students of all ages who have incurred brain injuries. Hopefully, educators will recognize many of these approaches and will begin to feel better equipped to work with this population.

General Approaches

Morris J. Vogel (1991) wrote: "Learning Happens When It Matters." This is a statement for educators to think about. How can they make learning matter for students? What should the content be? How should they deliver the content? Answers to these questions are related to three important points advocated previously:

1. Educators must investigate the S$\longleftrightarrow$R components which comprise a student's total learning environment (see p. 133)
2. Educators should relate assessment and teaching approaches in order to analyze what a student can and cannot do and to develop appropriate lesson plans.
3. Educators should determine how to make content meaningful **and** functional for a student.

When professionals select teaching techniques, they should think about this information in more detail and consider the nine points that follow.

1. *Cognitive Problem Areas Guide Teaching.*
   Cohen's list of Cognitive Problem Areas (1986) which are highlighted below was developed to assist teachers in targeting teaching goals for students. However, it also can serve as a checklist that guides teachers toward developing effective and efficient instructional skills. In so doing, it alerts teachers to:

(a) broaden their *orientation* about educational programming.
(b) expand their *attention* to and knowledge of skills involved in the learning process in order to serve students with a variety of needs.
(c) develop tasks with diverse ways of *following directions.*
(d) approach *memory* and *retrieval* tasks differently.
(e) accommodate students' *overload* limits by adjusting lessons and communication in general.
(f) recognize and create different activities to address *thought organization, task organization,* and *expressive organization skills.*
(g) demonstrate *flexible thinking:* implementing program changes that keep

pace with students' functional changes; establishing individualized goals for students with ABI that involve teachers *staying on tasks or on topics* that are different from the teaching emphasis for other students.

(h) understand the importance of creative *initiation:* demonstrating an interest and assertiveness in developing strategies and other program adaptations, and

(i) cope with: the challenges of working on *generalization* skills with educational teams and with students; the *frustration* of dealing with students' variabilities; the *stress* (and *fatigue!*) involved in probing to determine students' educational needs; and the inconsistent approaches to teaching that the students' needs may require.

2. *Are Students Relearning Information? Are Teachers Replacing Lost Skills?*

· Teachers must ascertain whether students with ABI are *relearning* information that was lost due to the trauma or whether teaching must focus on developing compensatory strategies and on *replacing* skills that do not seem to be returning.

In general, when students with ABI are unable to perform, teachers may find that direct instruction is needed both to train procedures that were previously automatic and to teach content that was previously understood; and the emphasis of teaching may be on strategy development that is extremely individualized (see Strategy Development).

3. *Task Analysis Is Essential.*

Teachers should query: *"What skills are involved in this task?"* both when students are having difficulty and when students perform successfully. Discovering what students *can do* sets staff on a path of positive planning procedures, while understanding how learning impairments affect students' performance strengthens staff's abilities to organize lessons with appropriate $S \longleftrightarrow R$ ingredients. Once educators determine what is important for students to learn and when school staff become knowledgeable about teaching procedures that will meet particular students' needs, staff can use a variety of materials to carry out their plans, and they don't have to be bound to using traditional curricula.

It may take time to decipher students' cognitive impairments, since the cognitive skills that are called into play for a single activity can be closely connected. Figure 7.2 shows that the quality of attention or the ease with which a person attends correlates with how well an individual comprehends the content; a person attends and comprehends better when material is well organized; organized information is easier to remember as is information that is understood clearly; and so on. The interrelationships of information-processing skills such as those depicted here are important for educators to explore when they use task analysis to put together the S$\longleftrightarrow$R features for teaching activities. Ylvisaker (1991) explains, for instance, that an apparent expressive language problem may be rooted in areas such as attention, organization or memory or it may be stress related or due to the influence of medication.

Task analysis also should determine whether students' skills are at the *acquisition, maintenance/mastery or generalization levels of learning* (Bos & Vaughn, 1988; Mercer & Mercer, 1989). Furthermore, teachers must recognize that students with ABI often learn and perform more slowly and need more practice time than their classmates in order to build skills at any stage along this continuum. Therefore, it is appropriate for lesson plans and I.E.P. objectives to include practice activities some of which have to be quite repetitive. Although these students may lag behind others in accomplishing goals, if they unlock previously known information during the learning process, their knowledge base can expand significantly and their skills may surpass their peers'. Both situations will impact on their group compatibility and will influence the types of materials and the amount of individualization teachers need to use with them.

Teachers may need to attend to the emotional aspect of the learning process, as students with ABI can have moderate or catastrophic emotional reactions to the changes in their abilities, and these are likely to impair school performance. In such cases, teachers can help students deal with critical losses, move through stages of denial, make changes that will accommodate their present competencies, and, hopefully, gain a revised sense of self-esteem, as they acknowledge their new achievement levels.

4. *Teaching Goals Include: Prioritizing, Structuring and SLOWING DOWN.*
   Since it seldom is feasible to make students *all better* all at once, educators should not attempt to address many problems at the same time. Once students' strengths and needs are identified, school staff must choose program areas to focus on initially. Then staff must determine how to structure the learning process for particular individuals.

As has been said, students with ABI learn better when they can apply skills or procedures to daily activities that have meaning for them. Therefore, educators may have to *slow down*, change their orientation, and work with content that is not necessarily associated with curricular programs. For instance, if it is important that students learn a particular activity, such as playing a game with peers, professionals must think about the skills involved and teach these skills in relation to the game-playing process. The game can be motivating for students; the process can build socialization skills or it may improve expressive organization and flexible thinking. On the other hand, if it is important for students to learn a particular process (organizing different materials to work more effectively), instructors must select tasks (which could include games) that require this skill.

Tasks that are considered routine can be complicated for students with ABI. Teachers may need to train such school-related behaviors as: working independently, finding a locker or a location in the school building, gathering materials for different classes, reading a schedule, or copying and planning how to complete assignments.

Of course, content from formal curricula is important for students to learn, but educators may have to adapt or change their goals in relation to the use of curriculum materials in order to make the content meaningful and to meet students' individualized goals. They may need to teach lost or weak concepts that are basic to particular Reading or Science lessons; or they may have to train processes students need in order to complete assignments correctly, e.g., referring to context for answers vs. making up responses (see Specific Techniques).

5. *Teaching Highlights What Is Important.*
   Since students with ABI learn very little incidentally, all teaching should underscore what is important for them to attend to. It should highlight significant content, and make students who have metacognitive awareness think about the thinking process and about the skills that are needed to perform tasks.

The purpose of each task (or parts of tasks) should be explained to students according to their levels of understanding. The use of *cognitive vocabulary,* such as the following, assists students *and* staff in focusing attention on task goals: (a) "Let's think about how this activity is *organized*"; (b) "How many different parts does this worksheet have? You have to be *flexible* and change from reading answers to writing them. Let's practice doing this." (c) "You are going to work on *initiation* today. Show me how to start this task?" (d) "What skills are you using to make this model airplane?" This teaching approach helps teachers and students avoid getting trapped in a task and overlooking the purpose of the activity. For instance, they can plan to use work sheets focusing on following oral directions. Or, they can recognize that a card game is being used to work on students' reading comprehension and on answering questions and staying on a topic.

When all members of a student's interdisciplinary team use cognitive labels in this way, the student begins to see relationships between the different parts of the school program. Using the same approach to *thought organization* in speech therapy and in the classroom, for example, provides extended learning periods for a student to understand more clearly how to apply one technique to different tasks.

6. *Teaching Approaches Resemble Those in Specialized Instruction.*
   This author (Cohen 1985, 1986, 1991) and others (Begali, 1987; Deaton, 1987; DePompei & Blosser, 1987; Lehr, Lantz & Doranzo, 1990; Rosen & Gerring, 1986; Savage & Wolcott, 1988; Ylvisaker, 1985) state that students with learning disabilities and those with acquired brain injuries benefit from the following teaching approaches many of which already have been mentioned: task analysis; multisensory approaches to learning; strategy development; instruction focused on individual learning styles and on skill integration; programs that develop socialization and academic abilities; and an emphasis on functional academics and practical learning experiences. Cohen (1991) also explains the importance of: developing active learning situations in which students demonstrate what they know and can do; teaching the process of an activity; and giving students varying degrees of responsibility while guiding them towards thinking and performing independently (see Specific Techniques).

It is important to make brief mention of some other techniques that are used frequently by special educators and that benefit students with ABI at any stage or level of learning. They are: *backward chaining and having students learn and perform through imitation, from a model, or independently and from memory.* In backward chaining, which incorporates elements of task analysis, the instructor does most of the task for the student and initially asks the student to perform the last step. This takes pressure off of the student, provides interaction between student and staff, allows the student to get a sense of task participation and task completion, and permits the student to be positively reinforced for doing a part of the task well. The student's task responsibilities (from end to beginning) are increased gradually accommodating problems in many cognitive areas including overload, attention, comprehension, organization, memory and skill integration. Moreover, staff realize it is their responsibility to carry out parts of tasks **for** students while beginning to train significant procedures the students need to learn.

Some students need to imitate behaviors that teachers demonstrate in order to learn how to respond or perform. This technique can shape students' verbal and motor responses as well as their thinking patterns. However, other students may learn adequately from a model rather than from explicit demonstration. For example, the latter may look at a completed puzzle or at a picture with arrows indicating how to physically move around a playing field and understand how to perform these activities. The highest level of learning which often is difficult for students with ABI to achieve is when students can remember information, problem solve independently and figure out how to proceed through tasks without teacher intervention.

7. *Adaptations Can Affect Grades and Graduation.*
   Adaptations that are necessary for students with ABI affect all educational decisions.

   When staff develop program components that differ from those used customarily by school systems, they must also think about how they are going to evaluate students' performance within those components. If students attend school part-time or take only some of the classes required for achievement in certain subject areas, how much credit should they receive? If complicated schedules prevent students from participating in Reading five times a week or if their goals, and, therefore, the work that they hand in, are not the same as those on which grading systems are based, what should their grades be? These decisions hinge on educators' abilities to establish achievement levels and evaluate quality of performance within a framework that has atypical educational standards.

Grades and credits are very important to school staff, students and family members. Educational systems have given students credit for cognitive therapy they received in rehabilitation facilities; and, once students return to community schools, they accumulate credits whether they are in mainstream or specialized programs. However, it can be difficult for the above individuals to rationalize that good grades for accomplishing individualized goals in school may not indicate that students are ready to move on to the next educational level.

Discussions about the benefits of maintaining rehabilitation goals and developing students' thinking and learning skills will help all concerned determine what the next step for a student should be. This information may be especially useful when reviewing programs for students who are about to move on to new levels of education, e.g., to middle school, junior high school, high school, or college. If students are not ready to move on, staff can commit to extending their current programs and yet arrange to have them participate in the eagerly anticipated graduation festivities even receiving certificates or diplomas that are unsigned.

8. *Transitioning Aids Students and Staff.*
   P.L. 101-476 states that transition programs should be in place for junior and senior high school students preparing them for life in the community, on the job or at institutions of higher learning. It is likely that students with ABI will need extra refinements in such programs. Bergland (Ch.8) details Life Skills programs which use

some of the teaching approaches mentioned here to train work-related and independent living abilities as well as leisure time and social skill competencies. While students may need step-by-step training in any area, community staff also will need to learn both what specific individuals with ABI can do and what adjustments should be made for them.

It often is more effective to move students slowly into selected parts of new school or community programs. Training students and staff ahead of time in skills and strategies that are needed for limited activities in the new settings assures that (a) the students will perform successfully there and (b) staff, who are working with the students for the first time, will gain a more positive view of the students' qualifications and capabilities. When students enter programs gradually in this manner, they are more likely to be *included* as integral parts of the whole rather than *integrated* respectfully but thought to stand apart from the whole.

Behavior Management

Many discussions about educational programming describe behavior management techniques as being related to but different from teaching techniques. However, the premise set forth here is that behavior management and teaching techniques are vitally intertwined. The general teaching approaches just presented, as well as others that will be mentioned later, can shape students' behaviors in academic and other situations. These approaches assist educators in determining why students behave the way they do and what their educational needs are.

Using this mind-set, then, the following four considerations should be included in basic teaching guidelines:

1. "Behavior management" is a broad term and should be applied to all aspects of student performance.
2. Those who interact with students affect how the students behave.
3. Students' behaviors are not always intentional.
4. Many behaviors can be structured and adapted.

Traditional behavior modification techniques work well with some students. Students who learn from these programs which are based on reinforcing appropriate behavior and ignoring inappropriate behavior are able to attend and remember information, understand cause-effect relationships, and have some ability to control their behavior and make proper judgements. Cohen et al. (1985) explain that such programs may be ineffective with students who have cognitive impairments.

These students cannot learn incidentally. In fact, they often become anxious when appropriate behaviors are not outlined for them. They need to be told clearly what the expected behaviors are ("Take out your writing books . . . Talk when your name is called . . . "); and, sometimes, these behaviors need to be taught step-by-step.

In other words, educators should regard direction giving as a behavior management technique. Rules, too, can delineate what students are to do, and they can be general or quite explicit as need be. But posting rules or providing directions may not be enough; students with ABI often have to be taught to refer to them, to understand the pertinent language concepts, and to translate the instructions into behaviors that are related to particular activities. Moreover, teachers may find that students with ABI need reminders to follow behavioral guidelines for certain tasks—or parts of tasks—for extensive periods of time. In fact, some students always may need cues and may never learn to perform totally independently (see Strategy Development).

When thinking about behavior management, then, professionals can plan to build students' abilities by individualizing reinforcers and reinforcement schedules in relation to tasks and by providing direct instruction and feedback on specific aspects of student performance. Students with specific cognitive weaknesses will benefit from the more direct teaching approaches which will insure that they will not have to figure out or remember what they are to do and that they will be able to receive positive reinforcement and, hopefully, become more self-assured while developing appropriate school behaviors.

   9. *Developing or Refining Socialization Skills.*

Students with ABI often have difficulties with interpersonal interactions which are a part of one-to-one or group activities of any kind. Their deficits in the psychosocial areas are felt to be the most long-lasting (Hall & DePompei, 1986; McClelland, 1986; Rosenthal, Griffith, Bond & Miller, 1990; Waaland & Kreutzer, 1988) and are extremely troublesome for the professionals who work with them as well as for the individuals and their families.

Educators must recognize and may have to teach the skills needed to understand and effectively contribute to social interactions, such as:

   1. *attending* to subtle verbal and nonverbal behaviors.
   2. *understanding, remembering, retrieving and expressing language concepts* that may involve idiosyncratic, idiomatic and colloquial statements.
   3. *self-control* and *judgement* in relation to thoughts, actions, and emotions.
   4. *flexibility* related to topics and activities that change rapidly.
   5. *generalization skills* to note similarities in social formats, since the content of two social situations is never exactly the same.
   6. *initiation skills* which are needed to interact.
   7. rapid *rates of processing and performing.*

8. *self-monitoring* and *profiting from feedback* in order to adjust behaviors to meet group or interpersonal demands.

It may be acutely clear that students' inappropriate, immature or inadequate social behaviors interfere with performance in school and other settings. On the other hand, people may misread the abilities of students with ABI who have basic conversation skills and appear initially to "fit into" social situations. Problems that arise with their personal relationships or group tasks may be due to their not being able to correctly perceive, interpret, or respond to what is going on around them. The teaching approaches presented in this chapter will assist educators in assessing and improving social behaviors that students need to have in particular life experiences.

Specific Techniques

Even though educators have knowledge about programs, placement decisions and general teaching approaches that will benefit students with ABI, they still have to determine how to teach specific content to these students. This section will present teaching approaches that address some of these instructional areas. The approaches have been used successfully with students with ABI and often can be integrated into activities that typically occur in classrooms. They are meant to be suggestions only. Hopefully, they will stimulate the reader's ideas about other techniques that could be implemented as well.

Program and teaching adaptations mentioned previously describe teachers' strategies that improve students' learning environments. In addition, teachers can devise strategies for students to use in order to function more independently. In either case, lesson plans should be structured to:

1. Delineate student and teacher behaviors building on what students can do in relation to specific activities.
2. Teach students to *think about* what they are doing.
3. Establish active learning situations in which students demonstrate what they know and can do rather than merely answering affirmatively (or otherwise) when asked if they understand.
4. Provide instruction around the process of an activity.
5. Train students to "generalize the use of" a particular technique, i.e., to use one technique in different situations. This is different from teaching students to see patterns in processes and to understand the concept of generalization, which is difficult for those with ABI to do.
6. Help students gain skills to function independently.
7. Reflect ultimate goals of moving students from specialized learning situations to more integrated, mainstream environments.

8. Incorporate or adapt familiar teaching styles; and
9. Attempt to include new approaches that benefit students with ABI in assignments for other students.

STRATEGY DEVELOPMENT

The overall goals of most education programs are to teach students to think and work independently. Students who achieve these goals usually are strategic thinkers who can reason and problem solve and can learn fairly automatically. However, students with ABI have significant difficulties in these areas.

Strategies help these students slow down, focus their attention on pertinent information, and plan what they should do. Strategies can structure the thinking process; and when they are printed forms which students can refer to, they become concrete guides which shape students' behaviors. They certainly further students' chances of performing independently.

For example, the form below (Figure 7.4) directs students to think about the process of doing a task. It highlights the task elements that students

FIGURE 7.4

Structured Thinking Form

Task _____

Time Constraints _____

Materials Needed:

_____ ☐
_____ ☐
_____ ☐
_____ ☐
_____ ☐
_____ ☐
_____ ☐

Steps Involved:

1. _____ ☐
2. _____ ☐
3. _____ ☐
4. _____ ☐
5. _____ ☐

Self-Evaluation

_____
_____
_____

should think about and provides an organized progression for task preparation. It also incorporates self-monitoring procedures, e.g., students check the boxes after completing the form to indicate that they have written correct information, and then they evaluate their overall performance. One should note the variety of skills that are required for this activity not the least of which are flexibility and sequencing.

The literature contains illustrations of strategies that help students clarify, organize, remember, and express information (Burns, Cook & Ylvisaker, 1988; Blosser & DePompei, 1989; Cohen, Joyce, Rhoades & Welks, 1985; Cohen, 1991; Haarbauer-Krupa, Henry, Szekeres, & Ylvisaker, 1985). Strategies also can assist students in developing other school-related behaviors, such as taking turns in a group, proceeding through a lunch line, reading a schedule, going to the correct location for a lesson, organizing written work, or recording and completing assignments. Frequently, the above "expected" school behaviors are troublesome for students with ABI, and the tasks have to be analyzed and taught step-by-step.

When students are armed with effective strategies, their stress levels decrease and their motivation to participate in school activities increases. Studies have shown that even preprimary and primary children benefit from strategy use (Burns, 1991); they may not understand why strategies are helpful, but they can learn to use concrete guidelines or habituate behavior patterns that lead to improved performance. Students whose functional abilities are around the ten-year level, however, are cognitively mature enough to use metacognition (Feuerstein, 1980) and think about the thinking process. They can understand the cognitive requirements of tasks and appreciate the value of using strategies to compensate for weak or lost skills. Once they are taught to use strategies independently, they assume some problem-solving responsibilities in relation to their own performance and begin to consider how W–H strategy components relate to specific situations, a job which was handled previously by their teachers: they think about WHO is involved, WHAT has to be done, WHERE they are to perform, WHEN performance is expected, HOW it should be carried out, and WHY certain behaviors are necessary.

Strategies can be taught in different ways. In addition to following the general teaching techniques and suggestions for lesson plan development already suggested, strategy training should involve: (a) talking with students about the purpose of particular strategies and about how strategies will assist students in carrying out various tasks; (b) soliciting students' commitment to learning and using specific strategies; (c) focusing on the content and the process or format of a strategy; (d) establishing students' self-monitoring skills so they can evaluate and/or adjust either their performance or the strategy formats (see Developing Executive Functions); and (e) teaching students and families to apply strategies to functional activities outside of school.

When staff develop single strategies that can be used in more than one situation, students have an opportunity to learn a procedure well and to begin to implement it more automatically. Too many procedures can confuse and overload students and cause them to be uncertain as to when to use what format. In this regard, the author of this chapter attempts to indicate how the W-H strategy can be used pervasively and effectively by students and staff.

Teachers often are uncertain about when to introduce strategies to students with ABI. This teaching technique should be used whenever students have difficulty functioning. Instead of stressing students by waiting to see if they will perform better over time, teachers should encourage them to participate in successful learning experiences that incorporate strategic assistance. Depending on students' capabilities, teachers may choose to fade certain teaching and learning supports. But they should heed this caveat: strategies may need to be reinstated to accommodate students' characteristic inconsistencies and new procedures may be needed to keep pace with the unpredictable advances or regressions in students' performance levels.

Instructional Interventions: Program Goals

The following material briefly outlines specific teaching interventions as they relate to educational goals of students with ABI. Many techniques can be used successfully for different purposes. The type of interventions promote active learning experiences that structure and enhance students' thinking; but, again, the specific teaching activities are meant to be only suggestions that will prompt educators to create their own approaches.

DEVELOPING ATTENTION/CONCENTRATION

In a sense, teachers are always working on attention! Attending skills need to expand as processing requirements of tasks become more complex.

1. Teaching must relate attending to the stages of information-processing (Bos & Vaughn, 1988) highlighting information and skills that are needed at each stage.
2. Educators should relate teaching attending to aspects of the input, elaboration, output, and motivation components of the cognitive map described by Feuerstein (1980).
3. Highlighting can involve methods such as: (a) telling students what to attend to ("Think about the *WHO*... or the *WHERE*... "); (b) providing written cues (stars, arrows, color signals) or gestures that

alert students to attend to material; or (c) furnishing strategy cards that direct students to: "Find the directions" . . . "Follow the numbers down the page" . . . "Keep working". . . . These procedures may need to be used frequently during a task and for long periods of time.

4. Different tasks will teach students to focus, divide, shift, and sustain attention. For instance, editing and tracking tasks can train students to focus attention on specific content, and computer and word-processing tasks also can train students to divide, shift and sustain attention. When students attend poorly, teachers must assess the type(s) of attention that activities require.

5. The quality of attention (or distractibility) influences whether students can learn in groups or whether they need to be taught individually. It impacts on students' abilities to stay on-task and on-topic, to follow directions and to complete assignments.

6. When building attending skills, staff should give students tasks that they know how to complete and gradually expand students' on-task behavior.

7. Students who do not attend well may be overloaded by the length or complexity of tasks. Teachers should assess whether attending improves when tasks are shortened or when material is made more understandable, i.e., think about the relationship of attention, comprehension, organization and memory.

8. Attending skills impact on the rate of processing, on students' abilities to pick up cues from the environment and on their development of self-awareness.

9. Reinforcement schedules can build attending skills.

10. Attention can be negatively affected by stress and fatigue.

11. Medication can restrict or improve attending behavior.

QUESTIONING vs. TELLING STUDENTS WHAT TO DO

Questioning encourages students to think independently; telling students what to do often solicits a more passive response in which students assume a dependent role.

1. Different kinds of questions require students to have different thinking skills: (a) *Open-ended questions* require students to remember and retrieve information and to be able to formulate a response. Examples: "Where did the dog go?" . . . "What happened on the playground?" . . . "What did we talk about yesterday?" (b) *Multiple choice questions* provide the response content and require individuals to recognize the correct information—retrieval and expressive language skills are not necessary. Examples: "Did the dog go to the kitchen or the

bedroom?"..."Did you play a game or ride on the swings?"..."Did we discuss the election procedures or the candidates?" (c) *Yes/no questions* require memory skills but no expressive organization skills. Examples: "Did the dog go to the bedroom?"..."Did you have a sandwich for lunch?..."

2. Questions can stimulate students to think about any topic and to use cognitive/processing skills and focus on: main ideas, details, sequencing, strategy use, cause-effect, feelings, memory, or problem-solving.

3. Questions can stimulate students:

   (a) to begin to work: "What are you supposed to do?"..."What should you do first?"..."Where do you find out what to do?"... "Should you _____ or _____?"

   (b) to respond: "Where do you write the answer?"..."How will you do this?"..."How can you make that into a sentence?"..."Where can you find the answer?"

   (c) to stay on-task: "What do you do now/next?"..."Where is #2?"... "Look at the page. Are you finished?"

   (d) to use a strategy: "What could help you do this?"..."Did you use your strategy?"..."What is the first step in your strategy?"..."Which strategy should you use?"

4. Students with ABI may become stressed and overloaded when questioned. Since it is more difficult for an individual to answer a question than to complete a sentence, teachers may have to move from questioning to statement-completion tasks to find out what students know. Examples: "the dog went to the _____"..."During recess you played _____"... The democratic candidate was _____" (see Training Memory and Retrieval).

FOCUSING ON COMPREHENSION AND LANGUAGE SKILLS

Usually individuals' comprehension levels are judged by how they express themselves orally, in writing, or through movement or gestures. Students with ABI may demonstrate poor comprehension due to impaired thinking skills. But they also may understand material and have knowledge to use and yet be unable to indicate this due to problems with initiation or to poor oral, fine-motor, or gross-motor skills. Therefore, teachers must probe to find out what students know.

1. When students do not respond or when expressive responses are incorrect, teachers should assess their receptive knowledge (what they know but may have difficulty expressing). Techniques: (a) give students response choices and have them point to or mark the correct

printed information or repeat the correct oral information; (b) present parts of a printed or picture story out of sequence and have students sequence the parts correctly; and (c) tell students who have poor initiation skills when and how to perform (orally, in writing, through gesture or movement).

2. Poor answers may be due to impaired expressive organization skills (see: Teaching Organization).

3. Teachers may have to build language/comprehension using the Language Experience Approach (Bos & Vaughn, 1988; Smith, 1991): providing content and situations that will develop specific concepts.

4. Games and recreational activities are motivation vehicles for reinforcing concepts that are associated with the game content (counting; using prepositions, e.g., "on," "over," "under"; connecting feelings with written or pictured counterparts).

5. Teachers must relate comprehension and language capabilities to attending, memory, organization and overload elements.

TEACHING ORGANIZATION

(Of Thoughts, of Tasks, of Expression)

Organization skills are factors which are basic to good performance. Teachers must think about the three areas of organization when planning instructional tasks.

1. Strategy forms, charts or exercises can be used to develop each area of organization.

2. The W–H strategy helps students organize information in different ways (Cohen et al., 1985; Cohen, 1991; DePompei & Blosser, 1991). Examples: (a) Used as a Sun Diagram (topic in the center, concepts placed as rays around the circle), it targets and organizes aspects of topics to think about, talk about or write about. (b) It helps students internalize the diagram and recall the image to assist them when needed. (c) Used as an outline for written expression, the concepts are listed individually in blocked off areas providing cues about content students should write in each block as they progress down the page. (d) The strategy cues can help students do other things such as find solutions to problems (WHO? ... WHAT? ... WHY? ...) or organize assignments (WHO for? ... WHEN due? ...).

3. Thought organization is central to understanding temporal sequences, e.g., time-telling, seasonal concepts, schedule plans (relating: activities to time of day/days of week; associating clothing and weather

with seasons; connection materials used in classes with schedule notations).

4. When the information in #3 is depicted and used on a clock, calendar or schedule form, it may become a task organization activity. Teaching must emphasize spatial organization, identify the steps of the tasks and, of course, relate the information to functional procedures.

5. Games and recreational activities are motivating vehicles for task organization (gathering materials; learning steps in the game; taking turns; finding the beginning, end and other important locations on the game board).

6. Expressive organization tasks can include: (a) sequencing words into sentences and sentences into stories (part-whole relationships); (b) learning formats that include specific "scripts" to begin and end conversations; (c) following guidelines to elaborate conversations (see #2); (d) taking time to plan what to say vs. rambling on in a confusing manner; (e) discerning messages relayed non-verbally; (f) understanding and using tone of voice appropriately; and (g) counteracting memory or retrieval problems by using approaches described in the next section.

TRAINING MEMORY AND RETRIEVAL

Memory skills are enhanced when teachers present material that is meaningful to students, use a multisensory approach to learning, and manipulate information in various activities in order to strengthen concepts. Strategies can help students attend, clarify, and organize information for long-term storage. However, if memory is severely impaired, storage will not occur, and this makes it difficult for students to build and maintain knowledge day-to-day.

1. If students cannot retain information, teachers should "put their memory out in front of them," i.e., give them concrete material to refer to (recognition vs. retrieval). This provides language and ideas that they can use to demonstrate other thinking capabilities. Techniques: (a) Give students a bank of words to use to fill in the blanks or create sentences; (b) provide sentences or pictures as assists in developing oral or written ideas; (c) provide detailed study guides; (d) have students use information they have procured through note-taking or tape-recording content.

2. Teaching tasks may vary in effectiveness depending on the kinds of memory they require (visual, auditory, semantic, personal, episodic, and motor).

3. Techniques to strengthen information are: role play, pantomime, and tasks which include motor performance and "getting the feel for" ideas or procedures; discussions; repeating or rehearsing content; establishing conceptual or personal associations; stimulating images that code information; categorizing material; and monitoring students' overload limits (see Developing Executive Functions).

4. Techniques to enhance retrieval of information are: (a) teaching students to "take thinking time" and search for information (make associations, categorize . . .); (b) using strategies such as the W–H format in which the components stimulate recall of the *topic;* (c) teaching students to identify and use sources of information (log books, schedules, assignment sheets, alphabet boards, texts . . .); (d) providing visual or auditory cues (related pictures, phonemes or phrases and acronyms or mnemonic assists); (e) correlating the amount of content with students' overload limits; and (f) probing memory content through sentence completion or multiple choice formats vs. asking open-ended questions.

CONTROLLING IMPULSIVITY/BUILDING SELF-CONTROL

Teachers must help students who behave impulsively to: slow down, change some of their automatic and inappropriate performance patterns, avoid getting into unsafe situations, and ultimately benefit from learning and socialization experiences.

1. Students may need exaggerated cues to break behavior patterns. Techniques: Raise a STOP sign or use an open-handed "stop" signal at significant moments. These can shift to more subtle cues delivered by "firm" or casual glances, finger raising, physical cues (touching the student), or having students listen for specific information (their names) before responding.

2. Teachers may need to assess and build competencies in any of the skill areas discussed here in order to change students' behaviors.

3. Teaching must focus on highlighting what students should think about and do and provide practice activities in which teachers and students: model correct and incorrect behaviors, role play, use prepared scripts that improve interactions, and evaluate and give feedback on performance.

4. A meaningful reinforcement program is essential to establish behavior change.

5. The goal for students is self-control, not necessarily giving accurate

responses to curriculum content; though the latter often accompanies the former.

6. Denial prevents students from recognizing their problems and modifying or changing their behaviors. Denial can result from poor thought organization skills and/or impaired comprehension. Not understanding cause-effect, for instance, influences responses requiring judgement and the ability to understand consequences. Techniques used in role play and videotaping performance with and without strategy use can help students (and families) recognize the value of working on behavior change.

7. Developing structured, organized procedures and rules and routines, and prompting students frequently to use them can produce changes in behavior.

8. Teachers need to help students with ABI control emotional lability or exaggerated emotional responses that result from their injuries. Techniques: (a) Stimulate students' awareness of controlling their emotional responses (mood swings that interfere with school performance; excessive laughter; feeling sad and crying); (b) pair supportive understanding with instruction connecting emotions and emotional control to specific situations; (c) encourage students to look for and follow behavioral cues that their peers demonstrate.

SHAPING FLEXIBILITY AND PROBLEM SOLVING SKILLS

Students with ABI are comfortable with consistency and uncomfortable when changes are required in behavior or thought processes. Their weak thought organization skills prevent them from determining alternative ways of thinking through situations. Teaching strategies can direct students to become more flexible.

1. Teaching can have students: (a) attend to change (note different activities on work sheets or different steps in routines); (b) prepare for different activities (put work in folders; take out different material); (c) respond to change signals (buzzers, schedules, clocks); (d) shift content topics (have transition discussions about new topics); or (e) make decisions based on several options.

2. Teaching techniques to develop flexible thinking and problem solving skills are: (a) provide a problem solving strategy that delineates and organizes the procedural steps for students (identify the problem, discuss and list relevant details; brainstorm about possible solutions and evaluate their effectiveness; select the best solution and carry out the plan; evaluate the outcome); (b) use material that includes and

trains students to use alternative ways of thinking about a subject; (c) ask students to think about "one more way" of doing something or to "tell something else about" an object or event (make lists to refer to); (d) teach cause-effect in relation to specific occurrences; (e) have students determine what is involved in assuming different roles in the classroom (line leader, discussion leader, schedule keeper) and provide behavior strategies and scripts as needed; and (f) use infringement of rules as a basis for problem solving (What went wrong? . . . How can you fix it? . . .)

DEVELOPING EXECUTIVE FUNCTIONS

Self-Monitoring; Taking Responsibility; Moving Toward Independent Work

Students with ABI often are dependent and unsure of what they can do and do not assume responsibility for their behavior. As they learn to monitor their performance, they develop awareness of: what they are presently able to do, when they can work independently, when they need help, what kinds of assists will be beneficial for them, and where they are making progress as they recover from their injuries.

1. Training students to ask for help when they "shut down" or "get stuck" involves building awareness of their abilities and limitations. Training techniques may focus on learning in imitation or from a model or moving from direct teacher instruction to the use of strategy cards with specific scripts ("I need help.") or with direct cues ("Ask for help.")

2. Teachers can develop self-monitoring skills for students of all ages. Young children can learn to check performance against directions given and to think about *how* to do something and about the appropriateness of responses. Selective monitoring focuses the attention of older students on the purpose of tasks and on the quality of their performance. Techniques: (a) develop charts, tally systems, etc. (with student cooperation, if possible) that produce concrete evidence of their performance; (b) have students predict performance goals and compare them to behaviors demonstrated; (c) provide supportive discussion, feedback, and direction to students.

3. Develop self-regulatory skills by having students: (a) use Cognitive Behavior Modification and self-talk procedures (Meichenbaum, 1977); (b) repeat teachers' instructions for self-direction; (c) problem solve

by assuming the role of a self-coach (Haarbauer-Krupa, Henry, Szekeres & Ylvisaker, 1985); and (d) use metacognitive approaches to learning.

4. Teach students to use input-control, alerting others: when the pace of conversation is too rapid or long; when content is confusing or needs to be repeated; or when others should give students thinking time in order to process information.

5. Build independent skills in stages along a continuum: (a) provide one-to-one instruction to teach the information and skills; (b) supply direct teacher cues (through questioning, pointing to particular content to focus students' attention, telling students what to do next); (c) move to cues on strategy sheets (that begin to make students responsible for their own behavior), e.g., written directions for each step, arrows to cue students to move from item to item, examples of response formats); and (d) teach students gradually to assume responsibilities independently with or without assistive materials.

MODEL METHODS

Using Curricula To Teach Cognitive/Processing Skills

The teaching approaches set forth in this chapter can be integrated into existing classroom programs. As a matter of fact, teachers can use an individual task to train several skills that students with ABI need to learn. For example, (a) in any group lesson, students can work on such things as: thought or expressive organization, impulse control, or shifting attention; and (b) math problem solving can be turned into a reading lesson or a situation in which to implement a strategy.

Reciprocal Teaching techniques described by Palinscar and Brown (1988) and Palinscar and Klenk (1992), the cognitive strategy instruction principles detailed by Harris and Pressley (1991), and Feuerstein's Instrumental Enrichment Program (1980) present teaching approaches that encourage students to: interact with peers and teachers; participate in cooperative problem solving; focus attention on specific topics; develop critical thinking skills; risk asking questions and presenting their own thoughts to clarify information; use strategies to improve performance; and apply curriculum content and strategies to functional life experiences. These approaches also build effective skills for teachers, such as: modeling, questioning students to encourage independent thinking; using task analysis; encouraging role play situations as well as predicting and self-monitoring; and applying thinking abilities and aspects of content to everyday situations.

Professionals have to work hard to figure out how to make information make sense to students with brain injuries. These students have forced us to investigate the thinking process more closely. As a result, we can deliver better educational programs for all students. It is encouraging to see that cognitive approaches to thinking and learning are taking hold in educational circles and that corresponding materials are being developed to aid educators. In this spirit, this author has attempted to provide practical teaching guidelines that will make sense to educators and that can be used with relative ease in school settings.

REFERENCES

Adams, L., Carl, C.A., Covino, M.E., Filbin, J., et al., (1991). Concept paper: Traumatic brain injuries. *Colorado Department of Education,* Denver.

Arffa, S., Fitzhugh-Bell, K., and Black, F.W. (1989). Neuropsychological profiles of children with learning disabilities and children with documented brain damage. *Journal of Learning Disabilities, 22,* 635–640.

Barth, J.T., Gideon, D.A., Sciara, A.D., Hulsey, J.D., and Anchor, K.N. (1986). Forensic aspects of mild head injury. *Journal of Head Trauma Rehabilitation, 1,* 63–70.

Baumeister, M., and Morris, R.K. (1992). Rural delivery model for vocational education. *Teaching Exceptional Children, 24,* 40–43.

Baxter, R., Cohen, S.B., and Ylvisaker, M. (1985). Comprehensive cognitive assessment. In Ylvisaker, M. (Ed.), *Head injury rehabilitation: Children and adolescents.* San Diego: College Hill Press.

Begali, V. (1987). *Head injury in children and adolescents: A resource and review for school and allied professionals.* Brandon, VT: Clinical Psychology Publishing.

Blosser, J.L. and DePompei, R. (1989). The head-injured student returns to school: Recognizing and treating deficits. *Topical Language Disorders, 9,* 67–77.

Blosser, J.L. and DePompei, R. (1991). Preparing education professionals for meeting the needs of students with traumatic brain injury. *Journal of Head Trauma Rehabilitation, 6,* 73–82.

Boll, T.J. (1983). Minor head injury in children. Out of sight but not out of mind. *Journal of Clinical Child Psychology, 12,* 74–80.

Bos, C.S. and Vaughn, S. (1988). *Strategies for teaching students with learning and behavior problems.* Boston: Allyn and Bacon.

Burns, P.G., Cook, J. and Ylvisaker, M. (1988). Cognitive assessment and intervention. In Savage, R.C. and Wolcott (Eds.), *An educator's manual: What educators need to know about students with traumatic brain injury.* Southborough: National Head Injury Foundation, Special Education Task Force.

Burns, M.S. (1991). Comparison of two types of Dynamic Assessment and static assessment with young children. *International Journal of Dynamic Assessment and Instruction.*

Chadsey-Rusch, J., Rusch, F.R. and O'Reilly, M.F. (1991). Transition from school to integrated communities. *Remedial and Special Education, 12,* 23–33.

Cohen, S.B. (1986). Educational reintegration and programming for children with head injuries. *Journal of Head Trauma Rehabilitation, 1,* 22–29.

Cohen, S.B. (1991). Adapting educational programs for students with head injuries. *Journal of Head Trauma Rehabilitation, 6,* 56–63.

Cohen, S.B., Joyce, C.M., Rhoades, K.W. and Welks, D.M. (1985). Educational programming for head injured students. In Ylvisaker, M. (Ed.), *Head injury rehabilitation: Children and adolescents.* San Diego: College Hill Press.

Congressional Record, *Education for All Handicapped Children Act, Vol. 121.*

Cook, J. (1991). Higher education: An attainable goal for students who have sustained head injuries. *Journal of Head Trauma Rehabilitation, 6,* 64–72.

Deaton, A.V. (1987). Behavioral change strategies for children and adolescents with severe brain injury. *Journal of Head Trauma Rehabilitation, 20,* 581–589.

DePompei, R. and Blosser, J. (1987). Strategies for helping head-injured children successfully return to school. *American Speech-Language-Hearing Association, 18,* 292–300.

Feuerstein, R. (1980). *Instrumental enrichment: An intervention program for cognitive modifiability.* Baltimore: University Park Press.

Fuld, P.A. and Fisher, P. (1977). Recovery of intellectual ability after closed head injury. *Developmental Medicine and Child Neurology,* 495–502.

Haarbauer-Krupa, J., Henry, K., Szekeres, S.F. and Ylvisaker, M. (1985). Cognitive rehabilitation therapy: Late stages of recovery. In Ylvisaker, M. (Ed.) *Head injury rehabilitation: Children and adolescents.* San Diego: College Hill Press.

Hall, D.E. and DePompei, R. (1986). Implications for the head injured reentering higher education. *Cognitive Rehabilitation, 3,* 6–8.

Harris, K.R. and Pressley, M. (1991). The nature of cognitive strategy instruction: Interactive strategy construction. *Exceptional Children, 57,* 392–404.

Lehr, E., Lantz, J.A., and Doranzo, J.F. (1990). *Psychological management of traumatic brain injuries in children and adolescents.* Rockville, MD: Aspen Publishers.

Lidz, C. (1991). *Practitioner's guide to dynamic assessment.* New York: Guildford Press.

McClelland, R.J. (1988). Psychosocial sequelae of head injury—Anatomy of a relationship. *British Journal of Psychiatry, 153,* 141–146.

McDonnell, A., McDonnell, J., Hardman, M., and McCune, G. (1991). Educating students with severe disabilities in their neighborhood school: The Utah elementary integration model. *Remedial and Special Education, 12,* 34–45.

Meichenbaum, D. (1977). *Cognitive-behavior modification: An integrative approach.* New York: Plenum.

Mercer, C.D. and Mercer, A.R. (1989). *Teaching students with learning problems.* Columbus: Merrill.

National Association of State Directors of Special Education, Inc. (1991). *Individuals with Disabilities Education Act: 20 U.S.C. Chapter 33.* Potomac: EDLAW, Inc.

National Joint Committee on Learning Disabilities (1992). School reform: Opportunities for excellence and equity for individuals with learning disabilities. *Journal of Learning Disabilities, 25,* 276–280.

Osborne, A.G., Jr. (1992). Legal standards for an appropriate education in the post-Rowley era. *Exceptional Children, 58,* 488–494.

Palinscar, A.S. and Brown, A.L. (1988). Teaching and practicing thinking skills to promote comprehension in the context of group problem solving. *Remedial and Special Education, 9,* 53–59.

Palinscar, A.S. and Klenk, L. (1992). Fostering literacy learning in supportive contexts. *Journal of Learning Disabilities, 25,* 211–225.

Rispens, J., van Yperen, T.A., and van Duijn, G.A. (1991). The irrelevance of IQ to the definition of learning disabilities: Some empirical evidence. *Journal of Learning Disabilities, 24,* 434–438.

Rosen, C.D. and Gerring, J.P. (1986). *Head trauma: Educational reintegration.* Boston: College-Hill Press.

Rosenthal, M., Griffith, E.R., Bond, M.R., and Miller, J.D. (1990). *Rehabilitation of the Adult and Child with Traumatic brain injury,* (2nd Ed.). Philadelphia: F.A. Davis.

Rothman, R. and Viadero, D. (1991, October 9). Thinking about thinking: An education week special report. *Education Week.*

Sailor, W. (1991). Special education in the restructured school. *Remedial and Special Education, 12,* 8–22.

Savage, R.C. (1991). Pediatric brain injury and public law 94–142. *NeuroDevelopments: Newsletter of the Pediatric Brain Injury Resource Center, 1,* 3, 10.

Savage, R.C. and Carter, R. (1984). Re-entry: The head injured student returns to school. *Cognitive Rehabilitation, 2,* 28–33.

Savage, R.C. and Wolcott, G.F. (Eds.). (1988). Eds: *An educator's manual: What educators need to know about students with traumatic brain injury.* Southborough: National Head Injury Foundation, Special Education Task Force.

Segalowitz, S.J. and Brown, D. (1991). Mild head injury as a source of developmental disabilities. *Journal of Learning Disabilities, 24,* 551–558.

Semmel, M.I., Abernathy, T.V., Butera, G., and Lesar, S. (1991). Teacher perceptions of the regular education initiative. *Exceptional Children, 58,* 9–24.

Silver, L.B. (1991). The regular education initiative: A déja vu remembered with sadness and concern. *Journal of Learning Disabilities, 24,* 551–558.

Smith, C.R. (1991). *Learning disabilities: The interaction of learner, task, and setting* (2nd Ed.). Boston: Allyn and Bacon.

Telzrow, C.F. (1987). Management of academic and educational problems in head injury. *Journal of Learning Disabilities, 20,* 536–545.

Vogel, M.J. (1991, September 25). Learning happens when it matters. *Education Week.*

Waaland, P.K. and Kreutzer, J.S. (1988). Family response to childhood traumatic brain injury. *Journal of Head Trauma Rehabilitation, 3,* 51–63.

Whinnery, K.W. and Fuchs, L.S. (1992). Implementing effective teaching strategies with learning disabled students through curriculum-based measurement. *Learning Disabilities Research and Practice, 7,* 25–30.

White, S. and Bond, M.R. (1992). Transition services in large school districts: Practical solutions to complex problems. *Teaching Exceptional Children, 24,* 44–47.

Williams, D.L., Gridley, B.F., and Fitzhugh-Bell, K. (1992). Cluster analysis of children and adolescents with brain damage and learning disabilities using neuropsychological, psychoeducational, and sociobehavioral variables. *Journal of Learning Disabilities, 25,* 290–299.

Ylvisaker, M. (1985). Ed.: *Head injury rehabilitation: Children and adolescents.* San Diego: College Hill Press.

Ylvisaker, M. (1991). Traumatic brain injury in children: New Disability Category. *The Clinical Connection, 5,* 1–5.

Ylvisaker, M., Chorazy, A.J.L., Cohen, S.B., et. al., (1990). Rehabilitative assessment following head injury in children. In: Rosenthal, M., Griffith, E.R., Bond, M.R. and Miller, J.D. (Eds.) *Rehabilitation of the Adult and Child with Traumatic Brain Injury,* (2nd Ed.), Philadelphia: F.A. Davis.

Zigmond, N. and Baker, J. (1990). Mainstream experiences for learning disabled students (project meld): Preliminary report. *Exceptional Children, 57,* 176–185.

Chapter 8

TRANSITION FROM SCHOOL TO ADULT LIFE: KEY TO THE FUTURE

Martha M. Bergland

INTRODUCTION

Acquired Brain Injury (ABI), or Traumatic Brain Injury (TBI), in the medical/psychological literature, is relatively new terminology to education, but of increasing relevance to educators in terms of meeting student needs and the mandates of recent transition legislation. As the prevalence and incidence of ABI among young children and adolescents has increased, so has the demand for educational intervention and transition services. Students with ABI anticipating transition from secondary education to an adult status are increasing in numbers (Begali, 1987; Cook, 1991; Rosen and Gerring, 1986; Savage, 1991).

Despite a growing knowledge related to the difficulties inherent in the education of students with ABI (Holmes, 1989; Lehr and Savage, 1990; Savage, 1987, 1991; Wehman, 1992; Ylvisaker, 1985), there are few existing studies specific to ABI and transition from school to adult life (Bergland and Thomas, 1991; Filley, Cranberg, Alexander and Hart, 1987; Kriel, Krach, Bergland and Panser, 1988; McCabe and Green, 1987).

However, recent disability-related legislation has recognized and provided for comprehensive transition services and designated ABI/TBI as a specific category of disability eligible for special education services. With these changes, special educators or TBI specialists will increasingly provide and exchange information with colleagues, generate instructional services and activities, and work cooperatively with related service providing agencies, programs, parents, and students to meet transition planning needs.

The purpose of this chapter is to address the transition legislation and issues encountered in making the progression from high school to adult status as successful as possible. It is not intended as a *cookbook,* since such an approach would be contrary to individualized education and the nuances of ABI. Specifically, ABI/TBI will be presented in the context of transition legislation and the necessary coordination between special educators, families, vocational rehabilitation, postsecondary personnel, and other interagency services for students with disabilities.

According to estimates, a traumatic brain injury occurs every 16 seconds nationwide and two-thirds of those injured are between fifteen and twenty-five years old (Kalsbeek, McLaurin and Harris et al., 1980; Rosen and Gerring, 1986). Injuries can result in mild, moderate, or severe impairment and often present a complex interplay of physical psychological, and social impairments. Deficits in cognition, behavior, communication, and consequent psychosocial functioning contribute most to difficulties and can continue in varying degrees after physical recovery (Eiben, Anderson, Lockman, Matthews, Dryja, Martin, Burrill, Gottesman, O'Brian and Witte, 1984). Educational progress and status are frequently altered with former *"normally"* achieving students being placed in special education settings and those with prior disabilities sustaining further setbacks.

Cognition or information processing deficits, particularly short-term memory losses, impair the ability to learn new information and, consequently, tend to compromise academic performance. Similarly, changes in behavior and higher level *executive* functions can affect performance, esteem, and social relationships. Self-mediation and abuse or overuse of alcohol or drugs constitute additional problems for some students.

Ozer (1988) has identified the most common physical and mental sequelae which interfere with learning ability, psychosocial functioning, and transition. These include:

1. Physical, motor, and sensory deficits.
2. Decreased memory and learning of new information.
3. Impaired attention and concentration, distractibility.
4. Altered visual, spatial and/or auditory processing; inability to transfer skills.
5. Slower cognitive functioning and communication.
6. Difficulty with organization, planning, prioritizing, and judgment.
7. Difficulty with concept formation, abstraction, generalization, problem solving.
8. Impaired self-control and/or social judgement.
9. Fatigue; lack of strength and endurance.
10. Need for structure/supervision.
11. Problems with depression, intolerance, impulsivity and inflexibility; hyperactivity euphony.
12. Problems with goal setting and planning.

It is important to differentiate between subsets of students with ABI, those injured during childhood and those injured in adolescence, entering the transition phase. Although physical/cognitive impairments may be similar, important developmental and psychosocial differences exist. Time favors the younger student in terms of adjustment and compensation, whereas the adolescent incurs losses during a critical developmental and life transition phase. Consequently, the older student may have limited access to educational interventions directed toward learning and preparation for adulthood with a disabling condition.

According to Savage (1991), problems in accurate identification, classification, and appropriate placement of students with TBI are key issues which interfere with meeting student needs. While students with ABI have physical or cognitive limitations which often overlap those of other disabling conditions, some characteristics are unique to ABI. For example, while a learning disability may be a consequence of ABI, the sudden onset of disability, academic, social, and personal losses and, sometimes, the extreme nature of cognitive impairments, differ. Changes from previous levels of functioning, including alterations in style and rate of learning, self-image, and social status have suddenly and often dramatically changed in a less than positive direction. Students tend to maintain their preinjury identity and the older student, in particular, may not fully recognize or appreciate the need for changes in academic placement, social behavior, or participation in special education. These are sensitive and pressing issues for the adolescent moving toward autonomy and adulthood; disability-related stresses, particularly cognitive impairments, further impede the process for the student with ABI.

TRANSITION LEGISLATION

The impetus for transition planning evolved from a growing awareness of the failure of many young people with disabilities to assume a satisfactory role in adult life after completion of high school. Problems noted were a high unemployment rate, psychosocial difficulties, social isolation, and a general failure of students to become integrated participating members in the fabric of their community (Wehman, 1992). The need for transition and a model was first outlined in the 1980s at the federal level by Will (1984), with transition legislation following.

The then-effective Education for all Handicapped Children (Act-P.L. 94-142) required an IEP and also mandated the provisions for transition planning. However, the legislation lacked specificity as to the definition and nature of services constituting *transition planning;* hence, numerous and varying models evolved across states. Students with ABI and learning needs or other needs could become eligible for services under the category of learning disability, physical and other health impaired, or developmental disability (first chapter, Savage, 1991). Unfortunately, these categorical designations do not address many of the specific needs of students with ABI and resulting transition plans are often insufficient in scope and detail. Due in large part to the efforts of parents, consumers, rehabilitation professionals, and educators, a growing recognition of both the number of students with ABI in the education system and a budding awareness of the unique needs of students with ABI emerged (Bergland, 1988; Cohen, 1991; Savage, 1987, 1991).

The Individuals with Disabilities Education Act, P.L. 101-476 (IDEA), an amended and revised version of P.L. 94-142, has designated TBI as a specific category under the definition of disabilities and clarified the nature and services related to transition. According to the federal definition,

> Traumatic head injury is an insult to the brain, not of a degenerative or congenital nature, but caused by an external physical force that may produce a diminished or altered state of consciousness, which results in impairment of cognitive abilities or physical functioning. It can also result in the disturbance of behavioral or emotional functioning. These impairments may be either temporary or permanent and cause partial or total functional disability or psychosocial maladjustment.

As in the earlier 94-142 legislation, students with disabilities, identified as needing services, are required to have an individualized Education Plan (IEP). Transition services, to be included in the Individualized Education Plan (IEP) no later than age sixteen or age fourteen, in appropriate instances, were mandated for all students with disabilities, including those with TBI or ABI. IDEA defines transition as

> A coordinated set of activities for a student, designed within an outcome-oriented process, which promotes movement from school to post-school activities, including post-secondary education, vocational training, integrated employment (including supported employment), continuing and adult education, adult services, independent living, or community participation. The coordinated set of activities shall be based upon the individual student's needs, taking into account the student's preferences and interests, and shall include instruction community experiences, the development of employment and other post-school adult living objectives, and, when appropriate, acquisition of daily living skills and functional vocational evaluation (20 U.S.C. 1401 (a)(19).

Several concepts and components of transition services are pivotal in achieving adult outcomes appropriate to the student with ABI. Services, programs, or instruction presumes a long-range planning process and, as such, must be started early enough in the secondary years to effect a desired adult outcome. This is a critical issue for students sustaining injury during the junior or senior year. Activities are to be coordinated by a suitable designee, usually a teacher or special educator. Services and interventions necessary for a smooth transition between school and adult life are to be assured through coordination and planning with appropriate interagency providers. Given the complexity of injury and improvement and the varied professionals and support staff involved, it is necessary that all involved team members and linkage providers are knowledgeable of ABI.

Coordination implies teamwork and cooperation at the local district, and state levels. Home teams usually consist of the student, parent, special educator, and teacher. Generally, committees or teams, comprised of members from all possible facets of transition are organized at the state and local levels. Such groups typically provide for the overall education, coordination, and guidance of transition programming. Linkages with community and facility service providers, who typically work with students after high school, must be established during the secondary planning phase. Postschool activities include, but are not limited to, postsecondary education, vocational training, integrated and supported employment, adult services, independent living, and community participation. Such linkages are necessary, but not always available for students with ABI. Ideally, linkages include those with vocational rehabilitation counselors, rehabilitation centers staff, job training and partnership act representatives, human services or social services caseworkers, students with disabilities specialists in postsecondary settings, independent living centers or specialists in postsecondary settings, independent living centers or specialists, community vocational service representatives, and residential facility staff.

Determination of the activities or services needed to achieve outcomes presumes a relevant assessment of both student and environmental factors. Areas of consideration include instruction, community experiences, employment development, adult living, daily living, and functional vocational evaluation. Based on assessment of needs, transition or readiness skills are to be developed in the areas of academic, vocational, community living, and reactional functioning. For students with ABI, assessment for transition purposes may require more frequent evaluation than mandated due to continuing recovery, learning problems inherent in ABI, and generalization of learning across situations. Of potential importance for some students are technological devices and services.

TRANSITION MODELS AND LINKAGES ACROSS STATES

Although no comprehensive nationwide studies document the extent and nature of transition services and models specific to ABI, some state transition plans and services specific to ABI/TBI are available for discussion (Wright and King, 1991). State transition programs generic to all disability populations and designed to comply with state or federal (IDEA) legislation are typical. The development of statewide comprehensive programs to meet the transition needs of students with ABI are still in the beginning stages. Where available, services for ABI/TBI are developed through grants or other funds by organizations such as education systems, human service agencies, Independent Living Centers, and state Head Injury Association chapters. The recent legislation and the award of statewide systems change grants to eleven states, may produce state programs with components specifically addressing ABI needs. Several states have initiated programs for TBI and have positions for specialists, trained in brain injury, at various agencies. These are worthy of mention, although in somewhat abbreviated form.

In Minnesota, the state passed watershed legislation in 1987 to address the transition needs of all students with disabilities as they are completing the secondary education experience and moving toward adult life. Individuals with ABI, as well as all other students with disabilities, are eligible to receive services if they meet the eligibility criteria for special education and have an IEP. These generic transition services, consistent with IDEA mandates, are well organized at both state and local levels.

The state transition program consists of a coordinating board, through the state Special Education Department, Unique Learners Section. The State Transition Interagency Committee provides training and direction to a statewide system of Community Transition Interagency Committees at the district level. The state committee develops compliance programs and establishes statewide transition committees to create materials which will assist school districts in the development of transition committees, teams, and interagency linkage systems within each school district (Corbey, 1992).

The Division of Rehabilitation Services (DRS) is a primary state linkage and maintains a cooperative agreement with the public education system to facilitate transition. The staff consists of specialists in transition and in TBI/ABI. A Rehabilitation Services Administration demonstration grant provided training related to rehabilitation for persons with severe TBI. Following training, a TBI specialist is available in each of the state regional offices. A DRS representative serves as a member of state and local committees and assists in planning and service delivery for students with ABI.

In addition, other specialized services are administered through related agencies such as Department of Human Services and the state Head Injury association. The Minnesota Head Injury Foundation has and continues to play a pivotal advocacy role in increasing awareness of ABI needs, promoting the development of legislation related to ABI, and coordinating the various service components in the state. Independent Living Centers have recently been granted funding (1992) to provide specialized independent living training to students in transition and frequently provide skills training to students with ABI. An advantage of the ILC service is the option to return for further skill development at any time in the future since the centers were developed to meet long term ongoing disability needs. In instances of differences of agreement in IEP or ITP plans, Minnesota provides for a conciliation conference, mediation services, and a due process or administrative hearing to reconcile differences between family and educators.

Some states, such as Massachusetts, have programs for young adults with severe disabilities who have graduated from special education or who are twenty-two and ineligible for services. The local school systems refer students to the appropriate human service or disability-related service or to the state Bureau of Transitional Planning if the student has unusual or multiple disabilities. The state designates a "transitional lead agency" or coordinator which assembles a team including all involved agencies, parents, etc., and develops an ITP.

Transition planning services in Kansas are provided to students with severe disabilities at age sixteen or those preparing to leave school within two years. The Department of Social and Rehabilitation Services is the entry point for students transitioning to adult life, with the Kansas Rehabilitation Services, a division of the department, designated as lead agency. A State Transition Committee with representative agencies, educators, and consumers, guides program development statewide. The committee provides assistance to a local transition council in implementing transition planning and coordination of services. Local agencies make referrals to appropriate transition counselors at the state level. The transition plan developed by parents, the student, teachers, and local community staff is part of the student IEP. No statewide ABI transition programs are available, however. The Head Injury Foundation of Kansas works as an advocacy organization for parents and individuals with ABI and some local community colleges provide entry services specific to ABI/TBI.

Transition in rural areas presents a special challenge to team members. Existing models designed for metropolitan or urban settings are often ill-suited to widely dispersed geographic populations. The transition planning components in Colorado have a six-year federal grant to replicate Colorado's Transition Model statewide in a manner consistent with specific community and student needs. Local interagency transition teams and governing boards plan with concerned parties and incorporate Transition into the Special Education Planning process. The plans for Parent/Family Education and the Empowerment component of the program are particularly advantageous to students and parents with ABI. As a partnership plan, both families and educators consider factors necessary to transition, such as interagency purposes and functioning, necessary planning and documentation, and steps needed for future service provision and maintenance of ongoing services when students and families are no longer in the education system.

Guidelines for promoting understanding of ABI and effectively meeting the needs of students are available through the Colorado Department of Education, Special Education Services Unit (Adams, Carl, Covino, Filbin, Knapp, Rich, Warfield, Yenowine, 1991).

Meeting Transition Needs

Specific and Practical Approaches

Adequate transition planning for students with ABI presumes an involved team composed of student, parent, special educators, teachers, other professionals, such as psychologists and neuropsychologists, and, when appropriate, available local linkage systems. Needs to be addressed in the IEP for the purposes of developing an ITP and determined through assessment and planning with local linkage systems must take into consideration the student's physical, cognitive, and preferential needs.

As stressed by Stowisckek and Kelso (1989), student assessment is inadequately used as a means of guiding the decision making process, instruction and intervention. At present, there is no consensus regarding an assessment protocol and few instruments for data gathering specific to ABI/TBI within the educational setting (Telzrow, 1991). Several authors (Milton, Scaglione, Flanagan, Cox and Rudnick, 1991; Telzrow, 1991) have noted both the limitations of available traditional methods and the desirable characteristics of a comprehensive TBI/ABI assessment. Traditional, standardized approaches, such as neuropsychological, speech pathology, and psychoeducational assessments by qualified outside consultants and school psychologists are important and, usually, necessary data sources. Unfortunately, these results may be unavailable or insufficient for adequate IEP and ITP planning. The data, in part, may reflect "old learning" (e.g., WAIS–R results), be specific to the test situation, fail to identify the nuances of current performance, or lack the predictive value to develop prescriptive interventions or goal setting needed for transition. Although similarities in impairment are reported at a global level across students with ABI, specific deficits and patterns of functioning are idiosyncratic. For these and related reasons, a comprehensive, multimethod, dynamic assessment is necessary.

Data reflecting pre and postinjury physical, cognitive, psychosocial and academic functioning, including medical information (sequelae of injury, time since injury, recovery of impaired function, and medications or restrictions) are necessary areas to be addressed in a comprehensive assessment. Cognitive processing, communication skills, psychosocial skills, psychomotor abilities (Cook, Berrol, Harrington, Kanter, Knight, Miller and Silverman, 1987), as well as the academic, vocational, community/independent living and recreational abilities mandated in the federal regulations are important areas of evaluation. Excellent coverage of a comprehensive cognitive assessment is presented by Baxter, Cohen, and Ylvisaker (1985).

Utilizing a multimethod approach incorporating standardized and norm-based instruments as well as a functional approach (required by IDEA), and obtaining information from as many sources as possible has the advantage of identifying abilities and deficits under a range of conditions and rendering information useable for prescriptive or planning purposes. Possible strategies include:

Multimethod Data Gathering Approaches
Standardized Norm-Based Tests
  1. Neuropsychological
  2. Cognitive—Language
  3. Psychoeducational
Functional/Ecological Assessment (Any Area of Functioning)
  1. Observation and Rating Scales
  2. In Situ or Simulated

Since performance may vary due to disability or situational variables, obtaining information in classroom, non-classroom settings, and naturalistic environments, such as the home or vocational setting, is a further benefit of using several methods of assessment in planning for transition. Teacher provide valuable information on current functional, academic, and psychosocial performance through observation and evaluation of classroom behavior and learning style.

Broad areas of assessment and methods, specific to ABI/TBI, as initially reported by Ozer (1988) and later expanded (Bergland, 1991; Bergland and Hoffbauer, 1992) are summarized below.

By necessity, assessment will be an ongoing process, particularly for the older student, in order to reconcile plans to continued improvements and life circumstances. Reassessment every six months, instead of the one year mandatory requirement, may better meet individual student needs.

TRANSITION ACTIVITIES AND LINKAGES

Identifying and developing a system of services, instruction, and programs consistent with student abilities, needs, and preferences and adaptable to student changes is a major transition task. Linkages may be established at any point in time during the transition planning phase (age 16 or 14, if appropriate), depending on individual student needs. The timing and selection of transition activities (instruction, services, programs) will depend, in part, on the nature and severity of physical and cognitive needs and require, to some extent, an estimate from community ABI specialists as to the hypothesized level of future functioning. The suitability of a specific linkage or future settings may be, at best, imprecise and require greater flexibility or activity than many providers can readily accommodate.

The transition specialist or special education teacher designated to assure that objectives are completed or reevaluated on an "as needed" basis plays a primary role in educating team members about ABI, appropriate resources, and coordinating the services of various involved community interagency services. In states with generic transition services, such as Minnesota and Kansas, interagency representatives participate in local planning meetings to assist in explaining the service and initiating the desired service or program in which the student will be participating. Parents are encouraged, and mandated by IDEA, to become active participants in IEP and ITP planning. Parents can also obtain needed information regarding proposed activities, agency programs, and documents needed for service later on in the transition process.

Linkages are particularly crucial in the phase prior to leaving the secondary environment. Interagency collaboration through committees or cooperatives are available to planning committees for this purpose. Interagency linkages and agreements, detailed by Wehman (1992), are necessary to ensure the setting of appropriate post high school goals, arrange for appropriate accommodations, and provide for follow through to the completion of stated goals. Coordination of educational systems and the various linkages is essential to assure continuity of service and to minimize overlap; these function most effectively when organized at the state and local levels (Wehman, 1992).

In general, it is desirable to evaluate the appropriateness of the potential service or setting, including:

1. staff experience with and knowledge of the ABI, especially cognitive and behavioral correlates since these often are mistaken for willful misbehavior.
2. programmatic appropriateness for student needs
3. supervision as needed
4. advocacy
5. interconnections with other appropriate services/providers and commitment to establishing contacts with other agencies once the individual leaves this program.

Weighing the relative value of selecting instruction or training from an interagency organization is warranted. For example, independent living skills training is provided through high school courses in many states. While this may be adequate for some students with ABI, others may need or desire further training and contact with peers. Participation in community support groups, such as those provided at ILC's can provide the advantages of a consumer perspective and a self-advocacy focus; peer counselors, often individuals with ABI, function as trainers. Furthermore, students may experience a sense of security in a less threatening environment and feel at liberty to discuss important issues of sexuality and intimacy.

It is important for transition specialists and community providers to be familiar with other disability-related legislation for consideration in transition planning as follows:

1. IDEA–P.L. 101-476, Parts B, C, D, E
2. Rehabilitation Act of 1973: Section 504
3. Higher Education Act-1992
4. ADA
5. Carl Perkins Applied Technology Act 1990
6. Technology Related Assistance for Individuals with Disabilities Act 1990 (P.L. 100-407).

For example, the recently enacted Higher Education Act restricts loan eligibility to full time students. This may constitute a significant barrier to higher functioning students with ABI, who need loan assistance to complete a postsecondary program.

A desirable characteristic of transition programming for students with ABI is assessment and instruction over time to account for variabilities in performance, awareness of performance, feedback on tasks, and evaluation in a situational or environmental context. Flexible, step-by-step planning throughout the transition process is preferable, since this allows for adaptation and revision. A recent publication profiling successful High School transition programs (Gaylord, 1991) included an exemplary program in the St. Paul, Minnesota public school system which includes components suitable to some students with ABI. Project Explore is a curriculum-based, transition assessment process developed for use at community, vocational, independent living, and recreational training sites. During the process, work-related behavior, specific work skills and functional academic skills are assessed twice a semester over a six-month period. Adequate performance and improvement areas are then identified and the process altered accordingly. Upon completion of the process, students are provided with a personal transition file and action plan for use after high school.

It is particularly important to ensure that a case manager, whether vocational counselor, social worker/case worker, or parent, is designated to monitor overall service delivery after the student with ABI has exited the secondary education system. Transition linkages in three areas, postsecondary education, vocational rehabilitation, and social case work services are of critical importance and will be discussed further.

TRANSITION AND POSTSECONDARY EDUCATION LINKAGES

Selecting a post high school education option is difficult. Although improvement can continue, many of the cognitive skills necessary for success remain impaired by injury with consequent difficulties in performance and coping in an academic setting (Holmes, 1988; Ozer, 1988). Furthermore, academic and social behavioral expectations are generally higher than those required of secondary level. Bergland (1991) cited the following factors as important to the success of students with ABI at the postsecondary level:

(a) Verbal/Language Abilities
(b) Memory
(c) Learning Rate and Style
(d) Self-Regulation and Management: Initiation, Maintenance, and Action

(Executive Functions) Planning, Judgement and Problem-solving

Behavioral and Emotional Control

(a) Stress Identification and Management
(b) Risk/Vulnerability Management
(c) Fatigue/Energy Recognition and Management
(d) Interdependence: Structure and Supervision
(e) Social Interaction and Integration
(f) Adaptive Leisure and Recreational

Resources and Skills

(a) Environmental Awareness and Responsiveness

Despite questions regarding the appropriateness of higher education (Hall & DePompei, 1986), studies continue to document successful postsecondary educational experiences for individual students with mild, moderate, and severe ABI (Cook, 1991; DePompei, 1987). Having made the decision, linkages with postsecondary institutions are crucial to avoid unnecessary delay and failure. Where possible, connections should be established with the Office of Students with Disabilities or similar services available at public institutions nationally to facilitate an exchange of information and transition planning. The specialist can act as a conduit of information for the high school transition specialist, student, family and related team members regarding both physical and program accessibility and support for the student on campus (Bergland and Hoffbauer, 1992). Specifically, the following information would be useful in transition:

(a) physical accessibility of the campus, including dormitories and classrooms
(b) academic supports, including program flexibility and faculty/staff awareness
(c) support for social integration and personal counseling
(d) support for career counseling, placement, and similar specialized services

Layout and accessibility of buildings and classrooms obtained through maps can assist in determining physical access, distance, and possible fatigue factors relative to student needs. Similarly, transportation arrangements and access to health services need to be considered. Dormitory versus other living arrangements needs to be evaluated in terms of the student's independent living skills, need for physical assistance, and degree of self-control and advocacy in view of the relatively unstructured campus social environment. The Office of Students with Disabilities at the University of Minnesota, Minneapolis, tailors services to these and learning needs of students with ABI through connections with secondary transition specialists and through assistance with course work and faculty student interactions.

A particularly useful exchange of information between the transition specialist, team, and campus specialist will specify the student's current learning style, successful compensation strategies, and rate of learning as well as areas in which behavior might be misunderstood or problematic. The need for note takers, tape recordings, and/or other cognitive strategies can be established in advance of actual course work. Important questions include determination of: (1) the extent to which the student can understand and express learning or other accommodation needs to the instructor; (2) general awareness of ABI/TBI among staff and faculty; (3) the availability of syllabi and texts or course materials prior to instruction; and (4) general faculty flexibility in altering tests and the format of assignments. Of particular significance is the determination of student self-advocacy and capacity for interdependence. In many instances, teamwork and problem solving by student, faculty and campus specialist or other professionals will be necessary in reaching transition goals. This may constitute a challenge to students unfamiliar with service or support systems. Linkage representatives can further assist in apprising the team of social supports available on campus, since social integration or reintegration is often difficult for students with ABI (Holmes, 1988).

The potential for campus support available for career planning and placement following graduation can be determined through postsecondary linkages. Important questions to be answered include the availability of career planning services, the determination of special career services for students with disabilities, and experiential or internship opportunities while enrolled in the program. Any proposed training or career choice will necessitate consideration of the impact of wage earning on the students future medical and other benefits. Where available, services which smooth the transition from postsecondary settings to work for students with disabilities, such as the program at Bakersville College in California (Wall and Culhane, 1991), are an added benefit to students with ABI.

Establishing suitability gradually, by taking an introductory class while still in the secondary setting or starting with one or two classes, are options which will be required for some students to ensure flexibility and possible transition plan changes. It is desirable to identify and ascertain the availability of other linkages and options in the event that a particular postsecondary program does not prove feasible.

Many institutions are not prepared to accommodate unique student needs despite the increasing number of students with ABI attending postsecondary education (Begali, 1987; Cook, 1991; Rosen and Gerring, 1986; Savage, 1991). Fortunately, some programs specific to ABI at the vocational, two, and four year postsecondary levels have already been established. For example, the *ABI Handbook* provides extensive program standards for students with ABI on over ninety-nine campuses in California (Cook, Berrol, Harrington et al., 1987) DePompei, (1987 and Ozer (1988) suggest further specific strategies to promote success at the postsecondary level.

The Lakewood Community College in Lee's Summit, Missouri is one example of a program tailored to the needs of students with ABI (Jenison, 1992). Project Able is a structured curriculum for students with Head Injury and Learning Disabilities designed to enable independent learners. Students take a required sequence of personal development, orientation, study skills, and career planning courses. Credits may be applied toward an Associate in Arts degree. Classes are limited to twelve students and support sessions and study sessions are required. A support group for parents and significant others is available. Students are usually referred through linkages with Vocational Rehabilitation or other appropriate agencies.

Unfortunately, specialized programs and adequate supports are not available to meet unique student needs in all geographic locations. Future students with ABI may expect a wider range of supports since the inclusion of TBI in IDEA will stimulate further development of services at institutions not formerly prepared to address their needs.

Transition and Employment

Making the transition to adult status, specifically to direct employment and training settings, is problematic for many students with disabilities, but particularly so for students with ABI/TBI (Bergland, 1988; Kriel et al., 1988; Wehman, 1992). Transition planning directed toward vocational objectives should be specified and initiated early in the transition process to adequately establish postinjury vocational needs and development. To improve transition outcomes, coordination with community vocational resources is essential. Linkages in this area can include those between the transition team/student and:

1. Vocational Rehabilitation Agencies
2. Job Training Partnership Act (JTPA) and Private Industry Councils
3. Private Sector (employers in particular)
4. Workshop or Related Rehabilitation Facilities
5. Families and other Advocates
6. State and County Social Work Providers

Students injured late in the secondary program, as well as individuals with severe limitations, may benefit from extended vocational or academic programming and postpone graduation until the mandatory age of twenty-two. Vocational evaluation, required by IDEA, can be achieved through interest and aptitude tests, work samples, functional and simulated or real work activities. Experiential or "hands-on" approaches, such as student work study or Jobs and Training Partnership Act (JTPA) employment offer an addition benefit, in allowing observation and functional assessment of student work behavior and in providing a baseline for skill development and modification. In vocational and community skills development, independent living and daily living, a behavioral analysis, including a cognitive task analysis, is indicated to adequately address, remediate, or compensate for injury-related skill deficits or excesses (Calub, Burton, DeBoskey and Hooker, 1989). Consideration of various options as well as student abilities, feelings, and self-image must be explored in the transition process, since many students will be altering earlier vocational expectation and choices.

Empirical evidence documenting employment is scant for students with ABI in transition (Bergland and Thomas, 1991; Kriel et al., 1988; McCabe and Green, 1987). However, a common pattern with ABI is that many individuals who initially secure employment eventually experience difficulty maintaining job tenure due to cognitive, behavioral, and social skills problems (Wachter, Fawber and Scott, 1987; Wehman and Kreutzer, 1990).

One option, Supported Employment (SE), which was originally designed for populations with moderate to severe disabilities, provides the advantage of inclusive work in a natural setting with available support for skill development over time, if needed. A job coach may teach initial skills, determine job specific cognitive, technological, and social needs, and return for additional intervention if necessary. Team members and providers will need to consider the most appropriate SE option, individual job, enclave arrangements, mobile work crews, or bench work model in view of personal preference, abilities, TBI-related factors and program availability. Linkages are established with vocational rehabilitation or, in some instances, with the agency or facility providing supported employment. Recently, the appropriateness of SE for some persons with ABI/TBI has been supported by research. West, Kregel, and Wehman (1991) report a favorable outcome utilizing the individual placement model and conclude that SE can be an effective means of entrance into competitive settings for persons with moderate to severe BI. Although Supported Employment may be an appropriate choice for students with ABI with moderate to severe disabilities, there are several caveats as noted by the authors. In more severe injuries, a long-term commitment to SE may be anticipated by team members, since job termination and dropout are not unusual. In general, second placements were more successful than first time placements, demonstrating the need to plan for SE programming over time.

The workshop or work activity, often utilized to meet the vocational needs of persons with more severe ABI-related needs (McMordie, Barker and Paolo, 1990) is viewed as the least desirable option by many educators and rehabilitionists. Condelucci (1990), for example, stresses the impact of separation, isolation, and the negative dynamics that occur in workshop settings. The student with ABI may resist placement in workshop settings because they view the placement as evidence of "illness" or other negative disability stereotypes and frequently express anxiety and discomfort in this environment. However, many settings currently attempt to normalize work experiences and several offer programs specific to ABI as well.

Several states utilize JTPA services to provide employment experiences or work programs for students with disabilities while still in high school. These experiences are invaluable for students with ABI, since work skills and abilities may continue to change following injury. Work programs offer an opportunity to evaluate work skills and cognitive behavioral social functioning and can contribute to obtaining real work experience, skill attainment, and confidence. Job coaching and on the job training capabilities are additional advantages of many youth work programs.

A key linkage system for students making the transition to adult life is the federal state rehabilitation system, the Division of Rehabilitation Services, or Vocational Rehabilitation Services (VR) as it is called in some states. Rehabilitation counselors can provide counseling, case management, and funding for vocational evaluation, job placement, job skill training, job seeking skills, and other vocational activities. The counselor should be knowledgeable of ABI and is central in service coordination. As part of a state federal system, vocational rehabilitation requires "accountability" in that services provided are expected to lead to an improvement in vocational or employment status and they are frequently time limited. VR counselors may form "mini linkages" in purchasing and coordinating services, such as evaluation, training, or supported employment from other community programs or vendors.

Whether vocational options are initiated early or late in the transition process, it is important to ensure continuity of service. Case service managers or special educators should have access to all reports/documents generated regarding the individual's abilities and activities. Programmatic changes or student improvements or setbacks require flexibility in the transition plan and must be reported in a timely manner to provide for revisions or replanning. As well, linkages with transportation, housing, and financial assistance must be assured, since breakdowns in these areas can undermine the best vocational objectives and plans.

TRANSITION AND SOCIAL WORK/RESIDENTIAL

The social worker or case manager assumes a primary role in assuring that financial and medical needs are established and maintained for the duration of service needs. As such, the case specialist may become involved at any point following injury and is a critical component of the transition team and eventual linkages with residential, workshop, supported employment, competitive employment, and postsecondary training or education. Securing and maintaining funding through local or county sources and assisting with federal disability and income programs (e.g., RDSI, SSI, Medicare) and state medical services are imperative to facilitative transition process. In some states, such as Minnesota, TBI Case Resource Specialists are available on a statewide basis through the Human Services Department (Minnesota Department of Human Services, 1992). The specialists provide assistance to local counties in facilitating assessment of health care and human service needs, assuring the development of an adequate individualized plan, and providing the necessary assistance to facilitate community placement for the individual. Specialists can also assess and coordinate state Medical Assistance in areas such as home care, use of funds, quality of service, and ensure that services are cost effective and accessible.

Adequate case management and coordination in postsecondary education training settings can prevent the loss of financial aid packages or benefits. It is equally important in the maintenance of necessary medical, income, or housing supports when the student assumes a paid employment position. The manager can assist in the determination of special "work incentive programs, such as PASS, that allow for continuation of benefits while employed.

LONG-TERM NEEDS AND ISSUES

Many of the unresolved issues for students with ABI overlap and parallel those identified for adults with ABI in rehabilitation. Menz and Thomas (1990) identify education, advocacy, funding, and needed systemic change as ongoing issues. In the context of transition, duplication or noncoordination of services and inadequate training and long-term funding are major policy issues in need of resolution. Of equal importance, is inclusion of family and significant others in the planning process and outcome.

Professionals, parents, and consumers have demonstrated the need for systems and policy changes directed toward education, programming and funding required to adequately address ABI/TBI needs (Savage, 1991; Manier, 1991). Supported employment, for example, is a major need for students with moderate to severe limitations; however, funding is frequently time-limited. As a consequence, the service option may be eliminated altogether, staff trained in ABI may be lost and the new contractee or vendor may lack expertise in ABI. Likewise, the timing of needs and availability of services are often incompatible. Students needing attention to cognitive, socialization, or loss-related issues, may find interventions lacking at the needed time; situations frequently resulting in additional frustration, setbacks, and misplacement for the student. Service availability is often lacking at the local level and students are placed on a wait list or referred out of their community and separated from their primary support group; again, a significant barrier for students with ABI, since important social and cognitive gains or opportunities may be lost.

It is generally recognized that community programs and the necessary community living supports are not funded on a consistent or long-term basis. Not only is ABI underfunded or poorly addressed in the above areas, but providing services to adolescents with chronic illness or disability receives lowest priority in service provision according to a recent national survey (Jorissen, 1992).

Limited expertise or a lack of specific training in ABI/TBI among school psychologists, educators, support staff, and vendors or community support programs involved in transition has been well documented (Manier, 1991: Savage and Carter, 1984). Interpreting or misattributing typical sequelae or consequences of brain injury to willful behavior or noncompliance is commonly reported (Savage, 1987). Research and education regarding ABI and other related factors, such as ethnicity, minority, and young women's needs are nearly nonexistent.

Although statistics are not available for students with ABI in transition, it is well documented that most individuals with ABI reside with the family. Families, as primary care givers, are significantly stressed by injury-related demands and a lack of adequate services (Brown and McCormick, 1988). Family involvement can add significantly to the success of transition efforts. However, the stresses, in terms of financial, social, emotional, and energy demands are not always well understood or appreciated by nonfamily members. Strategies to assist families with respite care, intervention, and planning for transition is needed on a national level. Planning efforts stressing partnerships in planning and creative problem solving lessen the effect of additional strain and stress on family energy and resources often required by transition activities. In addition, care should be taken not to invalidate or misinterpret family concerns about the student's future placement; these are concerns common to any family dealing with a member with unique needs in an environment short on available services and information. Continuing strategies directed at providing an educational interchange between families and transition team members, with families providing education about student needs and educators providing information and coordination of services and options are needed.

Despite the challenges associated with transition to a meaningful lifestyle for students with ABI, changes and improvements are occurring at the state and local levels. A move toward reconciling some of the above limitations and providing comprehensive systems training for TBI/ABI is currently under way at the federal level through proposed legislation, The Traumatic Brain Act of 1992 (S.3002) and TBI Act of 1992 (S.2949). The concerted efforts of all involved in transition planning will continue to play a primary role in empowering students with ABI to assume their rightful position as valued citizens in our society.

ABI/TBI ASSESSMENT FOR IEP & ITP PLANNING

(Bergland, 1991; Bergland and Hoffbauer, 1992)

Medical

1. Physical, motor and sensory abilities, medications and physical limitations, including fatigue, strength and endurance.

Academic/Information Processing/Communication

1. Neuropsychological Assessment: Areas and degree of impairment in information processing and cognitive functioning (i.e., remote and recent memory, current learning style, ability to focus in and sustain attention as well as shift attention, etc.).
2. Psychoeducational Assessment: General intellectual ability, mathematics, writing, and reaching achievement levels.
3. Communication: Specific areas of speech impairment (i.e., aphasia, dysarthria), language deficits (i.e., disorganization, inaccurate use and lack of inflection).
4. Functional/Classroom Assessment: Ability level in subjects taught, participation in discussion, initiation and maintenance of nondisruptive behaviors, and use of compensatory skills. Punctuality and task behavior as might be required in a vocational/educational setting. Ability level in library research, term or research papers and lab experiments in formats similar to those required in a postsecondary setting. Extent to which skills are acquired and integrated and identification of effective cognitive strategies/modalities.

Psychosocial Skills

1. Self-esteem, self-image, and awareness of disability and problem areas.
2. Self-management of disability, related stresses, concerns, and tasks.
3. Changes in social abilities and relationships (e.g., friends, family, teachers).
4. Social problems and strengths: Unacceptable behavior, rejection, and isolation. Potential or opportunities for social networking and positive social behavior. Social strengths such as humor, persistence, or participation.
5. Changes in academic and extracurricular activities.
6. Safety, vulnerability, sexuality, alcohol/other drug abuse.
7. Ability to self-monitor and self-regulate emotions and behavior.
8. Ability to be a self-advocate; exercise rights; express needs, preferences, and likes; know and use community resources.

Independent and Community Living Skills/Recreation

1. Assessment of self-care, home management, transportation recreation and finances.
2. Need for driving/safety evaluation.
3. Attendant care and/or supervision: Areas and degree of assistance needed.

4. Past and current recreational/leisure skills and adaptive skills.
5. Ability to initiate, organize and structure tasks.

Career and Vocational Planning

6. Vocational evaluation: Interest, ability, skill and aptitude areas. Speed and quality of performance. Consistency of positive work behavior.

Functional work evaluation: Job performance in a natural setting, over time. Task analysis inclusive of cognitive components.

1. Supported employment suitability.
2. Psychosocial functioning in the career/job setting.
3. Technology, modifications/adaptations to equipment and materials, compensatory strategies and aids needed in a vocational/career setting. Includes prosthetic memory and learning aids such as recording/signal devices, notebooks, coding systems, and computer/word processor.
4. Career exploration and experience: Opportunities for post-injury work experiences, job shadowing, job trials and volunteer activities.

Environmental Assessment

1. Site or linkage assessment: Staff knowledge of TBI/ABI in potential settings and linkages. Physical, programmatic, and attitudinal accessibility of settings. Time limits and documentation.

REFERENCES

Adams, L., Carl, C., Covino, M.E., Filbin, J., Knapp, J., Rich, J., Warfield, M.A., & Yenowine, W. (1991). *Guidelines paper: Traumatic brain injury.* Denver: Special Education Services Unit, Colorado, Department of Education.

Baxter, Cohen & Ylvisaker (1985). Comprehensive cognitive assessment. In M. Ylvisaker, (Ed.), *Head injury rehabilitation: children and adolescents* (pp. 247–274). San Diego: College-Hill Press.

Begali, V. (1987). *Head injury in children and adolescents: A resource and review for school and allied professionals.* Brandon, VT: Clinical Psychology Publishing.

Bergland, M.M. (1988). *Head injury in adolescence: Psychological functioning and transition to adult status.* Unpublished doctoral dissertation, University of Wisconsin, Madison.

Bergland, M.M. (1991). *Learning disabilities and head injuries: Similarities and differences.* Workshop, Higher Education consortium on Learning Disabilities-Spring Conference, Minneapolis, MN.

Bergland, M. & Hoffbauer, D. (1991). Students with TBI: Transition to postsecondary settings. *Teaching Exceptional Children,* (In Press).

Bergland, M. & Hoffbauer, D. (1992). *Knowledge and support: Understanding postsecondary students with Traumatic Brain Injury (TBI).* Unpublished manuscript.

Bergland, M.M. & Thomas, K.R. (1991). Psychosocial issues following severe head injury in adolescence: Individual and family perceptions. *Rehabilitation Counseling Bulletin, 35,* 5–22.

Brown, B., & McCormick, T. (1988). Family coping following traumatic head injury: An exploratory analysis with recommendations for treatment. *Family Relations, 37,* 12–16.

Calub, C., Burton, J., DeBoskey, D.S., and Hooker, C. (1989). *A cognitive rehabilitation system: Evaluation, treatment and generalization.* Tampa, FL: DeBoskey and Associates.

Cohen, S. (1991). Adapting educational programs for students with head injuries. *Journal of Head Trauma Rehabilitation, 6,* 56–63.

Condeluci, A. (1990). Community factors and successful work re-entry. In P. Wehman & J. Kreutzer (Eds.), *Vocational rehabilitation for persons with traumatic brain injury* (pp. 307–321). Rockville, MD: Aspen Publishers.

Cook, J. (1991). Higher education; An attainable goal for students who have sustained head injuries. *Journal of Head Trauma Rehabilitation, 6,* 64–72.

Cook, J., Berrol, S., Harrington, D., Kanter, M., Knight, N., Miller, C., & Silverman, L. (1987) *ABI handbook: Serving students with acquired brain injury in higher education.* California Community College Chancellor's Office, Disabled Students Programs and Services.

Corbey, S. (personal communication, 1992). Transition Specialist, Minnesota Interagency Office on Transition Services. St. Paul, Minnesota.

DePompei, R. (1987). *Attending college: An attainable goal?* Presented at National Head Injury Foundation, Ohio Association State Conference, Cambridge, Ohio.

Eiben, C.F., Anderson, T.P., Lockman, L., Matthews, D.J., Dryja, R., Martin, J., Burrill, C., Gottesman, N., O'Brian, P., and Witte, L. (1984). Functional outcome of closed head injury in children and young adults. *Archives of Physical Medicine and Rehabilitation, 65,* 168–171.

Filley, C.M., Cranberg, L.D., Alexander, M.P., and Hart, E.J. (1987). Neurobehavioral outcome after closed head injury in childhood and adolescence. *Archives of Neurology, 44* 194–198.

Gaylord, (1991). (Ed.) *Transition strategies that work.* St. Paul, MN. Minnesota Department of Education.

Hall, D.E., and DePompei, R. (1986). Implications for the head injured re-entering higher education. *Cognitive Rehabilitation, 4,* 6–8.

Holmes, C.B. (1988). *The head-injured college student.* Springfield: Charles C Thomas.

Holmes, C.B. (1989). Head-injured college students: Prevalence, reasons for college withdrawal, and suggestions from head-injury rehabilitation facilities. *Journal of Postsecondary Education and Disability, 7,* 72–77.

Jenison, M.E. (1992). Project able: Factsheet. Lee's Summit, MO. Longview Community College.

Jorissen, T.W. (1992). Adolescents not a priority. *Connections, 3,* 1–3.

Kalsbeek, W.D., McLaurin, R.L., Harris, B., et al. (1980). The national head and spinal cord survey: Major findings. *Journal of Neurosurgery, 53,* S19–S31.

Kriel, B., Brach, L., Bergland, M. and Panser, L. (1988). Severe adolescent head injury: Implications for transition into adult life. *Pediatric Neurology, 4,* 337–341.

Lehr, E., and Savage, R.C. (1990). Community and school integration from a developmental perspective. In J.S. Kreutzer and P. Wehman (Eds.), *Community integration following traumatic brain injury,* (pp. 301–310). Baltimore: Paul H. Brookes.

Manier, D.S. (1991). *Special educator's knowledge of traumatic brain injury.* Unpublished Research Paper, Menomonie, WI. University of Wisconsin-Stout.

McCabe, R.J.R., and Green, D. (1987). Rehabilitating severely head-injured adolescents: Three case reports. *Journal of Child Psychology, 28,* 111–126.

McMordie, W.R., Barker, S.L. and Paolo, T.M. (1990). The financial trauma of head injury. *Brain injury, 2,* 357–364.

Minnesota Department of Human Services. (1991). *Case management resources for survivors of traumatic brain injury.* St. Paul, MN: Department of Human Services.

Menz, F.E. and Thomas, D. (1990). Unresolved issues in the rehabilitation and community-based employment of persons with traumatic brain injury. In D. Corthell (Ed.), *Traumatic brain injury and vocational rehabilitation* (pp. 225–247). Menomonie, WI: University of Wisconsin-Stout Research and Training Center.

Milton, S., Scaglione, C., Flanagan, T., Cox, J., and Rudnick, F. (1991). Functional evaluation of adolescent students with traumatic brain injury. *Journal of Head Trauma Rehabilitation, 6,* 35–46.

Ozer, M. (1988). *The head injury survivor on campus: Issues and resources.* Washington, D.C.: Health Resource Center.

Rosen, C.D., and Gerring, J.P. (1986). *Head trauma: Educational reintegration.* San Diego: College-Hill Press.

Savage, R.C. (1991). Identification, classification, and placement for students with traumatic brain injuries. *Journal of Head Trauma Rehabilitation, 6,* 1–9.

Savage, R.C. (1987) Educational issues for the head-injured adolescent and young adult. *The Journal of Head Trauma Rehabilitation, 6,* 1–9.

Savage, R.C. and Carter (1984). Re-entry: The head injured student returns to school. *Cognitive Rehabilitation, 2,* 28–33.

Stowitschek, J.J. and Kelso, C.A. (1989). Are we in danger of making the same mistakes with ITP's as we made with IEP's? *Career Development for Exceptional Individuals, 12,* 139–152.

Telzrow, C.F. (1991). The school psychologist's perspective on testing students with traumatic brain injury. *Journal of Head Trauma Rehabilitation, 6,* 23–34.

Wachter, J., Fawber, H., and Scott, M. (1987). Treatment aspects of vocational evaluation and placement for traumatically brain injured individuals. In Ylvisaker, M. and Gobble, E. (Eds.). *Community re-entry for head-injured adults* (pp. 259–300). Boston: College-Hill Press.

Wall, C. and Culhane, H. (1991). Project employment: A model for change. *OSERS: New in Print, 4,* 17–21.

Wehman, P. and Kreutzer, J.S. (1990). *Vocational rehabilitation for persons with traumatic brain injury.* Rockville, MD: Aspen Publishers.

Wehman, P. (1992). *Life beyond the classroom: Transition strategies for young people with disabilities.* Baltimore: Paul H. Brookes.

West, M., Kregel, J., and Wehman, P. (1991). Assisting young adults with severe TBI to get and keep employment through a supported work approach. *OSERS: News in Print, 4,* 25–30.

Will, M.C. (1984). Let us pause and reflect—but not too long. *Exceptional Children, 51,* 11–16.

Wright, B. & King, M. (1991). *Americans with developmental disabilities: Policy directions for the states. Report of the Task Force on Development Disabilities.* National Conference of State Legislatures. Chicago, IL.

Ylvisaker, M. (Ed.) (1985). *Head injury: Children and adolescents.* San Diego, CA: College-Hill Press.

Chapter 9

EDUCATIONAL ISSUES IN PROVIDING APPROPRIATE SERVICES FOR THE STUDENT WITH ABI

PATRICIA L. JANUS

Educational systems face a multitude of issues in providing appropriate services for the student with acquired brain injury. While some states, such as Iowa, Maryland, New York, and Kansas have made notable strides in responding to the needs of students with ABI, the majority of states are at an early state of development in this area. This development is largely due to P.L. 101-476 (1990), the Individuals with Disabilities Education Act, which added traumatic brain injury to the list of disabilities which may qualify students for special education services.

School systems are discovering that while they may have myriad of resources, such as teacher, speech pathologists, psychologists, and occupational and physical therapists, few have developed adequate levels of expertise in ABI to meet student needs. In order to implement appropriate services for these students according to the mandates of special education law, educational professionals will require training and knowledge in the area of brain injury. Furthermore, as students with ABI often exhibit a changing profile of needs as they recover from injuries, school system administrators will need to promote a creative, flexible use of professional support and material resources. A substantial task in the best of circumstances, this becomes even more of a challenge during a time when school systems are confronted with serious fiscal constraints.

In two national surveys of state directors of special education, the need for staff training and information was identified as the primary issue to be addressed in providing services to students with ABI (Janus, Goldberg 1991, 1994). Specifically, state directors targeted the need for staff development and more information at all levels, including administrators. Topics for training included causes and prevention of ABI, teaching and behavioral interventions, short- and long-range implications of ABI, minor brain injury, and transition.

State and local education agencies are responding in varying degrees and ways to the challenge of educating staff in ABI. These include:

— Conducting conferences and workshops sponsored by state departments of education, sometimes co-sponsored with local rehabilitation hospitals and/or state chapters of the National Head Injury Foundation.
— Forming a state task force on ABI (generally, multi-agency).
— Distributing printed material to local education agencies.
— Funding local school system projects, some through state grants.
— Signing cooperative agreements with state chapters of the National Head Injury Foundation.
— Developing written guidelines on ABI.
— Providing technical assistance from state agencies.
— Developing training and prevention programs.

It is encouraging to note that in 1991, approximately 50 percent of the states had conducted conferences on brain injury, with an increase to 80 percent in 1994.

It is also interesting to note that while the 1994 survey indicates that the issues in providing services to students with ABI have basically remained the same as those reported in 1991, the growth in legislative and educational efforts at the state level since 1991 has been steadily improving. The federal definition of TBI was not widely recognized in 1991. However, between 1991 and the present, many states have developed or are in the process of developing guidelines for identification and program implementation. Progress is also noted by the number of states collecting statistics on TBI and using it as an educational disability on the IEP. In 1991, only seven state education agencies indicated that they collected statistics on TBI. By 1994, this number had risen to 37. Likewise, in 1991, only six states indicated that they were using TBI as an educational disability code, compared to 36 in 1994.

In addition to staff training, other issues noted by state education agencies in providing services to students challenged by acquired brain injuries include:

— The wide array of services, especially medical services needed by students.
— Medical vs. educationally-related support services.
— Dealing with a medical problem in an educational setting.
— Developing cooperative efforts with other agencies and organizations for smooth reentry to school.
— Need for coordination of services between agencies.
— Improving communication between medical and educational personnel.
— Funding.

- Appropriate, accurate identification; undiagnosed, misdiagnosed, unreported ABI.
- Conducting evaluations and accurately interpreting test results.
- Identifying/developing appropriate services and settings within the public school.
- Appropriate IEP development and need for frequent reviews and IEP modifications.
- Technology needs.
- Problems with differing eligibility criteria among programs and agencies.
- Getting services to students living in rural, remote areas.
- Improving collaboration with parents; providing support to families.
- Peer education.
- Increasing public awareness.
- Prevention.
- Increasing awareness of mild brain injury.
- Lack of professional pre-service training programs in brain injury at the university level.
- Transition; increasing appropriate community-based services and options.

A survey of special education directors from the school systems in Maryland (Janus, 1990) revealed similar concerns in providing services to students challenged by brain injuries. These included:

- Identification of students with ABI.
- Adequate staff for program modifications.
- Opportunity to plan with sending agency.
- Dealing with problematic behaviors.
- Inservice training.
- Differences between congenital and acquired brain injury.
- Initial testing and reevaluation.
- Coding for services.
- Transitioning from high school.
- Insufficient related services.
- Involving other agencies in sharing program responsibilities.
- Funding.
- Need for nurses.
- Liability.
- Physical care.
- Transportation.
- Accessibility and emergency exit plans.
- Lack of rehabilitation facilities in the local community.

— Unrealistic expectations.
— Family support services.

This variety of concerns can be grouped into the following major categories. Strategies are suggested that can be helpful in addressing these needs.

ISSUE: STAFF TRAINING

Most school systems have a lack of professionals who adequately understand the causes and consequences of ABI. With insufficient and/or inaccurate information providing appropriate services and support can be adversely affected. To meet this need, both general information on ABI and specific information on the student returning to school after a brain injury should be included in training.

Strategies

Attend and/or organize training conferences on ABI. Training should include information on mild brain injury and be shared with general educators as well as special education professionals.

Provide for the training of a multidisciplinary team in your school system that can assist in the reentry process and serve as a resource to others. At a minimum, this should consist of an administrator, teacher, psychologist, speech pathologist, occupational and physical therapist, nurse, and vocational or transition support teacher.

Obtain and distribute published information on various types of acquired brain injuries. Begin to develop a library of resources. There are a growing number of texts available. The National Head Injury Foundation publishes a guide for educational personnel called the *Educator's Manual* as well as a large number of other relevant publications, videos, and tapes. A complete listing can be obtained by contacting the National Head Injury Foundation and requesting their catalog of educational materials.

Arrange school assembly presentations by students with ABI and their family members.

Contact legislators and community leaders to support research and training efforts.

Advocate for preservice education on ABI at the university level.

Network with medical and rehabilitation professionals in your area. Invite them to inservice staff.

ISSUE: SCHOOL REENTRY

Returning to school and community life after a brain injury should be viewed as a process that begins on the day of admission to a rehabilitation facility. Reentry can only be successful when both the school and hospital dedicate sufficient resources to this process and communicate with one another. Understanding the similarities and differences between the hospital and school environments is critical to re-entry planning.

Strategies

Identify a contact person/case manager at the school and the hospital to exchange information on a regular basis.

If geographically feasible, school personnel should visit the rehabilitation facility prior to the student's discharge. Likewise, rehabilitation staff should visit the school setting. Videotapes are helpful when this isn't possible. As the student gets closer to discharge, it is helpful for the rehabilitation staff to simulate elements found in the school setting. This might involve using the student's textbooks from school, working in a small group, and decreasing the amount of 1:1 reinforcement to assess attention to tasks.

Use schedule modifications when necessary—half days, rest periods, and days that may be split between school and an outpatient setting. Consider the student's orientation difficulties related to changing classes. Use check-in points, charts, buddies, checklists, and assignment books.

Involve the hospital staff in planning the student's return to school. Make sure records and evaluations are current and complete to make educational decisions. Determine accessibility, transportation, and emergency exit plans for the student who is physically disabled as a result of injury.

Provide information to the hospital on special education programs and educationally vs. medically-related services. For a period of time, many students with ABI may require extra speech, occupational and physical therapy, and possibly counseling in addition to what the school system provides.

Provide and obtain a list of resource people and phone numbers.

ISSUE: IDENTIFICATION, EVALUATION, AND PLACEMENT

Because of the federal definition of TBI, identification of children with brain injury and data collection have steadily improved. The federal definition of TBI includes injury from external causes and is the definition most adopted by state education agencies. Of 37 states collecting statistics on students with TBI, 30 are using the federal definition while seven have included internal and external causes of brain injury in their state definition of TBI (Janus and Goldberg 1994). While this statistic is encouraging, it also points out the need for reexamination of the current definition of TBI. A uniform definition of TBI at the state level is critical if accurate statistics and research on effective intervention methods are to be collected. The collection of accurate statistics is also affected by the newness of the TBI classification as an educational disability. Before IDEA, students with TBI were being served in many school systems under another disability category. Some states have indicated confusion about whether they should go back and change the disability code to TBI.

Students with more severe injuries are known to the school due to the extended period of time they are absent. However, schools are not always notified of those students who experience milder injuries. Whatever the severity when identified, assessment and placement decisions must involve individuals with a knowledge of brain injury. Without appropriate expertise, assessment results and residual needs may be misinterpreted, exacerbating the issues faced by both student and staff. It is critical when making placement decisions that the student's attention span, distractibility, frustration tolerance, and need for structure be considered. These students will often benefit from a more restrictive setting, such as home instruction or a special class, upon their initial return to school with a gradual reintroduction to a less restrictive setting as they are able to tolerate more stimulation. Placement decisions must be individual and subject to change, based on the presenting needs of the student at the time.

Strategies

Provide information on mild brain injury to parents and professionals. If school personnel are notified of a mild injury, they should observe the child for any changes in his learning behaviors.

Use current information to make educational decisions. Don't repeat testing of information that is available, up to date, and appropriate from the hospital. Often, the hospital can complete a neuropsychological exam prior to the student's discharge. If additional testing is required and administered by school personnel, they need to be knowledgeable in ABI.

Once the student is placed, conduct regular reviews and make changes as indicated. Consider fatigue, length of day, amount of structure, and stimulation the student can accommodate.

Inservice staff and peers, as necessary. Use a team approach that integrates series and promotes joint ownership for the student's mastery of objective.

ISSUE: FUNDING

In some instances, providing services for the student with ABI may be very costly, especially when the student may require extensive therapy, help with daily living skills, and assistive technology. Funding may involve a variety of sources and a creative, cooperative approach among agencies.

Strategies

At reentry planning meetings, determine educationally relevant therapy needs. Remember that insurance companies may continue to be involved in securing devices and providing rehabilitation therapy.

Seek out civic organizations, government programs, and special interest groups that may provide funding.

Consider conducting or helping in a fund raising event.

Contact state agencies designated to support assistive technology.

Establish liaisons early with adult service agencies.

If a student's needs are in a state of change, do not be too hasty in securing an expensive device that the student may rapidly outgrow. Communication between rehabilitation agency and the school or workplace is essential on this issue when preparing for a student's return.

ISSUE: PARENT AND PEER SUPPORT

As students move through various levels of treatment and professionals along the way, parents remain the constant figures at their sides. At the time of reentry, they have usually gained a great deal of understanding of ABI and their child's needs. This information can be very helpful to the school. Peers, as well, need to be informed to understand changes in their classmate and assist in their reentry.

Strategies

Involve parents in educational planning and problem-solving. Where appropriate, be consistent with the use of strategies at home and in school.

Offer support and understanding by answering questions and providing written information on special education services and summaries of parent conferences.

Refer parents and siblings to support groups.

Educate peers about their classmate's brain injury and involve them in providing support and problem-solving.

ISSUE: PREVENTION

While the incidence of acquired brain injury cannot be totally eliminated, it can be greatly reduced with education and increase use of safety measures. The Janis and Goldberg survey (1994) revealed that 29 states were involved in some kind of prevention effort to decrease the incidence of ABI.

Strategies

Advocate for legal mandates and school system policies that require helmets for bicycle and motorcycle use and promote safety in sports and playground equipment.

— Promote use of seatbelts and carseats.
— Provide education on the effects of drug and alcohol.
— Conduct parent training courses.
— Support efforts to reduce child abuse resulting in brain injury.

It is encouraging to note the progress that has been made legally, medically, and educationally in responding to the unique needs of individuals with ABI. While much has been accomplished, much remains to be done. To progress further will entail cooperation across a variety of agencies and a willingness to share what is learned from both our successes and failures.

REFERENCES

Janus, P. and Goldberg, A. (1991). *Survey of state directors of special education on traumatic brain injury.* Unpublished manuscript.
Janus, P. and Goldberg, A. (1994). *Survey of state directors of special education on traumatic brain injury.* Unpublished manuscript.

Chapter 10

ADVOCACY AND THE PARENT—PROFESSIONAL PARTNERSHIP

PATRICIA L. JANUS

There is always more than one victim when a child experiences a brain injury. While the life of the child may be instantly changed, family members also experience an abrupt interruption in their normal routine and are thrust without warning into a world for which they are not prepared. While struggling with a variety of emotions, they must assimilate a new body of knowledge relative to medical condition, rehabilitative potential, school reintegration, and life planning for their child who may be permanently changed, physically, cognitively, and emotionally.

Family members play an important role in the child's treatment and education. Their attitudes, interactions, and skills in advocating can significantly influence the recovery process. Knowing how to advocate involves the family's ability to represent their child's needs and interests to people who are responsible for how programs are delivered. It is dependent on knowledge and the ability to establish a cooperative working partnership with the professionals involved in their child's treatment.

All individuals connected to the recovery process need to recognize the issues involved in fostering effective advocacy. This begins with understanding the variety of emotional responses to crises and the family's needs for support, information and involvement in treatment activities.

EMOTIONAL RESPONSES TO TRAUMATIC BRAIN INJURY

Recovery from a brain injury may require a long period of time and does not always result in a complete return to the child's preinjury status. During the recovery process, family members will progress through a variety of emotional reactions before they arrive at a realistic acceptance of postinjury needs and potential. The family's adjustment will be influenced by social, psychological, and financial resources, its adaptability, stability, prior vulnerability, perception of problem, and problem-solving capabilities (Slater, Rubenstein, 1987).

The reactions that family members experience in response to their child's injury are often similar to the reactions when a child is born with a disability. However, for those whose child is injured after birth, these reactions may actually be intensified as parents must grieve the loss of a child as they have known him/her for a number of years. Most often, reactions will include shock, anxiety, denial, anger, guilt, and sorrow.

While all of these reactions are normal, they will vary in the time they last for each individual. In addition, individual family members may actually have different reactions to the same situation. One may respond with grief, another with anger directed toward the cause of the injury, while another will exhibit a take charge attitude. It is also common for several emotional reactions to be experienced at the same time. Family members may find that communication with each other is hindered by anxiety about the future. Any preexisting family problems may be intensified as issues related to their child's recovery are encountered.

The first likely reaction at being notified of a severe injury is shock as family members convene at the hospital, not knowing whether their child will live or die. This may be followed by a period of relief and gratitude that the child has survived, then helplessness and anxiety. Other common reactions include numbness, denial, anger, guilt, and grief. Most individuals experience all of these emotions on their way to acceptance and understanding of the situation. Kubler-Ross (1969) found that denial, anger, despair, and depression are all part of the grieving process and necessary before acceptance is possible.

In the early stages of recovery, denial is a common response and a normal part of the adjustment process. While the child is in a coma, parents may hold on to the hope that he will wake up and be himself again. Mary Romano (1974) refers to this as the "Sleeping Beauty" myth. When residual effects are severe, parents may be unable to face the reality of the problems and deny their existence even when the symptoms appear obvious. Likewise, in mild injuries, parents may deny the existence of cognitive and emotional needs, as the child lacks physical symptoms. Blazyk (1983) reports the absence of observable physical handicaps results in much misunderstanding of problems by family members and the community. Because the child looks and sounds like himself prior to injury, it may be difficult for individuals to recognize residual nonphysical changes in behavior and even professionals who are uncomfortable with the child's condition. Even when individuals do attempt to help parents face the reality of the situation, they may find their attempts rejected.

Another common response is blaming others, such as the doctor, therapist, or teacher for problems the child is experiencing. A teenage friend was responsible for the alcohol, the doctor made an error, or the therapist didn't use the right techniques. Anger resulting from frustration may be turned against a professional person or even against the entire profession he/she represents. The anger may eventually be directed toward the injured child who is not progressing as the parent desires or toward a family member who is perceived as nonsupportive.

As parents realize the extent of what has occurred, they usually experience mourning or grief. This stage of mourning precedes acceptance of the situation. When residual effects are severe and lasting, parents grieve for those lost hopes and dreams they may have had for their child. Family members should recognize that emotional reactions such as denial and sorrow are a normal part of the adjustment process. However, where defenses remain strong, they may negatively impact the parent's ability to provide support for their child in a constructive way. In these instances, professional counseling should be sought.

Adapting to an acquired injury will frequently involve a change in roles for family members and an alteration in all their lifestyles. A traumatic brain injury disrupts a child's normal development toward independence. In fact, for adolescents, the injury may cause a regression to an earlier stage of dependency and immaturity, requiring parents to take on the role of primary caregiver again. The daily care that may be necessary for feeding, dressing, and personal hygiene can be exhausting and dramatically disrupt family functioning. Financial resources may be stressed and career plans or travel plans may be temporarily or permanently affected.

Each individual has his/her own way of coping with traumatic events. Some parents react by focusing on the medical and educational factors associated with the child's needs. Their time is consumed dealing with the daily requirements of care such as medications and supervising therapy exercises. Little time or energy is then left for their own or their child's emotional needs. When coping mechanisms differ significantly among family members, paired with the time consuming needs of the recovering individual, marital or familial stress may escalate and require professional intervention.

Because there may be many unanswered questions for an extended period of time, it is important that family members pay attention to their own physical needs, such as getting rest and eating regularly. Extended family members and close friends should be notified to provide emotional and physical support. They can assist in running errands, caring for siblings or pets, or preparing meals.

Many individuals find it helpful to keep a journal for personal and/or legal reasons. A journal can provide an emotional release as well as address the legal implications of the situation. Detailed information such as facts regarding the cause of the injury, names and accounts of witnesses, and professionals contacted may be needed at a later date. Journal entries should reflect when individuals are contacted, their position and affiliation, and a summary of the contact. Depending on the circumstances of the injury, it may be advisable to contact an attorney regarding issues such as liability and insurance coverage.

As parents work through the mourning process and gradually come to accept the implications of the child's injury, the need for defense mechanisms becomes less important. Some parents actually report positive effects on family functioning, even with the additional stress placed on the family by the injury. They indicate they are less likely to take one another for granted, are more respectful, and more available for support. The family may be more united and communication among family members may increase (Slater, Rubenstein 1987).

EMOTIONAL RESPONSES OF SIBLINGS

Siblings experience many of the same emotional responses as their parents. Like their parents, providing them with information regarding the injury will increase their ability to cope effectively with their sibling's condition and changes in the family's interactions. Parents need to spend some time, even if briefly, talking with their children on a regular basis and keeping their routine as normal as possible. If siblings are unable to visit, parents should encourage them to send messages via letters, cards, photos, or tapes. When they do visit, they should be prepared for what they will see, explaining in advance the medical equipment in use and condition of their sibling.

Siblings should be encouraged to talk about their feelings and ask questions. They may resent the attention and time that their brother or sister requires and the resulting disruption in their normal routine. Sibling support groups provide an excellent opportunity for other children in the family to obtain information and express their fears, concerns, and frustrations. If support groups aren't available, being able to talk to another child or teenager who has been in a similar situation is also helpful.

INFORMATION AND TRAINING

It is important to remember that not all parental reactions are emotionally based. Some are due to lack of information regarding the effects of brain injury and what the child can realistically be expected to accomplish. It is here that the parent will turn to professionals for help. The more knowledge parents possess at each stage of their child's recovery, the better they will be able to understand and advocate for their child's needs. Rogers and Kreutzer (1984) urge a proactive approach and conclude that providing information is important for preventing family crises. Family priorities include the need for a clear and kind explanation of the individual's condition and treatment, discussion of realistic expectations, and emotional support (Mauss-Clum, Ryan 1981).

In addition to physical needs, parents should be informed about possible long-term cognitive and behavioral needs. This is especially relevant in mild injuries, where physicians may primarily evaluate physical status alone, giving false sense of security that everything is back to normal once physical recovery is achieved.

During the course of treatment and education of their child, parents come into contact with a variety of professionals representing a multitude of disciplines. These can include medical personnel such as physicians and nurses; speech, occupational, and physical therapists in both rehabilitation and educational settings; and classroom teachers. Psychologists, psychiatrists, social workers, nutritionists, and school administrators may also be involved. Each transition, from preinjury status to acute care, from acute care to rehabilitation, from rehabilitation to school, from fifth grade to sixth, from school to adult life, brings new anxiety as additional people in different systems are encountered.

During the acute and early rehabilitation stages, the stress level of parents may be so high that they avoid or are unable to grasp the information being presented to them. Because parents may be overwhelmed initially, it is likely that information will have to repeated more than once. Professionals should be aware of this need for repetition and present the information directly and clearly. Professionals should also be available to answer questions and provide family members with written information to read. Frequently, families complain that the intensive support network disappears shortly after the acute stage of recovery, making them feel alone and helpless. Professionals need to help the patient and his family identify other avenues of support through all stages of recovery and reintegration into community life.

Some helpful strategies for parents to employ include tape recording information, taking notes for future reference, and requesting that a friend who is less emotional and more objective accompany them when information is being presented. Videotapes of treatment strategies are also helpful resources to parents and other professionals. Parents should be viewed as team members and taught to reinforce treatment goals at each stage of recovery.

PLANNING FOR SCHOOL RE-ENTRY

The return to school after an extended period of medical treatment may mark the beginning of another overwhelming and exhausting time for parents, especially if their child requires special education services not needed prior to injury. Having spent a number of weeks or months learning the language and procedures of rehabilitation, parents must now deal with another unfamiliar world with its own procedures, jargon, and more new people. Once again, they will need to acquire a body of knowledge that facilitates effective decision making and problem solving. This includes an understanding of federal law and state regulations regarding special education and local school system procedures and programs.

Upon a child's admission to a medical or rehabilitation facility, the school system should be immediately notified. Contact persons should be identified at each facility in order to establish a communication network. Parents should be aware that the school system needs this lead time if it is going to be prepared for their child upon the time of discharge, or a gap in service may result as educators scramble to construct an appropriate program without adequate information. Conducting the meetings and processing the paperwork for special education services, should the child require them, can often take months.

While students with severe injuries are generally known to the school system due to extended absence and severity of residual needs, those with mild injuries may not be identified. Incidents of mild brain injury, even when no hospitalization was involved, should also be reported to the child's school in case cognitive and behavioral difficulties appear in the future.

Prior to school re-entry, parents should have a clear explanation from physicians and specialists about their child's current and potentially permanent needs. If they are unsure about any aspect of their child's condition or treatment, they should request further information from the physician or specialist. School and rehabilitation personnel and family members should meet to discuss residual needs that may affect the child's performance in school, services that the child may require, eligibility criteria for special services, placement options, special education terminology and procedures, class size, staff training in traumatic brain injury, building accessibility, peer training, opportunities for personal and social development, transportation, and other issues related to the child's daily routine.

Parent information groups within the school system can also help in orienting parents to special education programs and services. Each state has a Parent Information and Training Center which is federally funded to provide information and support to parents. Parents can call their local school system and request where to contact these information groups and centers. Hospital or school social workers can usually arrange for parents to talk to other parents who have experienced a similar situation. Additional sources of helpful information may include the library, universities, health department, vocational rehabilitation centers, and adult agencies for the disabled. Organizations such as the National Head Injury Foundation and its local state chapters have a wealth of information to share with family members. Support groups are available through these and similar organizations.

Parents should realize that most educational professionals have not received training specifically related to brain injury. School professionals and parents will have to work cooperatively in helping one another learn about effective programming for traumatic brain injury and how it differs from other conditions. Parents may be able to supply educational staff with resources on brain injury such as printed materials and videotapes.

Parents need to be viewed as school team members, not in just contributing information about their child, but as active participants in decision-making. As they meet with educational personnel, it is recommended that they continue the practice of keeping a log of people and their roles, as well as copies of correspondence. Entries should be dated and arranged in chronological order. Including phone numbers and addresses of contacts is helpful for future reference.

A positive working relationship between parents and professionals depends on effective communication skills. Parents often need help to accomplish this successfully. Initially, it may be helpful for work with an advocate's support who has experience with the educational system. When preparing for meetings, parents should always be aware of the purpose of the meeting and familiar with the information that the school team will be reviewing to make decisions. Information they wish to share about their child should be organized into a logical presentation that communicates relevant information and demonstrates a mutual respect for each member's time.

While some students with brain injuries will be able to return to regular education immediately after their injury, most will require temporary or permanent program modifications or some level of special education services. Numerous studies indicate the adverse effect on educational adjustment for the majority of children with brain injuries (Telzrow, 1987). An indepth discussion of special education law is found earlier in the book. Several aspects are especially relevant to acquired brain injury, and are important for parents to understand in order for them to be effective advocates. These include parent participation in the special education process, the concepts of free appropriate public education and least restrictive environment, the relationship of evaluation to the development of the individual education plan, placement, extended school year services, and due process rights.

PARENT PARTICIPATION

For students to successfully return to school, parent input continues to have a positive impact when collaboration in problem solving and decision making occurs. The intent of special education law is clearly one of a team approach that involves administrators, specialists, parents, and whenever possible, the child himself. In many cases, parents are the most informed sources about their child, both pre and post injury, and while progressing through various treatment stages with their child, have become educated on brain injury.

FREE APPROPRIATE PUBLIC EDUCATION (FAPE)

All children, including children with traumatic brain injury, have the right to free appropriate public education (FAPE). This right is guaranteed by the Education for All Handicapped Children Act of 1975 (P.L. 94-142), amended in 1990 as P.L. 101-476, the Individuals with Disabilities Education Act (IDEA). This legislation ensures all children with disabilities a free appropriate public education which includes special education and related services, as necessary, to meet their needs. P.L. 99-457 extends entitlement of such services to preschoolers.

Special education is specially designed instruction to meet the unique needs of a child with a disability, provided at no cost to the parent. Inherent in FAPE is the concept of zero reject which assures access to free public education to all regardless of the severity of the disability. What this means for students with ABI is a guarantee that no matter how severe their residual needs, they are entitled to appropriate educational services.

Parents should be aware that special education services are available to their child until the age of 21 or until graduation from high school. Once a student graduates, he is no longer eligible for special education services. It may therefore be advisable to defer graduation in order to obtain educational services that are needed and appropriate. Parents may need to request deferment of graduation in writing, as follows.

Sample Letter to Defer Graduation

Dear (Superintendent of Schools),

Our daughter, (name) was involved in an automobile accident on (date), which resulted in a serious brain injury. She was in a coma and is now receiving treatment at the (facility).

(Name) was to graduate on (date) from high school. However, due to the uncertainties associated with her injuries, we are requesting that her official graduation be withheld in order to insure her eligibility for special education services. We understand that P.L. 101-476 provides for special education for students under the age of 21 without a high school diploma. We seek your assistance in ensuring our daughter's right to the appropriate educational services she may need as a result of this accident.

We are, of course, eager and willing to work with the school on this matter. Please feel free to contact us at (number).

Sincerely,

Copy: Director of Special Education

In particular, needed services may include transition services which are provided to help students receiving special education move successfully from school into community life. IDEA specifies that beginning at age fourteen, IEP's must consider the transition needs of students as they plan for the eventual move from school to adult life. This includes addressing those work and self-related skills that will promote independence in the adult world. The school system can help in linking students and their families to adult service providers before graduation. This process needs to begin early as entitlement programs cease to be available after graduation from high school. Receiving services from adult agencies is based on meeting eligibility criteria, not entitlement. In addition, there are generally long waiting lists of individuals for adult services. Another obstacle is the lack of professionals in adult agencies who have experience working with individuals with ABI.

LEAST RESTRICTIVE ENVIRONMENT

Special education law specifies that services should be provided in the least restrictive environment, that is the place where the child will have as much contact as possible with children who are not disabled while meeting the child's learning needs. Inherent in this is consideration of the child's home school as an appropriate placement. However, not all children will be able to resume class in their neighborhood school. Local education agencies must therefore ensure that a continuum of placements is available to meet the needs of students with disabilities. These include instruction in the regular classroom, special classes, special schools, home instruction, and instruction in hospitals or residential facilities.

Each student's placement is determined annually, based on his individual educational needs. Mainstreaming with normal peers may be an attractive option that parents want at the time of discharge as this signals a return to normal. However, children are usually not ready to assume preinjury placement upon discharge from rehabilitation programs. A premature return to the mainstream may result in overwhelming frustration and escalate existing needs (Burns, 1987). It is often advantageous to plan a gradual return to school starting with home instruction. Other options to be considered as tolerated include short school visits, a reduced day, and a modified full day schedule with rest periods throughout the day.

EVALUATION

In order for a student to receive special education services, certain state and federal criteria regarding educationally disabling conditions must be met. Parents can find definitions of these disabilities in their state regulations.

Local education agencies use an educational assessment process that involves a multidisciplinary committee to determine eligibility for special education services. A child may have one or more disabling conditions. One is usually identified as the primary disability because it has a greater impact on the child's educational progress. When the disabilities are determined to equally contribute to the child's problems, the child is usually identified as multihandicapped. Prior to IDEA, traumatic brain injury did not exist as a disability category. Students, therefore, received services under other categories such as learning disabled, other health impaired, mentally retarded, and emotionally disturbed.

It is important that parents participate in the eligibility process as committee members may not be familiar with traumatic brain injury. The evaluation process for determining special education eligibility usually consists of reviewing information currently available in the student's record and administering assessments, as necessary to determine if a disability affecting the child's education does exist. Observations of the child in different settings also yield valuable information.

A couple words of caution should be kept in mind during this process. First, because of the sometimes rapid changes in the recovering student, it is important that the information used to determine eligibility for special education and for reviewing progress is recent and accurate enough to make valid decisions. The information in the child's record is critical in making decisions. Parents should be familiar with it and comfortable that it gives a good picture of their child's strengths and needs.

Secondly, parents need to know which assessments are being used. Many standardized measurements assess information learned prior to the injury but do not shed light on the child's ability to acquire new learning. Formal test findings often minimize cognitive difficulties and may result in unrealistic expectations (Baxter, Cohen, Ylvisaker, 1985). In addition, testing is usually administered in a one to one, structured setting where the numerous distractions of a classroom are absent. The child's performance may differ significantly with the increased demands of a classroom. Parents should pay close attention to what the results mean, the validity of the results, and the qualifications of the test administrator. Input from rehabilitation personnel and/or an individual in the school system with experience in brain injury should be utilized in administering and interpreting test findings. If the child tires easily, it may be advisable to test him over several shorter sessions.

Parental permission is required before assessments can be administered. If parents have concerns about the adequacy of the evaluation conducted by the school system, they should request information from the local director of special education on procedures for obtaining an independent educational evaluation at the school's expense. It is important that this information be obtained prior to the independent evaluation. Without this information, there is a risk that the cost of the outside evaluation may not qualify for reimbursement. An independent evaluation is testing that is conducted by a professional who is not employed by the student's school system. School systems may request a due process hearing to show its evaluation is appropriate. If the hearing officer finds that the evaluation was appropriate, then the school system does not have to pay for the independent assessment. Parents always have the right to obtain an independent assessment. Parents always have the right to obtain an independent evaluation at their own expense. Information from independent evaluations must be considered when making program decisions.

INDIVIDUAL EDUCATION PROGRAM

When a student with a disability is found eligible for special education services, an individualized education program (IEP) must be developed. The IEP consists of long-range goals and short-term objectives to address a child's needs as determined by the evaluation process. It is jointly developed at a meeting by a multidisciplinary team, including the parent. Many systems prepare a draft IEP that is sent to parents to review prior to the meeting. This is a working document that parents should feel free to question and revise as necessary once the meeting is held.

The IEP document contains the child's present level of functioning in specific areas, goals and objectives to meet the child's needs, the type of special education program and related services necessary, amount of participation in regular education, and initiation and duration of services.

Special education regulations require that the IEP be developed prior to determining the child's placement. Parents should remember that the IEP must be individualized to meet the child's, not to fit preexisting programs. Flexibility and creativity in program planning are often required in providing appropriate educational services for the student with acquired brain injury.

According to law, the IEP must be reviewed at least once a year to discuss progress on objectives. While this is satisfactory for the majority of students, a child with ABI may experience significant changes during the first year of recovery. Therefore, the IEP must be reviewed at least once a year to discuss progress on objectives. While this is satisfactory for the majority of students, a child with ABI may experience significant changes during the first year of recovery. Therefore, the IEP should be written on a short term basis and review meetings should be held more frequently throughout the year to address changing needs and corresponding program revisions. The first review should occur at approximately six weeks.

Parents may choose to bring another individual to the IEP meeting. They are entitled to a copy of the IEP document and may tape record the meeting, if they desire. In addition, they may request a review meeting to discuss the IEP at any time.

RELATED SERVICES

Special education law specifies that students are eligible for related services, such as speech, physical therapy and occupational therapy, when they are necessary to assist a student to benefit from special education. Not all students receiving a special education program require related services. This is an important provision, especially as it relates to occupational and physical therapy. School systems provide educational based therapy related to the student achieving his educational objectives. Students may need to receive additional private therapy outside of the school system to address ongoing medical and rehabilitation needs.

PLACEMENT

School systems offer a continuum of placement options for meeting the needs of students with disabilities, ranging from regular education in home schools to home and hospital instruction.

Placement is determined after the IEP has been developed and approved by the special education committee. Several placement options are usually considered for meeting the students' needs. Parents should visit these placements to observe and ask questions about the curriculum, teaching methods, materials, class size, staffing ratios, accessibility of building and bathrooms, fire escape procedures, and the daily schedule of activities. The physical layout of the building should be examined in order to plan for possible problems with orientation. Less structured times such as playground and cafeteria should be assessed also. These are the times where the student with acquired brain injury may experience the greatest difficulty. Rosen and Gerring (1986) emphasize this point with the statement that cafeterias and corridors are mine fields for these students.

EXTENDED SCHOOL YEAR

For some students with acquired brain injury, a break in educational programming over the summer months can result in a significant loss of skills. Fortunately, extended school year services are available for students exhibiting the need for special education, related services or both beyond the regular school year. Extended school year services means an extension of specific services beyond the regular school year provided as part of a free appropriate public education in accordance with a properly developed individualized education program. A student's eligibility for extended school year services is determined by a multidisciplinary special education committee. The committee considers whether there is a likelihood of substantial regression of critical life skills caused by the normal school break and a failure to recover those skills in a reasonable period of time.

PROCEDURAL SAFEGUARDS— RESOLVING DISAGREEMENTS

Special education law guarantees parents specific rights and services, referred to as due process or procedural safeguards. Parents should receive a copy of these rights from their school system. Among these rights are active participation in developing the IEP, obtaining parental permission for release of records to other parties, parental access to information in the student's record, assurance of confidentiality, prior written notice of evaluation and placement activities, the right to have information presented in one's native language, and the right to an impartial due process hearing should differences be unsettled through informal means.

Since the passage of P.L. 94-142, parents and education agencies have used impartial hearing procedures to resolve disputes concerning identification, evaluation, placement, or provision of a free appropriate public education to a child with a disability. The parent or school system may request a local due process hearing which is conducted by an impartial hearing officer according to the requirements of federal and state law. An impartial hearing officer may not be an employee of the school system or any public agency involved in the education or care of children. At a hearing, the hearing officer reviews documentation submitted by both parties prior to the hearing date, listens to oral testimony, and then makes a decision based on findings of fact. The decision is final unless the parents or school system appeal it to their state department for a state due process hearing.

At the state level, an impartial state review board will examine the record of the local level hearing, seek additional evidence, if necessary, provide both parties the opportunity for oral and/or written arguments, and make a decision upon completion of the review. The decision of the state review board is final unless the parents or school system appeal the decision to state or federal court by filing a civil action.

While not mandatory, some parents use the services of an attorney to represent them at the hearing. Under the Handicapped Children Protection Act of 1986, parents may be able to recover attorney's fees from the school system if the hearing officer(s) decides in their favor.

A due process hearing need not be the only avenue for resolving educational disputes. Recognizing the complexity, expense, and adversarial atmosphere of these proceedings has caused many to examine the use of this method and look at alternatives for resolving special education disputes. One such option is a process called mediation. Many states use mediation as an intervening step prior to conducting a formal due process which parents may choose voluntarily. A state cannot require parents to mediate a dispute prior to requesting a hearing and choosing to participate in mediation will not interfere with the parent's right to a due process hearing. In many cases, mediation results in resolving differences without the development of an adversarial relationship. The obvious advantage in this is the need for school and parent to have an ongoing positive relationship, as they are both involved with the child for an extended period of time.

In mediation, an impartial mediator listens to the views of each participant and assists them in arriving at a mutually agreeable solution to the problem. Unlike hearing officers at a due process hearing, a mediator has no power to make a decision concerning a dispute. It is up to the parents and school system to present their positions and attempt to arrive at a mutual solution. The mediator's role is to facilitate the process by clarifying issues, summarizing positions, and offering possible alternatives to the parties for consideration. If an agreement is reached, it is written and signed by both parties. If agreement is not reached, the parties may choose to meet again for additional mediation or proceed to hearing. Either party involved in mediation may request that the process be stopped and the dispute submitted to a hearing. Should the dispute proceed to hearing, the mediator cannot be called as a witness.

Mediation Guidelines

In order for mediation to work, the process rules must be clear to both parties. Both parties need to agree to abide by the same rules, otherwise mediation will not be productive. The following are some basic rules, helpful not only in mediation but at any problem-solving meeting.

1. Information should be shared openly and honestly.
2. Issues should be stated and discussed in a fair manner, without anger and without making accusations about the other party.
3. Information obtained in the mediation session will not be used against the other party.
4. Mediation proceedings are confidential.
5. Each party is given an opportunity to speak uninterrupted and express their views.
6. The focus is on present concerns, not past problems.
7. The mediator will not be a witness in any future legal dispute.
8. Information and materials should be organized for clear presentation.
9. Both parties should think of possible ways of solving the problem.
10. Both parties should think about what they want the other party to do and what they are willing to do.

As an issue moves from the point of being identified to the point of a hearing, the process becomes more formal, expensive, and adversarial. Recognizing this, school staff and parents should attempt to resolve problems early through parent meetings and other informal methods that involve parents as decision making members. *Preventive medicine* goes a long way in education in preventing due process hearings. It implies the use of practices that help both the parent and the school to cooperate in planning an appropriate educational program and in developing an effective long term relationship. Inherent in this is recognition of the parental needs and family stresses in regard to their concerns about their child.

Steps in Problem Solving

Successful resolution of problems depends on an understanding of the issues and an exploration of options to solve the disagreement. As families and their children progress through various stages of recovery, many different problems and issues will be encountered along the way. It is helpful to follow an organized format in addressing each issue comprehensively.

1. Define the problem: Be as specific as possible in identifying the issues and whose problem it is. Collect data from program personnel and involve the student to the extent possible.
2. Brainstorm solutions: Encourage creativity and flexibility in identify-

ing a number of alternatives that may solve the problem. Involve a group of people for generating different approaches.

3. Evaluate and choose an alternative: List the pros and cons of each alternative. Consider what it will take to implement each in terms of time, money and personnel. After choosing an alternative, discuss expected outcomes and how success will be evaluated.

4. Implement the alternative.

5. Evaluate the results. Were expected results achieved totally, partially, or not at all? Was something learned during the process that can be applied to a different strategy? Remember, several alternatives may need to be tried before finding one that works.

SELF–ADVOCACY

Advocacy usually implies that one individual represents the interests and needs of another. However, this chapter would not be complete without recognizing the importance of self-advocacy. Self-advocacy, where individuals with disabilities assert their own rights and interests, is an essential component in facilitating maximum independence. As with family advocacy, self-advocacy must be viewed as an ongoing process that varies according to the individual's age and physical, emotional, and cognitive status.

Self-advocacy may be a difficult process for family members to encourage if they have previously maintained total responsibility for all decisions related to their child's medical treatment, education, and future planning. When appropriate, students should participate in meetings with medical and educational personnel. By getting the student involved in decision making, he/she can take greater control of life and be an active participant in defining independence.

Even at an early age, parents can encourage self-advocacy by promoting the self esteem of their child who may be misunderstood and possibly, rejected by his peers. Many students with ABI feel and actually are misunderstood, especially when there are no apparent physical changes. These students may recognize a difference in their thinking and feelings but because they appear normal physically, their claims of such are often dismissed. Parents should encourage their child to openly discuss his feelings. Interests and strengths should be capitalized, as well as efforts toward new goals. Giving the child choices and opportunities for involvement in problem solving and goal setting, both educationally and socially will contribute to a sense of self-worth (Nickerson, 1991).

There are a growing number of self-advocacy groups where individuals with disabilities learn from one another as they deal with similar life issues.

These groups usually have an individual or individuals who advise them and provide guidance in decision making.

PREVENTION

The National Head Injury Foundation reports between 50,000 and 90,000 people a year receive a brain injury which seriously limits their return to normalcy. While brain injury cannot be eliminated, informed individuals can make a difference in reducing the number of injuries that occur annually. Supporting organizations such as the National Head Injury Foundation and writing legislators to support the use of child safety seats, seat belts, and the helmet use by motorcyclists and bicyclists may save many individuals and their families from the devastating effects of a traumatic brain injury. Information on alcohol and drug use should be routinely available to students in an effort to educate them about the dangers of driving and substance abuse. Furthermore, many students who have experienced brain injuries and their family members are willing to share their stories at student assemblies as a means of advocating understanding and prevention of brain injury.

SUMMARY

Regardless of age, an acquired brain injury is an unexpected event which may result in physical, emotional, and financial burdens for the family. At every stage in the child's recovery and in planning for future issues as well, family involvement is one of the most effective ways to reach goals. While team members change from one setting to the next, parents are the one constant member. By giving them information, answering their questions, and encouraging their participation in interventions and decision making, professionals can have a positive influence on helping parents to assume advocacy roles. To the maximum extent possible, the child or adolescent who sustained the injury should also be involved in decisions affecting his life.

Providing sibling support and peer training are essential in promoting recover and in accepting changes that may result in family roles. Support groups can help by sharing problem-solving skills and coping mechanisms that worked for others in similar situations.

Many students with ABI will never recover to where they were before injury. However, with knowledge and support from caring individuals, both the student and his family can improve in their ability to adjust to postinjury changes.

REFERENCES

Anderson, W., Chitwood, S., & Hayden, D. (1990). *Negotiating the Special Education Maze: A guide for Parents and Teachers.* Rockville, MD: Woodbine House.

Baxter, R., Cohen, S., and Ylvisaker, M. In M. Ylvisaker (Ed.), *Head Injury Rehabilitation: Children and Adolescents.* San Diego: College-Hill Press.

Blazyk, S. (1983). Developmental crises in adolescents following severe head injury. *Social Work in Health Care, 8.*

Burns, P., & Gianutsos, R. (1987). Reentry of the head-injured survivor into the educational system: First steps. *Journal of Community Health Nursing, 4,* 145–152.

Curran, D. (1989). *Working with Parents.* Circle Pines: American Guidance Service.

Kubler-Ross, E. (1969). *On Death and Dying.* New York: MacMillan.

Mauss-Clum, N., & Ryan, M. (1981). Brain injury and the family. *Journal of Neurosurg. Nursing, 13,* 165–169.

Nickerson, M. (1991, Summer). Developing self-esteem in children. *Family Support Bulletin,* 21–22.

Rogers, P.M., & Kreutzer, J.S. (1984). Family crises following head injury: a network intervention strategy. *Journal of Neurosurg. Nursing, 16,* 343–346.

Romano, M. (1974). Family response to traumatic head injury. *Scandinavian Journal of Rehabilitation Medicine, 6,* 1–4.

Rosen, C., & Gerring, J. (1986). *Head Trauma: Educational Reintegration.* San Diego: College Hill Press.

Slater, E., & Rubenstein, E. (1987). Family coping with trauma in adolescents. *Psychiatric Annals, 17.*

Telzrow, C. (1987). Management of academic and educational problems in head injury. *Journal of Learning Disabilities, 20.*

Chapter 11

CASE STUDY
TRACKING BEHAVIORS:
THE REHABILITATION AND
EDUCATION CONNECTION

SALLY B. COHEN

BACKGROUND INFORMATION

Bobby was 9½ years old when he was rendered unconscious in a car accident and sustained a closed-head injury. He was flown by helicopter to a trauma center in a local hospital where he was found to have frontal, temporal, and basal skull fractures. CT scans taken periodically throughout his hospital stay showed diffuse swelling initially and hematomas that resolved gradually. In general, Bobby's brain damage left him with weakened physical abilities in his upper and lower extremities and with cognitive impairments.

After a four-week hospital stay, Bobby was transferred to a rehabilitation center. A transdisciplinary treatment program was developed for him by staff in the departments of medicine and nursing, physical therapy, occupational therapy, speech/language/cognitive therapy, social service, neuropsychology, and special education.

EDUCATION-RELATED REHABILITATION INFORMATION

Premorbid Education Information

Before his accident, Bobby was in a mainstream fourth grade class in his neighborhood public school. His homeroom teacher reported that he was a *straight A* student and was well liked by his peers. He was very conscientious about his work and tended to be nervous and overly concerned about whether he had completed all details of an assignment.

Performance in the Rehabilitation Setting

In general, Bobby's physical condition improved, and within three months he was able to ambulate independently using a walker. However, his cognitive impairments became more obvious over time. Bobby had lost big chunks of his knowledge base, some of which he was unable to relearn. In addition, his fleeting attention, disorganized thinking, extremely impulsive responses and poor memory made it difficult for him to understand what was going on around him. Consequently, his responses in treatment or teaching situations frequently were off target and his social behaviors often seemed peculiar and, at times, bizarre.

The treatment team identified behaviors and impaired skills that interfered with Bobby's present functioning and that ultimately could be problematic when he was discharged to home and school. Indeed, though they lessened in intensity, many of these impairments were still present several years later. (For the purposes of this text, the cognitive, processing abilities will be emphasized).

In therapy settings Bobby:

a. was confused and forgot where he was going
b. was impulsive and unaware of unsafe situations
c. had below age level visual-perceptual skills and poor visual attention
d. had difficulty following lengthy, spoken directions
e. could only attend and stay on topic briefly; was easily distracted
f. was off-task frequently
g. had trouble recalling labels/names and/or explaining things
h. rambled and could not come to the point
i. had poor memory skills
j. was extremely disorganized: had trouble working a page (knowing where to start a task, following directions or thinking and proceeding sequentially, continuing through to task completion)
k. was impulsive: talked out disruptively, could not control emotional outbursts, could not wait, needed immediate feedback or response or else would maintain disruptive talking.

Bobby received both individual and group therapy. Behaviors shaped in groups were considered to be essential for school and for successful social interactions. For instance, in occupational therapy or cognitive therapy groups selected goals were to: (1) improve attending skills; (2) expand thought organization and communication abilities as ideas were formulated and evaluated by group members; (3) strengthen self-control by learning to wait his turn, to think carefully about what he was going to say or do *before* he responded, and to slow down, follow directions and comply with task demands; (4) become more flexible by learning to handle an increasing number and variety of tasks; or (5) learn what he could do independently (with, perhaps, the use of a strategy), when he needed assistance, and where to find information or people who could assist him.

Bobby made significant progress in the rehabilitation program, and after six months as an inpatient and six more months as an outpatient, he was discharged to home and a community school setting.

Neuropsychological and Educational Assessments

In order to obtain a clear picture of where Bobby could fit into community school programs and of the adjustments that would be necessary, it was important to integrate information from his neuropsychological and educational assessment reports. The following assessment results helped to determine the final discharge recommendations.

(a) The neuropsychological assessment: Bobby's strengths were his understanding and use of language. However, his comprehension of information was uneven and generally below age level and deteriorated markedly when content became lengthy or complex. His short-term memory was impaired and required the examiner to deliver content in very short segments. He was easily distracted, causing him to lose information that could otherwise shift into long-term storage, and his ability to retrieve information from long-term storage was quite weak.

Bobby often needed directions repeated. Although he was quick to say he did not know an answer, when given time and encouragement, he demonstrated that he did know information and could carry-out procedures. He had difficulty processing visual information, problem solving, and understanding or making judgments about social situations. In addition, his understanding of his present levels of functioning and of his newly acquired impairments was shallow.

Scores from the Wechsler Intelligence Scale for Children-III:

1. Verbal I.Q.   80
2. Performance I.Q.   46
3. Full Scale I.Q.   62

(b) The educational assessment: Given tasks with a minimal amount of information, Bobby scored at the mid-second grade level in reading comprehension, math, and spelling. His distractibility, problems with memory, word retrieval, overload and inconsistent levels of comprehension affected his performance on academic tasks. His motor-planning for writing tasks was slow and labored, and spatial organization of written work was poor. He was unaware of the fact that he skipped words and lines when reading orally and needed cues to read more than the first paragraph of a one-page story. Though his conversation skills were good, word-finding problems were evident on formal testing tasks, and he often did not respond to open-ended questions. But, his performance improved when given a multiple choice format. Auditory memory for oral directions was poor, and a lack of visual attention to detail was noted when he did not follow changed process signs in math problems.

Suggested educational goals indicated that a high degree of individualization would be necessary and recommended that, in general, school staff should: capabilities could be very inconsistent; (2) assess whether he could work independently in a busy classroom; (3) give him short tasks initially and probe to see if comprehension and skills remained when tasks were gradually lengthened; (4) supply cues and vary task presentation to accommodate his memory and retrieval problems; (5) provide supervision and structure in unstructured situations that could overwhelm or confuse him, e.g., lunchtime, recess, and assemblies; (6) and carry on the informal and formal assessment process to target performance changes that could occur as he continued to recover.

PLANNING SCHOOL PROGRAMS IN THE COMMUNITY

In order to develop a school program that would benefit Bobby educationally and would continue his rehabilitation, treatment team members met and shared ideas with staff from his school district. The rehabilitation staff learned about classroom content and teaching formats in the schools and about the special services that were available to students. In turn, they explained to the school staff that although Bobby's cognitive and physical functioning were much improved, he was not able to think, work, socialize or move about at his premorbid levels.

For instance, he needed a great deal of structure and staff contact to get through a task. He not only needed written instructions to refer to and clearly defined task-steps that he could check off, but he also had to be reminded to use these approaches. While it took Bobby a long time to process information and to carry out tasks, he quickly became overloaded and, when presented with more than four sentences of written or spoken text, his comprehension broke down. In addition, he was learning to use memory strategies.

The rehabilitation and school staff developed the initial I.E.P. objectives defining program adjustments and teaching structures for Bobby. They determined that Bobby should spend 85 percent of his day in a Learning Support classroom where an individualized program would accommodate his cognitive/processing needs and strengthen basic academic skills in the areas of Reading, Math, and English/Language Arts. A speech pathologist would see him individually three times a week to connect his cognitive rehabilitation to academic functioning, e.g., the speech/language program would use classroom materials to focus on task and thought organization, to teach memory strategies, and to provide tutorial support and extra time to learn lesson content or school-related procedures. He would be included in fifth grade mainstream Social Studies and Science classes when staff felt he could comprehend lesson topics and attend satisfactorily in large or small learning groups.

Because Learning Support and Mainstream classes were integrated for Physical Education, adjustments were needed to insure his safety and to plan how to include him in activities as much as possible. Likewise, during recess and lunchtime (when several classes were grouped together) and in larger, mainstream classes such as Art, Music, Social Studies, and Science, increased structure or program adaptations probably would be needed. School staff would have to determine whether his time in more stimulating situations should be decreased initially and/or whether lesson plans should be individualized for him.

The Learning Support class with students Bobby's age was not at his neighborhood school. So, in addition to becoming a special education student for the first time, he would be attending a new school with many unfamiliar students. Whereas he previously had walked to school, he now would have to take a bus. Busing presented more issues for staff related to physical capabilities, overstimulation, judgment, and safety. Plans were made for a monitor to ride on the bus and train Bobby to get on and off, to go from the bus to his classroom in the morning, and, at dismissal time, to identify the bus, get on it, and sit in a designated seat up front by the driver. The monitor was to encourage social interaction between Bobby and his bus-mates and to protect him from getting jostled when students moved around quickly.

Rehabilitation-Related Education Information

Bobby did well during the first year of his new school program. In the Learning Support classroom, his reading comprehension for the three-page stories was at the fifth grade level. Mathematical computation was lower, at grade three. His work in the partial Social Studies and Science placements was adequate, as long as Learning Support staff helped clarify content and adapt assignment and tests for him. He was participating satisfactorily and fully in mainstream Art and Music classes. So, school staff decided to include him in mainstream sixth grade Language/Arts, Health, Social Studies, and Pre-Vocational classes the next year. He would remain in the Learning Support setting two periods a day for Reading, Math, and English.

Bobby and his parents had become comfortable with the more specialized school program, and his parents questioned his ability to handle increased academic and social demands in the mainstream. As it turned out, they had valid concerns. Bobby could not do more advanced work in less structured situations. Some cognitive impairments that had disappeared returned. He became confused easily in sixth grade academic and social situations. He was anxious and was not learning. The teachers were frustrated and did not know how to plan for him; and his family, realizing he was no longer receiving an appropriate educational program, put pressure on the school district to adjust his program.

The school district personnel did not feel qualified to make on-going program decisions that would be suitable for Bobby, so they hired a consultant skilled in programming for students with acquired brain injuries to: (1) adapt Bobby's program so that he would have successful learning experiences and (2) work with staff *over time* and develop cognitive approaches to programming that would benefit all students.

The consultant found that almost three years after his injury, Bobby's residual physical impairments made it difficult for him to participate in some school activities. He still had poor motor-planning skills and a slowed rate of fine-motor performance for writing and manipulative tasks. It took him longer to get around even though he used his walker well, and gross-motor problems prohibited him from participating fully in physical education classes.

It was apparent, however, that *his cognitive impairments were the most difficult for school staff to adjust to and to accommodate.* Teachers found the following behaviors hard to manage: his impulsive, interrupting, off-topic comments were excessive; he asked repetitive questions and didn't seem to benefit from responses he received; when he had trouble completing a task, he often tore up his work or scribbled over directions and texts; he did not hand in homework, could not keep up with the class and was not making progress; and his level of immaturity made it difficult for him to understand social innuendos of peers, and frequently schoolmates excluded him from social groups because he didn't seem to understand what was going on.

The consultant observed that: his *negative,* annoying behaviors occurred in large group situations or during discussions when he had difficulty attending and comprehending and became overloaded; there were very few activities that he could complete; he was not called on often; and he received very little positive reinforcement.

Then, working together, the special education supervisor, school principal, Bobby's teachers and the consultant shared ideas about Bobby's educational needs. Focusing on issues of inclusion, adapting mainstream and Learning Support programs, and establishing more intense team planning, they created a new program.

In a matter of weeks, Bobby's attending skills improved, his classroom responses became more appropriate, he was completing work, it was clear that he understood content and tasks he was given, and, in general, his social interactions were more successful.

Some program changes that shaped these positive school behaviors were:

1. Staff focused on providing *successful* experiences for Bobby which might be different from those given to other students. The goal: to increase attention and comprehension, shape more appropriate school behaviors, and build self-confidence.
2. Bobby's directions and assignments were shortened. Homework and in-class directions were written by staff or by Bobby, so he had them to refer to and could carry them out and meet teacher expectations.
3. He was given fifth grade reading material when possible.
4. An aide from the Learning Support classroom joined his mainstream classes and was trained to adapt assignments and clarify content and procedures for him.
5. Staff planned to call on him often and decrease his *wait-time* in order to keep him on-task.
6. Teaching approaches were targeted to decrease memory requirements for him, to organize tasks presented to him, to prepare him to participate in class, and to encourage him to think more critically about content. (See strategies described in this chapter.) He was trained to use his notebook as a resource for information he needed in school, e.g., to look in designated sections for assignments, class notes, and guidelines for doing specific tasks, such as organizing a work sheet or doing all steps in a mathematical process.
7. Rules to shape behaviors were explained to him and were written down for him to keep in his notebook. Then, selected behaviors were trained and practiced.
8. Team meetings were held with the consultant periodically throughout the year to evaluate details of both successful and problematic situations and to determine approaches to use or to revise in different settings. Increased staff communication was encouraged.

The increased individualization and cognitive approaches to programming did pay off! School staff were challenged by the adjusted procedures and became highly motivated and encouraged by their results. What's more, Bobby's family reported positive changes: he was calmer, happier, and more appropriate in situations outside of school.

The consultant worked intensively for one year with the school staff. Then the school district felt consultation time could be decreased and requested that the consultant come in three times throughout the following year to monitor program effectiveness while remaining on call to answer questions and provide assistance as needed.

The program planning process that was put in place to meet Bobby's needs strengthened the school team. Bobby continued to respond positively to teaching tasks well after the consultant's time with the district was decreased. Moreover, the individual team members having gained confidence in the value of the approaches used with Bobby began to use these approaches effectively with other students. In this way, the school district's goals to improve programming for one student and enhance the general skills of direct service staff for all students were achieved.

Additionally, all of the educators were keenly aware of an important premise that would influence their thinking as they worked with Bobby over the years, i.e., definitive predictions could not be made about his ultimate levels of recovery. What's more, there were on-going planning objectives that should affect teaching approaches: (1) staff could recognize that Bobby's school program may need more structure, limitations and changes than other students' programs and, perhaps, may require adjustments in standard programming procedures; (2) they should continue to create and monitor teaching techniques to improve his functioning; (3) they should empower him to see how strategy use will motivate him to participate in academic and social activities; (4) they should never assume what he can do, rather, they must evaluate his skills objectively; (5) they should assess his abilities (formally and informally) more often than they do for other students in order to target changes as he continues to recover; and (6) they should help him and his family understand how selected program components are appropriate for his educational rehabilitation.

Chapter 12

THE LAST WORD(S)

Alan L. Goldberg

Great strides have been taken toward providing appropriate services to children and adolescents who have sustained a variety of acquired brain injuries. Previous chapters have highlighted a variety of topics related to understanding injuries to the brain and educational issues relevant to the special population of individuals who have acquired brain injuries. Legal issues, school systems issues, practical issues for educators, advocacy issues, transitions, and issues concerning effective networking have all been discussed in preceding chapters. It is clear that information exists to enable proper education of students who have sustained brain injuries. And yet these students are often faced with significant challenges in attaining the necessary and relevant services.

In order to better understand some of the challenges, it is important to understand financial issues. Many school systems are facing financial crises. The political atmosphere of our nation is such that school bond issues and other new taxes face increased scrutiny from the public and uncertain passage in elections. Many school bond issues have faced defeat in recent years. With tightening budgets, specialized training, including in-servicing of staff, is diminishing. In many instances, dollars are allocated to categories of students where there are high volumes. This again speaks to the use of Acquired Brain Injury (ABI) as opposed to Traumatic Brain Injury as a category, as it is more inclusive. Proper advocacy can, and often does, lead to appropriate service delivery. The case of the squeaky wheel getting the grease provides an apt analogy.

Funding issues are also changing the manner of health care service delivery. While formal legislation concerning "health care reform" did not make it out of the last Congress, funders of services are aggressively working to change the manner in which health services are provided. Managed care is a major issue in health care delivery, with much attention being paid to functional, cost effective service delivery. Given funding pressures in the health care markets, inpatient stays are becoming much shorter and/or less frequent. It is common to see clients spend only two to four weeks in inpatient rehabilitation settings after significant brain injuries. Time frames for outpatient therapies are also being shortened, often due to specific policy limitations. The burden of care is placed on family members and the community at large. While our school districts are struggling to learn more about brain injuries so as to provide increasingly relevant services, they are faced with delivering services to much more significantly impaired individuals.

Challenging issues and perplexing dilemmas face all providers of services as we move into the next century. Yet, armed with knowledge, the law, positive attitudes, and frameworks for increased interagency cooperation, we can each play an active role in helping to ensure the best possible services for our charges who have sustained brain injuries.

We hope that you have enjoyed learning about acquired brain injuries and public education through your reading of this book. Feel free to share what you have learned so as to make this world a more user friendly one for those who have sustained brain injuries.

AUTHOR INDEX

SUBJECT INDEX